Prince of Forgers

The Imperial Library, Paris, France
(Bibliotheque Nationale)

Prince of Forgers

Joseph Rosenblum

1998
Oak Knoll Press

PRINCE OF FORGERS was published in 1998 by:
Oak Knoll Press 414 Delaware Street, New Castle, DE 19720 USA

First English language edition. Original French edition published under the title
Une Fabrique de Faux Autographes. 1870, Paris.

ISBN: 1-884718-51-5 U.S.A

Author and translator: Joseph Rosenblum
Typographer: Michael Höhne
Editors: John von Hoelle & Mary Hallwachs
Cover & Book Design: John von Hoelle & Michael Höhne
19th Century French Illustrations: J. Andrew Armacost Collection

Library of Congress Cataloging-in-Publication Data

Bordier, Henri Leonard. 1817-1888.
[Fabrique de faux autographes, ou, Recit de l'affaire Vrain Lucas. English]
Prince of forgers / translated from the original French by Joseph Rosenblum.
p.   cm.
Translation of *Une fabrique de faux autographes, ou, Recit de l'affaire Vrain Lucas / par Henri Bordier et Emile Mabille.*
Includes bibliographical references and index.
Added title page title Forging of false autographs, or, an account of the affair Vrain Lucas.
ISBN 1-884718-51-5 (hc)
1. Vrain-Lucas, Denis, b. 1818—Trials, litigation, etc. 2. Trials (Forgery)—France. 3. Chasles, M. (Michel), 1793-1880. 4. Autographs—Collectors and collecting—France. 5. Forgery of manuscripts—France. 6. Literary forgeries and mystifications. I. Mabille, Emile, 1828-1874. II. Rosenblum, Joseph. III. Title. IV. Title: Forging of false autographs, or, an account of the affair Vrain Lucas.
KJV130.V73B6713   1998
345.44'0263—dc21   98-14515
                                                                                  CIP

Printed in the United States of America

Table Of Contents

Other Works by Joseph Rosenblum

Shakespeare: An Annotated Bibliography

A Bibliographic History of the Book: An Annotated Guide to the Literature

Thomas Holcroft: Literature and Politics in England in the Age of the French Revolution

Edited works

The Plays of Thomas Holcroft

Lives of Mississippi Authors, 1817-1967 (with James B. Lloyd and Robert Linder)

American Book Collectors and Bibliographers. First and *Second Series*

Sir Walter Wilson Greg: A Selection of His Writings

Shakespeare

This translation is dedicated to the memory of M. Edward Clément,

who more than thirty years ago introduced me to the French language,

and

to my dear colleagues Laurie Lake White and Pamela McRae

green isles in the dark sea of life.

List of Illustrations

Acknowledgements

―――――――∙«(◉)»∙―――――――

I wish to thank Mark Schumacher of the Reference Department, Jackson Library, University of North Carolina at Greensboro, for his assistance on many occasions, Anna Maria P. McLin of the University of North Carolina at Greensboro for help with matters Italian, David Fein, again of UNCG, and Ed Montgomery of Interlink Translations (Chapel Hill, NC) for their assistance with Old French, John von Hoelle and Bob Fleck of Oak Knoll for their encouragement and aid, and the Interlibrary Loan department of Jackson Library for promptly and consistently securing necessary items. Reproductions of the original illustrations from *Une fabrique de faux autographes, ou, Récit de l'affaire Vrain Lucas* (Paris : L. Techener, 1870) were supplied courtesy of the University of Delaware Library, Newark, Delaware.

Foreword

━━━►«(●)»◄━━━

*I*n the shadows of the great boulevards of Western literature lurk the sinister masters of literary forgery. Their legacy of spurious literature has bedeviled our culture for over two thousand years, and many are the unwary who have fallen victim to their brazen practices. In America, we have had our fair share of infamous scoundrels. The cunning skills of the Mark Hoffmanns and Dorman Davids could stand shoulder to shoulder with Britain's boldest forgers; Wise, Forman, Chatterton, and Ireland.[1] However, when compared to the industry and audacity of Frenchman Vrain-Denis Lucas, these historic forgers become mere dabblers in the black arts of literary swindles. In sheer quantity, Lucas created and sold more books, manuscripts, and documents than all six of the aforementioned gentlemen combined!

Joseph Rosenblum's excellent and painstaking translation of the 1870 French edition of *Une Fabrique de Faux Autographes* by Henri Bordier and Emile Mabille brings to life one of the most incredible narratives in the annals of literary forgery. Bordier was an attorney and a leading expert on manuscripts at France's National Archives; Mabille was a librarian at the Imperial Library in Paris (today, the Bibliothèque Nationale). Both men testified at Lucas' celebrated trial in 1870. Meticulously, like a trial transcript, the lawyer and the librarian laid before their readers the facts of the case against Lucas. In doing so, they captured only part of the sheer enormity of Lucas' forgeries.

Professor Rosenblum's translation of the sometimes arcane, legal French, reveals Lucas as a man very much underrated by his peers. Though Lucas had little formal education, he acquired an early love of reading and books, especially history. As a young, self-schooled scholar, he inhaled the stored knowledge of the great library of Châteaudun, his birthplace.

For many years, Lucas worked as an honest law clerk, copying deeds and wills before obtaining a position with the venerable Law Courts at Châteaudun. However, his dream was to work with books. In 1852, at the age of 34, Lucas traveled eighty miles to Paris with a letter of recommendation for employment addressed to the Librarian of the Imperial Library. Unfortunately, his laudatory letter could not outweigh his lack of Latin or a diploma, and the presumptuous country peasant was turned away unkindly. Lucas tried to find

---

1 Thomas J. Wise, Harry B. Forman, Thomas Chatterton, and William Henry Ireland.

work at several publishing firms and, later, even in retail book shops. Once again his provincial demeanor and lack of higher education proved a severe handicap among the haughty Parisian literati.

Failing to obtain a position among the legitimate literary professions, Lucas became associated with the dubious genealogical firm of M. Letellier.

Monsieur Letellier was a first-rate scoundrel who fed on the vanity of France's socially conscious *nouveau riche*. He provided doctored family pedigrees for anyone able to pay his generous fees. With artfully forged documents, letters and bogus family Bible inscriptions, he created family links to illustrious ancestors for his naive but eager clients. As an apprentice literary forger, Lucas could not have had a better mentor than M. Letellier.

By 1854, the one-time respectable law clerk was a budding master at his new trade. Using old paper purloined from Paris' numerous libraries, and special, handmade inks, Lucas wrote his masterpieces. Some early examples of his work were published as source material for M. Conches'[2] great three-volume work, *Causeries d'un Curieux* (1864). Lucas' letters, with Montaigne's forged signature, threw new light on the history of their time. If these were among Lucas' first works, they must have given him a sense of power and exhilaration. He had fooled one of the prominent scholars of his day.

Over the next sixteen years, Vrain Lucas would create tens of thousands of autographed forgeries, selling over 27,000 to one collector who was a distinguished member of the Academy of Sciences. Using his prodigious memory for historical details and the public reading rooms of the august libraries of Paris, Lucas penned thousands of letters supposedly autographed by Pascal, Galileo, Descartes, Newton, Rabelais, Louis XIV, and other luminaries of science, philosophy, royalty, and literature. And remarkably, he sold his handiwork for hundreds of thousands of francs, a value equal to millions of dollars today.

However, Lucas' forgeries were not merely common literary intercourse between the famous; but they often revealed events of historical importance that could revolutionize French history. One series of his letters proved that Pascal had really discovered the laws of gravity thirty-five years before England's famed Sir Isaac Newton! Lucas' forgeries so flattered the pride of his fellow countrymen that their discovery created much excitement and controversy among France's leading scholars. Vrain-Denis Lucas, patriot and lover of history, would create for the French people the history they so richly deserved, or so he led many of the scholars at the Academy of Sciences to believe.

By 1866, Lucas' recklessness and disdain for credibility reached the point where he was writing autographed letters by Mary Magdalene, Alexander the

---

2 Felix-Sébastien Feuillet de Conches

Great and from Cleopatra to Julius Caesar, *in French on water-marked paper,* and selling them for thousands of francs. Had his audacity, industry, and knowledge of history finally entered the realm of incongruity? Or was Lucas mocking the learned men of France and their vaunted formal educations? After two years of debate, had not members of the Academy asserted that Lucas' Louis XIV letters were of "a noble simplicity no forger could have produced; the style of the letters proved that they could only have emanated from their professed author; whilst their freedom from such [historical] blunders as no forger could have avoided were a moral proof of their authenticity." The peasant from Châteaudun must have smiled ear to ear. Whatever the case, this self-taught scholar rocked the Olympian halls of French science before disappearing with his secrets and ill-gained wealth. Professor Rosenblum's long awaited translation of this French forgery classic is a must read for any collector interested in literary history. *Prince of Forgers* brings the full scope of this scoundrel's fascinating story to the English-speaking world for the first time.

John Lewis
Accomac, Va.

Mid 19th Century street scene of Vrain Lucas' Paris.

Introduction

⸻ ꞏ((◉)) ꞏ ⸻

O N 5 MAY 1888 *L'Illustration* BEGAN SERIALIZING Alphonse Daudet's novel *L'Immortal,* the main character of which is Pierre-Alexandre-Léonard Astier-Réhu, historian and member of the Académie française. M. Astier-Réhu is writing a book entitled *The Unknown Galileo,* "based upon most interesting, hitherto unpublished documents."[1] These documents have been sold to Astier-Réhu by a bookbinder named Albin Fage. Astier-Réhu's relationship with Fage dates from the latter's visit to the historian to inquire about a letter concerning Galileo written by Marie de' Medici to Pope Urban VIII. After Astier-Réhu had certified that the autograph letter was genuine, Fage declared that he also had "Pope Urban's reply, Galileo's letter of thanks to the [French] queen" and many other such documents.[2] To Astier-Réhu's question regarding the provenance of these treasures, Fage replied that they belong to "a certain aged maiden lady of noble birth, who was forced to sell, piece by piece, a very valuable collection which had been in her family since before Louis XIV."[3] According to Fage, in her possession is "an inexhaustible treasure of documents of the sixteenth and seventeenth centuries, varied, interesting, throwing a new light on the past, sometimes overturning with a single word or a date accepted ideas concerning men and facts."[4] Taken to England during the French Revolution, some of the papers had suffered water damage, but most remain in fine condition. Fage says that he plans to offer the manuscripts to various collectors, but Astier-Réhu insists on buying all of them himself, and he pays Fage as much as five hundred, a thousand, even two thousand francs for a single item. In the course of two years the historian pays 160,000 francs for these autograph documents. Numbering in excess of ten thousand, these manuscripts include autograph letters by Cardinal Richelieu, Colbert, Isaac Newton, Galileo, and Pascal. Also among these papers are three letters from the Emperor Charles V to Rabelais; for these alone M. Bos has offered 20,000 francs, but Astier-Réhu refuses to part with them. Yet another piece in the col-

---

1   *"The Immortal," to Which Is Added "The Struggle for Life."* Trans. George Burnham Ives. Boston: Little, Brown, 1900, p. 2.

2   Ibid., p. 199.

3   Ibid., p. 200.

4   Ibid.

lection is a letter from Catherine the Great of Russia to Denis Diderot on the subject of the Académie française, a document that Astier-Réhu secures from Fage just as the historian is preparing an address to that body, a speech that will be attended by the Grand Duke Leopold of Finland, Catherine's great-grandson. Astier-Réhu presents this letter to the duke. To the Academy itself Astier-Réhu gives a letter from the poet Jean de Rotrou to Cardinal Richelieu concerning the statutes of that body.

Astier-Réhu's wife is less sentimental about the documents than is her husband. Her son needs 20,000 francs, which she secures by selling to Bos the three letters of Charles V. Bos in turn sells them to Baron Huchenard, who detects an 1836 watermark on the paper, indicating that these cannot date from the sixteenth century. Astier-Réhu's book on Galileo is attacked by the Academy of Florence, as are the documents he included. Astier-Réhu is compelled to acknowledge that his manuscripts have all been forged. Fage is arrested and sentenced to five years in prison; Astier-Réhu drowns himself in the Seine the night after the trial.

Like Anatole France's "Scolastica," a story which is included as an appendix to the present volume, Daudet's novel is based on the activities of Vrain-Denis Lucas, Fage's prototype. The quotation from a letter of Charles V to Rabelais is taken verbatim from a Lucas forgery: "To François Rabelias, master in all sciences and good letters."[5] In some particulars Daudet exaggerated: Lucas was sentenced to two years in prison rather than five; Michel Chasles, the original of Astier-Réhu, outlived Lucas' trial by a decade and died a respected mathematician. In describing the forgeries, though, Daudet under-represented the quantity and nature of Lucas' efforts. Lucas created over 27,000 documents, and he did not restrict himself to the sixteenth and seventeenth centuries. Among the pieces that he sold to Chasles were six letters by Sappho, ten letters by Plato, twenty-eight by Pliny, ten by Seneca, three by Mary Magdalene, one by Alexander the Great to Aristotle, and another by Mohammed to the king of France. Lucas even created an entire manuscript of the *Roman de la rose*, containing 1,107 pages. The complete inventory of Lucas' fabrications, listed in the present volume, entitles him to be regarded as the most prolific forger of all time.

Chasles, a brilliant geometrician who in 1865 received the Copley Medal from the Royal Society (London) for his contributions to mathematics, almost certainly did not think that he was buying authentic documents executed by the supposed signers from antiquity through the Middle Ages, though Lucas probably hoped that his forgeries would be regarded as genuine. Lucas took pains to age the paper by submerging the documents in water—in his early

---

5 Ibid., p. 105. Compare with the text quoted on p. 36.

attempts he left the letters in water too long and so had to invent the story of the shipwreck—holding the manuscripts over a smoking lamp, or burning the edges. Lucas also made crude approximations of Carolingian script and archaic orthography, but his texts are all essentially in modern French. The kindest interpretation to be placed on Chasles' gullibility is that he believed that these letters had once existed (which is credulity enough) and had been preserved, transcribed, and perhaps translated by Alcuin and his scriptorium at Tours in the ninth century, and that in the sixteenth century they had been collected, once again transcribed, and at least somewhat modernized by Rabelais, acting with the encouragement of François I and Margaret d'Angoulême. Such seems to be the implication of the account that Chasles presented to the Academy of Sciences at the session of 13 September 1869 when he conceded that the documents in his possession were not authentic. Yet in making this statement he was relying on precisely those manuscripts that Lucas had forged to explain their existence.

The more recent letters, those dating from the sixteenth, seventeenth, and eighteenth centuries, Chasles did believe were original, and it is here that he exhibited the greatest willing suspension of disbelief. According to these thousands of documents supposedly executed by Pascal, Galileo, Newton, and other leading scientific and literary figures of the period, the credit for discovering the laws of gravity belonged to Pascal rather than to Newton, and the first moon of Saturn was found not by the Dutch Christian Huyghens but rather by Galileo. Like Astier-Réhu, Chasles was writing a book based on these revolutionary materials, and in July 1867 Chasles began publishing them in the *Proceedings* of the Academy of Sciences (Paris). He even donated twenty-three of his autograph documents to the Academy, including two letters from Jean de Rotrou to Cardinal Richelieu regarding the Académie française. Again Daudet's fiction understates the facts. The report here translated and the related documents appended recount the ensuing controversy, which engaged the leading scientists of nineteenth-century Europe and occupied the Academy of Sciences for over two years. Finally, on 13 September 1869, Chasles conceded that the documents were not authentic, but even then he could not believe that Lucas had forged them. One might imagine that a letter from Cleopatra to Julius Caesar could somehow have been repeatedly transcribed over the centuries and translated into French. As Horace Helbronner, Lucas' defense attorney, pointed out, though, Sir David Brewster, biographer of Newton, had found no trace of correspondence between the English scientist and Pascal; yet Chasles supposedly owned 175 letters from Pascal to Newton. Letters from Rabelais were known to be scarce; Chasles bought 1,367 of them. Only twenty genuine letters by Jean de La Bruyère were known in the mid-1800s; Chasles' collection contained 739. Classical and medieval texts might have been translated into French, but how explain Galileo's or Kepler's corresponding in French when Latin was the international language of scholarship, such that Newton composed his *Principia* (1687) in that language rather than in English? Nor was there any evidence that Galileo even knew French. Robert Grant's criticism of the scientific calculations presented in the forgeries appears in this volume among the documents related to the case; surely here a mathematician as learned as Chasles should have detected grounds for skepticism.

Lucas' uncanny ability to produce crucial documents at moments of crisis might also have given pause to one less willing than Chasles to be deceived. According to Lucas, the manuscripts belonged to an old man, a descendant of the comte de Boisjourdain who had assembled this remarkable archive. These documents were supposedly "scattered without order in the attic of a town house, in Paris." This lack of organization explained why Lucas, who claimed to be acting only as the agent of this old man, brought random letters from various people and periods rather than complete files. Of course, he brought Chasles whatever had been forged in the past several days; a search of his residence uncovered no cache of documents, whether authentic or fabricated. Yet when the occasion demanded, Lucas could put his hands on manuscripts that proved curiously apt. On 7 October 1867 Chasles produced three letters in the hand of Galileo dated January, May, and June 1641. The session at the Academy on 11 November heard a letter sent by Robert Grant of the Glasgow Observatory, who pointed out that (a) Galileo had been blind since 1638 and (b) one of these letters from Galileo spoke of the satellites of Saturn, the first of which was not discovered until 1655. On 18 November Chasles was able to introduce twenty letters asserting that Galileo was merely feigning blindness to receive gentler treatment from the Inquisition, and that he had constructed a telescope through which he had seen one of Saturn's moons. On 12 April 1869 Paul-Émile Breton de Champ pointed out that sixteen letters by Pascal and two fragments of a letter by Galileo, introduced by Chasles into the Academy's *Proceedings* back in 1867, had been copied from Alexandre Savérien's *Histoire des philosophes modernes* (Paris: Brunet, 1761-1767). On 19 April Chasles replied with three letters indicating that Savérien had copied his information from the original letters, which had once belonged to Madame de Pompadour and later had passed into the collection of Boisjourdain.

As the obituaries included here indicate, Chasles was not only highly respected as a mathematician but also much loved as a person. When Henri Bordier and Émile Mabille were asked by the court to examine the charge of forgery against Lucas, they faced a delicate task. Their report treats Chasles gently. Nor was Chasles the only one taken in by the documents. No less an historian than Louis Adolphe Thiers believed them authentic, as did certain members of the Academy. Indeed, on 5 April 1869 the permanent secretary of the Academy attested to their genuineness and rejected out of hand any possibility of fraud. Bordier and Mabille needed to prove to the court that the letters were spurious and that Lucas was their creator, yet they also had to explain how these palpable forgeries could have fooled Chasles and occupied the leading scientists of France for over two years. The report thus balances candor with kindness.

As Bordier and Mabille note, Lucas was not well educated. All his forgeries were in French because that was the only language he knew, and all were written on paper either because he had no skill in working with parchment or because parchment was too expensive or too difficult to obtain. Securing blank paper even a century or two old was hard enough; Lucas was one of those rare biblioklepts who sought to steal only blank leaves. Even so, like Fage, Lucas was indifferent to watermarks. Apart from producing a convincing ink and trying to use old paper (which, as already noted, he further aged synthetically), Lucas took few pains with his fabrications, beyond the extensive effort of producing so many. Perhaps he was too busy to try to imitate so many different hands and styles—the correspondents in his forgeries number in the hundreds. The report thoroughly documents the solecisms that abound in Lucas' work, errors that should have inspired skepticism in anyone accustomed to working with manuscripts.

To extenuate to some extent the credulity of Chasles and his supporters, Bordier and Mabille dwelt on Lucas' success with his ink, on his skill as a storyteller in imagining the Boisjourdain archive, and on his skillful use of sources so that the texts attributed to various people often actually embodied their words. To the lay reader the most glaring absurdities would have been the letters from antiquity, but of these the Academy had no knowledge. Nor did the Academy know the full extent of Chasles' hoard. He shared 381 letters out of the more than 27,000 that he had bought, and since these were largely transcriptions from scientific sources, they were relatively free from error—except for the impossibility that their contents could have been written by the people and at the dates Lucas assigned them. Bordier and Mabille more precisely identify the basis of Lucas' success when they write that Chasles, "naturally imbued with the desire to prove a thesis, saw only that which agreed with his argument." That "naturally" typifies the gentle treatment accorded Chasles. The Academy's inability to expose the forgeries more rapidly is also extenuated, being ascribed to "surprise" and to "the confidence inspired by the eminent glory of M. Chasles as a geometrician and … the respect commanded by his character." Bordier and Mabille further redeem the reputation of the Academy by noting that many members did reject the documents from the beginning. Why these individuals were not overwhelmed by surprise and Chasles' reputation, and why the others could not recognize what should have been clear to them, are matters left unexamined.

While the report thus pursues an agenda, it remains the most comprehensive account of this audacious forgery. Exactly when Lucas began his operations remains unclear, nor can one be certain as to why he sought out Chasles in 1861, though the sequel proved Lucas' choice to have been a stroke of genius. A lover of history as well as of old books and manuscripts, the thirty-four year old Lucas had come to Paris from the village of Châteaudun in 1852, hoping to secure employment in a library or bookstore. His limited education precluded such a post, and he ended up as an agent for a genealogical establishment that found, and no doubt also manufactured, pedigrees. Lucas' first known forgery was prompted by a request from the marquis Antoine-Théodore Du Prat, who was seeking documentary evidence of his descent from Antoine Du Prat, chancellor of France and cardinal. The Letellier archive that employed Lucas could not supply the desired material, but Lucas could. The fifteen letters that Lucas fabricated, and that are described in the Bordier-Mabille report (pp. 37–38) were published by the marquis in *Glanes et Regains* (gleanings and aftermaths) in 1865 (Versailles: Beau). This volume also contained two letters from Montaigne published the previous year by Felix-Sébastien Feuillet de Conches, regarded as the pre-eminent authority on French autographs. Yet these two letters were also the work of Lucas.

Like Chasles, these men were fooled because the forgeries flattered their vanity, in the one case genealogical and the other bibliophilic. Daudet's Astier-Réhu buys Fage's fabrications not only to further his research but also to prevent others from possessing the manuscripts. Bordier and Mabille say little about Chasles' collecting mania, but they note that when he learned of the sale of four notes to a M. Belley, Chasles hastened to purchase them for 200 francs. Lucas at one point offered to return all of Chasles' money in exchange for the documents; Chasles rejected the proposal. Chasles finally had Lucas arrested not because of all the latter's forgeries but because Lucas had failed to supply some 3,000 additional documents that Chasles had requested, and Chasles, believing still that these manuscripts actually existed, feared that Lucas was planning to sell them to others, perhaps even, horror of horrors, to foreigners.

Astier-Réhu is prompted by documentary greed and a desire to revenge himself on political enemies by writing a revolutionary account of Galileo. Chasles shared the first of these motives, and he possessed the second at least in so far as he hoped to alter the history of science. Perhaps an argument with Paul-Émile Breton de Champ over Euclid's porisms was a contributing factor. Chasles was also driven by a desire to render unto France the glory that England had unjustly snatched from her. Perhaps Lucas shared this patriotic zeal; perhaps he simply preyed on Chasles'. Ethnocentricity is apparent in giving Pascal the credit for Newton's discoveries, and it pervades the letters of all periods. Alexander the Great urges Aristotle to visit France because the Macedonian conqueror regards that region "as being that which has brought the light [of learning] into the world." Cleopatra writes to Julius Caesar that she plans to educate their son Caesarion at Marseilles (rather than Alexandria or Athens or Rome) because of the excellent climate and fine curriculum available in that French port. Mary Magdalene and her sister Martha agree with Alexander that "it must be from [France] that the light of learning must come." Charles Martel informs the leader of the Moors that a handful of French soldiers will suffice to defeat hoards of would-be invaders. Is it too much to suggest that these forged letters echo a national sentiment characteristic of the Second Empire?

Whatever else impelled Lucas, money was a primary concern. From 1861 to 1869 Chasles paid Lucas between 140,000 and 150,000 francs for the false documents and for books to which Lucas had given spurious provenances. It is unclear what became of this sizable sum; at his trial Lucas claimed that he had spent all but a few thousand francs. Yet he apparently had neither the time nor the inclination to squander what Chasles gave him. The prosecution described Lucas' Spartan routine:

> He would leave his house at eleven o'clock and lunched, sometimes at the café Riche, when he had money, sometimes at a small restaurant, when money was lacking. All day he would work at the Imperial Library, and at night he would return to his house after having dined. He would not speak to anyone, and he went only to the house of M. Chasles.

Perhaps he gave the money to his mistress, who found ways to spend it while he toiled. Lucas himself, as the presiding judge noted, worked like a monk. For at least eight years forgery was Lucas' job; and if he was well paid, in terms of effort he earned every sou. What became of Lucas after he served his two-year sentence is uncertain. Chasles continued to devote himself to matters mathematical.

Lucas' fecundity shames other forgers, but he was hardly a unique figure in nineteenth-century France. In one of those ironies in which Clio delights, Chasles in 1851 assumed the seat in the Academy of Sciences vacated by Guglielmo Libri, who had decamped to England in 1848 just before he was to be arrested for robbing French libraries that he had been appointed to inspect. Libri was not only a biblioklept; he also, like Lucas after him, forged provenances to disguise his depredations or to enhance the value of purloined material. Thus, he added "Di Dante Alighieri" to a fourteenth-century manuscript, and "Pippinus rex Francorum" to Merovingian documents.[6] From Châteaudun Lucas followed the Libri controversy, perhaps taking Libri as a role model. As soon as Chasles began publicizing his letters, many scientists suspected that they were forgeries, and the name of Libri was freely circulated as their author. Libri protested in a letter to the London *Times*, included among the related documents here; and of this crime at least he certainly was innocent.

Lucas' defense counsel noted another contemporary forgery. In 1864 Louis Marie Paul Vogt, comte d'Hunolstein, issued his *Correspondance inédité de Marie Antoinette*[7] (unpublished correspondence of Marie Antoinette) containing 132 letters. The third edition published that same year added nineteen more. All but two of these were spurious, yet for years Hunolstein retained confidence in their authenticity. In 1868 he published a fourth edition, which included a lengthy preface defending the letters. For these manuscripts he paid £3,400, or more than half the sum Chasles paid for his entire cache (which itself contained seventeen forged letters by Marie Antoinette). In the light of this forgery, Lucas' prices seem absurdly low.

This was also the period when Constantine Simonides traveled across Europe offering ancient manuscripts to collectors and libraries. In the early 1850's in Paris he befriended Marie Louis Jean André Charles de Martin du Tiral, comte de Marcellus, who was gathering material on the fifth-century A.D. Greek poet Nonnus. Simonides sought to assist by producing a biography of Nonnus by Demetrius of Magnesia, who did indeed write biographies of poets (who had the same names as cities), but who unhappily predated Nonnus by about five hundred years. To cite but one further example, in 1855 E. de Saint Maurice Cabany, Director-General of the Society of Archivists of France, published *Moredun: A Tale of 1210* (London: S. Low and Son) as being by Sir Walter Scott. Cabany claimed that he owned a writing desk containing Scott's manuscript. The novel, supposedly composed in 1826, refers to improvements made at Newcastle in the 1830's.

The post-Napoleonic period provided unparalleled opportunities for collectors, as monastic and aristocratic libraries were dispersed. Between 1825 and 1835, 12,000 autograph documents were sold at auction in France. In the next five years, nearly the same number, 11,000, were offered. The period 1841-1845 witnessed the sale of 15,000, and between 1846 and 1859 another 32,000 came onto the market.[8] As Lucas' lawyer observed, as sales proliferated,

6 P. Alessandra Maccioni Ruju and Marco Mostert, *The Life and Times of Guglielmo Libri* (Hilversum: Verloren, 1995), p. 211.

7 Paris: E. Dentu, 1864.

8 J. A. Farrar, *Literary Forgeries* (London: Longman's, Green, 1907), p. 215.

"Demand brought forth supply; soon documents were lacking, and the appetite of lovers [of autograph documents] being sharpened, forgery was known to satisfy it."

The story of Lucas and Chasles is thus fascinating but hardly unique. Forgery is as old as literature itself. In the catalogue of ships in Book II of the *Iliad* are the lines, "And Ajax led from Salamis twelve ships, and stationed them where the battalions of the Athenians stood" (lines 557-558). Aristarchus of Samothrace (c. 215-143 B.C.), head of the Alexandrian Library, rejected the Athenian allusion as a sixth-century B.C. interpolation designed to enhance the prestige of Athens. As Anthony Grafton writes in *Forgers and Critics: Creativity and Duplicity in Western Scholarship* (Princeton: Princeton University Press, 1990), "For 2,500 years and more, forgery has amused its uninvolved observers, enraged its humiliated victims, [and] flourished as a literary genre" (p. 5). From a pseudo-Sophoclean play, the *Parthenopaeus*, created in the fourth century B.C. by Dionysius the Renegade, to the Hitler Diaries and the spurious documents linking President Kennedy to Marilyn Monroe, greed and credulity have joined with other motives such as patriotism, filial piety,[9] or the imp of the perverse to bedevil scholars and entertain everyone else. If Lucas' story does not point a moral, it does adorn a tale.

A NOTE ON THE TRANSLATION

The letters forged by Lucas include some attempted archaisms. I have not reproduced these, but, for the most part I have retained the punctuation of the original. Most typographical errors I have corrected silently; my editorial emendations appear within square brackets.

---

9   For example, William Henry Ireland's desire to supply his father with a document in the hand of Shakespeare.

Forgeries
or
Newly Discovered History?

⟫⟪⟩⟪⟫

*P*UBLIC CURIOSITY was for a long time excited by an internal struggle that arose among scholars over papers newly discovered, according to which it would have been necessary to transfer to Pascal almost all the glory of Newton. This understandable curiosity has finally been satisfied. After two and a half years of exchanges, of objections, of refutations, and of doubts, the fraud, acknowledged by those who initially had defended it and by its author himself, has been revealed in all its details in the great day of judgement. The court of summary jurisdiction has put an end to it by condemning the author of the forgeries to two years in prison.

When the questions raised by this fraud have so vividly attracted attention, an obligation in some degree seems to fall on those who made the discoveries to make the matter known in full detail: this obligation is in no way to conceal from the educated public the information that they [the experts] possess. This is a sort of debt that they have to pay. It is perhaps also a useful lesson and capable of bearing fruit in the future. How can a praiseworthy, unbiased, purely literary passion completely blind a great mind? How is it possible that error should be so readily welcomed and truth so reluctantly upheld? By what methods could an unrefined hand succeed in creating such a delusion? What particularly are the facts and who are the people that the falsification affected? Such are the points that it is useful to clarify, and perhaps such information will cause people to take care in the future by casting light and publicity on this series of events.

A concern for learning and concern for the reader, future or present, are then the claims that we will invoke to obtain favorable notice, in exposing in the following pages our observations and our research.

I

The Discussion
at the Academy of Sciences

———=•《①》•=———

*I*T WAS ON 8 JULY 1867 that the Academy of Sciences heard, for the first
time, that is to say officially, during one of its sessions, of the autographs that would come to occupy its time for more than two years.
Finding that it was close to the two-hundredth anniversary of the founding of
the Academy, established in 1666, and that a lecture had been prepared on this
subject, M. Michel Chasles, one of the most illustrious scientists of our century, and who is said to be a geometrician of genius, M. Chasles saw in this circumstance the occasion to make a gift to his colleagues; he gave, to be deposited in the archives of the organization, four letters of [Jean de] Rotrou, of which
two were addressed to Richelieu, in which the poet was encouraging the cardinal, at least thirty years before 1666, to organize in Paris a society of writers and
scholars, patterned after that which Clémence Isaure had already established at
Toulouse. Following this announcement, the president of the Academy, M.
[Michel-Eugène] Chevreul, asked if it would suit M. Chasles, without the
Academy's waiting for a work of which he [Chasles] had spoken some time ago,
touching the discovery of the laws of gravity by Pascal, to be completed, to add
to his gift by speaking without delay some words about this great scientific
development. M. Chasles responded to this invitation by promising some rev-
elations in the next session, and in fact, on 15 July, he gave new proof of his generous nature by also giving to the Academy two letters of Blaise Pascal to the
English chemist Robert Boyle, as well as four notes or observations jotted on
small sheets of paper, and, a circumstance that must have seemed strange, all
four also signed *Pascal*. The Academy of Sciences inserted the texts of these six
documents into its printed proceedings of the session, as it had done for the
two letters of Rotrou [to Richelieu]. But almost from the beginning, this group
of documents raised strong doubts even within the Academy. At the following
session, 22 July (since it is each Monday, the morning of the session, that the
proceedings appear, with mathematical regularity, detailing what had been said

11

and done the previous Monday), one of the physicists of the Academy, M. [Jean Marie Constant] Duhamel, declared that one of the letters and several notes of Pascal relating to the general laws of gravitation seemed to him inexplicable, because they assume the use of measurements and the knowledge of formulas that had not yet been discovered and that would not be discovered until some time after the death of Pascal (which occurred in 1662); and M. Duhamel concluded with these words: "Even admitting the authenticity of the letters presented by M. Chasles, and even supposing that they had been published before the *magnum opus* of Newton (*The Principles of Natural Philosophy* [more precisely, *Philosophiae naturalis principia mathematica*, 1687]), they would not give anyone the right to say that Pascal was the first to prove the general law of gravity."

At the meeting of 29 July, M. Prosper Faugère, author of many works about Pascal, his writings, and his family (1842-1847), and M. Bénard, of Evreux, wrote to the Academy to protest against the documents in question, certainly, they openly declared, false and blatantly forged. M. Bénard called attention to mathematical expressions and certain calculations supposedly Pascal's that seemed to him [Bénard] copied from a certain modern treatise on cosmography; M. Faugère, who was obliged to follow the discussion for a long time more, proved the deceit by examining Pascal's life and works, where one finds not the slightest interest in astronomy, by pointing out numerous anachronisms in the dubious documents, finally by growing indignant at a consideration of the style that someone dared lend to the author of the [*Lettres*] *Provinciales* [provincial letters].

The circle of objections continued to grow, quickly gaining greater publicity, as M. Chasles soon increased his publication of new documents in the Academy's proceedings.

Naturally, the English scornfully rejected the attack brought against Newton's glory, and on 12 August the Academy considered an objection coming from Edinburgh and prepared by one of its associate members, Sir David Brewster, known since 1800 for his work on light, author of three volumes of biography and of documents concerning Newton. In his letter, this scholar bitterly exclaimed against any correspondence between Pascal in his declining years and Newton in his twelfth year, along with other supporting letters, documents that M. Chasles had published (29 July) following fifty-three new notes by Pascal (22 July). Sir David urged above all that, among Newton's papers, religiously preserved by Newton's descendants, there was not the slightest mention of Pascal, that even his name did not appear, and Sir David affirmed that these letters were "contemptible forgeries." Having asked to see the originals to compare with those papers held by the family, he returned (session of 30 September) the photographs that M. Chasles had sent him, while confirming with new force his original statement.

M. [Robert] Grant, director of the Glasgow Observatory, appeared at the same time to provide formidable support to M. Brewster. In a letter inserted into the *Proceedings* (12 September), he compared the best calculations that one could imagine available to Pascal as late as possible, that is to say the year of his death, 1662, with those that were available to Newton: (1) when he published the first edition of his work (1687), and (2) when he published his third and final edition (1726). Now, in examining the computations given to determine (1) the masses of the sun, of Jupiter, of Saturn, and of the Earth; (2) their densities; (3) the force of gravity on their surfaces, one sees immediately in the work of M. Grant, that Newton's results in 1686 were considerably inferior, in quality and precision, to what they became in 1726 in the same hands; whereas, according to the documents of M. Chasles, not only did Pascal present estimates far superior to those of 1687, but he gave figures identical to Newton's in 1726. While M. Chasles defended step by step, and often with apparent success, all the documents that he produced, the disagreement continued to spread and the number of opponents to grow. But the discussion presented above all the phenomenon of moving periodically from one point of debate to another, because, forced by enemy penetration of the first defense where they had established themselves, M. Chasles' documents sought another shelter, another story to resist [their opponents], and, again driven out, they sought a third, a fourth refuge; they would have thus sought to infinity if the entire world, without exception, had not finally opened its eyes.

To the first doubts formulated by M. Duhamel, M. Chasles immediately (29 July) replied by citing numerous letters that he owned; these proved all the relations of Pascal in his last years with the very young Newton, and, particularly, the investigations of the former into gravity. Among the number was this letter from Pascal to Newton, the tone of which has most appropriately been compared to that which might today be the banal phraseology of a barely literate schoolmaster:

> My young friend, I have heard with what care you seek to introduce yourself to mathematical and geometrical studies. . . . I send you various problems that were once the object of my thoughts concerning the laws of abstraction, so as to exercise your genius. . . . Work, study; but this should be done with moderation. This is the best way to acquire knowledge and to profit from the knowledge that one acquires. I speak to you from experience. . . . Learning, by slow degrees and with time, this is the most lasting, etc.

From the question of knowing whether Pascal had concerned himself with gravity (i.e., attraction, and not with abstraction), one then passed to a different question of knowing whether he had corresponded with *the young* Newton, and M. Chasles brought a new file of letters for support that he communicated the same day (12 August) that the first letter of Sir David Brewster was also communicated. Brewster's letter being dated the 6th, and having probably been shown to M. Chasles as soon as it reached Paris, it would not be impossible that the duration of four or five days would have sufficed for the forger to ward off the objections of Sir David Brewster; the mistake of abstraction for attraction, as well as the other errors, prove that he worked extremely quickly, and did not have the time to correct himself; but this batch of papers may also have been prepared long before, since for the most part their purpose was to explain the simultaneous presence of letters with very diverse sources, by creating the belief that Newton, so envious of Pascal and of Descartes that he silently appropriated their work, had sought after their death either to acquire the manuscripts that they had left, or to get their families to give him their letters, and that after his, Newton's, death, all the materials had been gathered into the hands of the French man of letters [Pierre] Desmaiseaux, his friend.

Until now Galileo had hardly been mentioned, in the documents of M. Chasles, although one hundred fifty letters or pieces already had been published in the *Proceedings*, concerning Pascal, and the communications of M. Chasles were growing increasingly incriminating against Newton; the kings of France and England themselves were drawn in [Louis XIV and James II— authors' note], when, at the meeting of 7 October, M. Chasles produced a group of new documents; these were letters of Galileo proving that the Florentine astronomer had involved himself with the law of gravity, with Pascal, then a young man of seventeen years, and had provided him [Pascal] with valuable estimates. This time, the forger had had the time to prepare supporting evidence, in composing these works of Galileo, because M. Duhamel had said, in the course of his first objection (22 July, p. 122), "The law of proportionality (of attraction varying according to masses) was deduced by Newton from that of *the fall of bodies, discovered by Galileo, and from various experiments he conducted himself relating to the oscillations of the pendulum.*" M. Duhamel had also said (12 August) that, if Newton had plagiarized from anyone, it would not have been from Pascal but from Descartes and from [Pierre de] Fermat. The file communicated by M. Chasles, in the meeting of 7 October, contained a letter from Pascal to Fermat, clearly meeting this last objection, three letters of Galileo, dated the months of January, May, and June 1641, and various letters by [Christian] Huygens, [Edme] Mariotte, Newton, the Cardinal [Melchior] de Polignac, and [Nicolas] Malebranche, all agreeing in confirming those of Galileo proving that Pascal had composed, using the observations of Galileo and writings of Kepler, a brief treatise containing the numerical values of the masses and densities of the planets, that would be reproduced by Newton in his 1726 edition of his *Principia*. But at the session of 11 November a new letter arrives from the Glasgow astronomer, M. Grant, observing (p. 788) that Galileo speaks, in 1641, (1) of the satellites of Saturn that had never been known and of which the first was not discovered until 1655; (2) of Galileo's sight that was growing weaker, "*when it goes, it goes more and more*," according to the writer's expression, when it is well known that Galileo was completely blind from the end of 1637 until his death, which occurred in 1642. At the following session (18 November), M. Chasles dispelled these serious objections by producing twenty letters of Galileo, of [Vincenzio] Viviani, Galileo's pupil, of Boulliau, [Giovanni Domenico] Cassini, Huygens, etc., proving that Galileo never was, until the last months of his life, completely blind; that he exaggerated his infirmity to secure consideration from the Inquisition; that he had constructed, towards the end of his life, a telescope with which one could observe the orbit of a satellite of Saturn; that having become unable to use this instrument himself, he sent it to his friend Pascal, and that from Pascal, through the agency of Boulliau, the telescope passed into the hands of Huygens; that Huygens was able to take advantage of it to make the precise observation of the first satellite of Saturn (in March 1655) and sub-sequently all the credit was given to him.

This time it was no longer just England, but also Italy, and Holland, that were stirred up in their turn; for one of the remarkable points of this affair is the unanimous sentiment that united the scholars of all these diverse countries in one spirit of indignation, those of France and of Italy that were supposedly tricked out in false credit, as well as the English and Dutch, who would have been stripped. M. Gilbert Govi, of Florence (*Proceedings* of 2 December), Father [Pietro Angelo] Secchi, of Rome (*Proceedings* of 16 December), M. Thomas Henri Martin, dean of the science faculty at Rennes, and author of a study of the life and work of Galileo (*Proceedings*, 9 December), seemed to agree to appear almost at the same moment to declare to the Academy that these let-ters contradicted everything that was known about Galileo, that the great Florentine astronomer never wrote in French; that the history of his telescope sent to Pascal was a fiction; and M. Harting, an astronomer of Utrecht, wrote (*Proceedings* of 9 December) to express his sadness that the well-known honesty and integrity of his compatriot Huygens had not protected him from these injurious imputations [of claiming as his own the work of others]. The Dutch, particularly hurt, recovered the journal containing the observations of Huygens and his brother regarding Saturn, and even the very telescope they had used.

The debate followed along these lines throughout the entire course of the year 1868, M. Chasles replying to all objections with unabated firmness and periodically opening his briefcase to allow new autographs to emerge, that were placed with the others in the *Proceedings* of the Academy of Sciences. The discussion was not finished at the beginning of the year 1869, but the forger could have hoped, at this period, that he would not be required new expenditures of imagination, because the Academy itself, through the voice of its permanent secretary, gave him the victory, in the session of 5 April 1869, in these words:

> An autograph letter from Galileo to Louis XIII, paraphrased by Louis XIV, *in his own hand,* in which the noted astronomer ingenuously explains to the king of France that he is not as completely blind as it is said, but he is careful not to dispel the fortunate misconception, which was providing the protection of the freedom he was being allowed, such a letter appears to me to be an historical document of incomparable worth.—The permanent secretary adds certain remarks on the obvious antiquarian character evidenced by the manuscripts placed before him on his desk, but he also recognizes, with M. Chasles, that the best guarantees of their origin are the intellectual signs that are evident from reading them. The authors of the letters and notices inserted into the most recent number of the *Proceedings* had written without affectation; but nobody could assume the role of placing himself in the position of writing at will from Galileo, from Milton, from Louis XIV, from Cassini, consistent with circumstances always more or less changing and obscure. *Style is the man,* and it would certainly be difficult for a wretched forger to raise himself to the noble simplicity of Louis XIV, speaking in a voice so often overpowering of the famous persecuted [astronomer] who had been the friend of the king's grandmother, the queen Marie de' Medici.—The other pieces in sufficiently large number that M. Chasles has entered into the *Proceedings,* in the course of almost two years, without the discovery of any inconsistencies that could not have failed to emerge from forgers, present in a manner no less evident the moral certainty of their authenticity.

But precisely at the meeting that followed this official approbation (12 April 1869), the truth became evident through a new development, and compelled the author to undertake new strategic moves. An engineer associated with the Observatory of Paris, M. [Paul Émile] Breton (de Champ), placed before the Academy sixteen notes of Pascal and two fragments of a letter of Galileo published in the *Proceedings* of 1867, that were nothing but passages taken literally from a work that appeared in 1761 and in following years under the title of: *Histoire des philosophes modernes* (history of modern scientists), by Alexandre Savérien, a naval engineer. The scholars had challenged in the name of pure knowledge and of the history of science the documents that were denying the authenticity of all facts heretofore believed; a happy accident at last had demonstrated the method of the forger: it appeared that he could no longer refuse to give up; but at the meeting of 19 April, M. Chasles replied that the certainty with which M. Breton regarded his discovery as a decisive proof of falsification was at once naive and hasty, that one should not forget that biographical encyclopedias are a bloodless product of notices and biographies already known, and that it was Savérien who copied these documents, not the reverse. For support he produced three pieces: (1) an undated letter from Montesquieu to Savérien offering, on the very warm recommendation of J.[ean] Bernouli, to recommend him in turn to Madame de Pompadour, "who possesses," says the letter, "one of the finest and richest collections of documents of all sorts"; (2) an undated letter of Savérien to the marchioness, announcing that he is "returning to her two hundred letters of Copernicus, of Galileo, [René] Descartes, [Pierre] Gassendi, Pascal, Malebranche, [Gottfried Wilhelm, Baron] Leibnitz, Newton, and other scientists …" after having examined them carefully and having made extracts that will be very useful to him, he says, for a history of ancient and modern scientists that he plans to undertake; (3) a letter from the marchioness placing her library and all that she possesses at the disposal of the writer.—It was after this statement of M. Chasles that M. [Urbain Jean Joseph] Le Verrier arose and promised to demonstrate scientifically the falseness of all the items produced by M. Chasles as far as they concerned the supposed borrowings that Newton had made from Pascal.

The debate continues several more months in this new aspect: if M. Breton (de Champ) argues that, for a man who had the library of Madame de Pompadour at his disposal, Savérien most surprisingly said nothing of the non-blindness of Galileo, of the great telescope with which he supposedly had the first view of a satellite of Saturn, and of so many other discoveries, M. Chasles replies (26 April) that Savérien did indeed have access to the marchioness' house, but that he had quickly been banished from her house as a Newtonian, as a friend of Voltaire, as a tactless person; and he produces letters to support these claims. If M. Breton shows that a supposed letter of Montesquieu relating to Newton was an extract from the eulogy for Newton by Fontenelle (3 May, p. 1000), that is, says M. Chasles, because that letter of Montesquieu had passed through the hands of Fontenelle before he drafted the eulogy printed in the *Mémoires de l'Académie des Sciences* [memoirs of the Academy of Sciences]. If then M. Le Verrier observes that Newton died in 1727, that the eulogy by Fontenelle was printed in 1729, and that it was only in 1728 or 1729 that

Montesquieu undertook a voyage to England, from which he did not return until 1731, such that he could not have written this letter until that latter date, but that in that case the letter could not have been copied by Fontenelle in 1727 or 1728, M. Chasles produces at the next meeting (10 May) seven letters, not only by Montesquieu, but by Bernouli, by Fontenelle, and by Maupertuis, according to which Montesquieu supposedly in 1727 and 1728 secretly made two voyages to England of which biographies had never spoken.

Finally, the Academy struck the decisive blow. In a series of meetings that took place on 21 June, [and on] 5, 12, and 26 July 1869, M. Le Verrier presented a dissertation treating in detail all the principal questions that had been raised by the documents of M. Chasles. [He addressed specifically] the relations between Pascal and Newton, those between Pascal and Galileo, the blindness of Galileo, [and] the discovery of the first satellite of Saturn. The author [Le Verrier] again raised all the historical questions, the question of handwriting, [the matter] of style. He exposed more than sixty letters or pieces printed by M. Chasles in the *Proceedings* of the Academy, as supposedly the autograph documents of Newton, of Pascal, of [François de] Malherbe, of Rotrou, of Montesquieu, of [Pierre Louis Moreau de] Maupertuis, of Louis XIV, of Viviani, of Leibnitz, and that were [in fact] merely fragments copied from various works by [Antoine Léonard] Thomas, Voltaire, the Duke [Louis César Le Baume Le Blanc] de La Vallière, Savérien, Father [Giacinto Sigismondo] Gerdil, [Jacques George de] Chauffepié, and others. In the last chapter [of Le Verrier's address], entitled *Of the Masses of the Planets; of the Force of Gravity at Their Surfaces and Their Densities; and of Comets,* he summarized the entire scientific argument. That is, he brought together the irrefutable arguments and diverse objections that had been put forward by M. Duhamel, M. Grant, or others, and those that he [himself] could add to them, in such a manner as to leave no trace of a single innovation that the autograph documents of M. Chasles had sought to introduce into the history of science.

Nevertheless, M. Chasles again would have sought to respond. On more than one occasion, during the course of this communication, he had announced that he would offer a reply, but one incident that occurred at the same time began to shake this confidence, unshakable until then, that he had in the authenticity of his autographs. The Academy was considering, in the course of the discussion, a letter of Galileo, dated 5 November 1639, held by the library of Florence, and that had at first been thought to be in Galileo's hand, but that was recognized to be only in the hand of Galileo's son. Had it been in Galileo's hand, it would have proved that Galileo , in 1639, as M. Chasles contended, had not been blind. Now, at the session of 3 May, M. Chasles announced that, among the two thousand letters from Galileo that he had in his collection, he was going to retrieve the original of that of 5 November, which was unquestionably, according to him, the draft in the hand of Galileo, since it was in the same handwriting as all the others; and he announced further that he was going to send a photograph of that letter to Florence, in order to submit it to expert opinion and thus to verify its authenticity. The official report of the examination made at Florence with all possible care (8 July) arrived at Paris on the tenth, and was communicated to the Academy during the session of July 12; it contained not only a statement contrary to that which M. Chasles expected, but a very fine dissertation, tending to demonstrate that the piece sent had been forged from the text of the last edition of the works of Galileo edited by M. [Engenio] Alberi, in 1856. Immediately, at the same session and at the next (19 July), M. Chasles declared that he had been mistaken in the consignment he had made, that it was another piece that was the good and true draft from Galileo, that he agreed to await the final judgment of the evaluation commission to which he was going to send this newly recovered piece. The piece was sent, despite the objection of M. Le Verrier, who had no trouble demonstrating that the "mysterious author" of these documents, as Le Verrier called him, had certainly had the time to be informed of the objections of the Florentine commission and to remake a better version of his piece; but the response from Florence was that the second version was no more authentic than the first, and that the commission believed it useless to proceed to other examinations of this series of pieces, the forgery of which appeared to them obvious.

At this latest set-back, the weapons finally fell from the hands of M. Chasles, and, at the meeting of the Academy of Sciences of 13 September 1869, he agreed to deliver that statement, which all the newspapers copied, by which he made known the full extent of the delusions that the accused had caused to be engendered in him, and had stayed in his mind for eight years. Nevertheless, even then, the deceit of which he had been the victim was not evident to him with total clarity, since he concluded his declaration with these words: "The collection extends to the earliest days of the Christian era, and even beyond; because it includes some letters and many notes from Julius Caesar and the Roman emperors, from the apostles, chiefly from Saint Jerome, from Boethius, from Cassiodorus, from Gregory of Tours, from Saint Augustine, from several Merovingian kings; a large number from Charlemagne as well as from Alcuin.... I do not at all guarantee these pieces. Whatever they may be, it is certain that their composition, *if they are not authentic*, must have demanded an extended effort, using many references; and if one considers that they match so well with others, from all periods up to the last century, and treat so many different subjects, one cannot believe that they are the work of one person, one forger, who, among other considerations, knows neither Latin, nor Italian, nor the slightest bit of mathematics or the other sciences with which a considerable portion of these documents deal. A mystery remains to be solved, and until it is, *nothing can be concluded with certainty.*"

As to the accused, for a long time he did not lose hope that he could continue forging and have access to M. Chasles. Even after the reading of M. Le Verrier's dissertation and the disastrous responses of the Commission of Florence, he went every day to the Imperial Library to study *La Chroagénésie ou génération des couleurs contre le système de M. Newton* [chromatogenesis or generation of colors contrary to the system of Mr. Newton], by Gautier [Jacques Gautier d'Agoty] (1749), the dictionary of Chauffepié [*Nouveau dictionnaire historique et critique pour servir de supplement ou de continuation au Dictionnaire historique et critique de M. Pierre Bayle*, Amsterdam: I. Chatelau, etc., 1750–1756—a new historical and critical dictionary to serve as a supplement or continuation of the historical and critical dictionary of M. Pierre Bayle; Bayle's dictionary first appeared in 1696],the correspondence of Galileo, the collection of autographs intitled *Isographie,*[1] and we found in the collection of M. Chasles one final witness to the efforts made by the forger up to the last moment to maintain his story and complete the ruin of Newton: it is the following letter addressed to this great man:

22 November 1688

Sir, I have read in times past certain manuscript fragments of your book dealing with the mathematical principles of natural philosophy [science] with all the care I was able. I once again read them recently, in order to tell you my feelings, as you asked me to do. As far as I am concerned, the work is perfect. You know precisely how to organize and how to use the materials that M. Pascal furnished you while, of course, adding to these much of your own. While this is obvious, I nevertheless regret one thing and allow me to make this confession, that is to say, forgive my outspokenness in making it to you, which is that you have tried too hard to dissimulate. You cannot be unaware that there remain traces of the writings of P(ascal) and G(alileo). I want to admit to you fully that I am aware of some of these writings; I have compared them with your work, and I have had definite proof that you must have had copies of these. There can be no doubt, and I regret one thing, which is that in seeking to dissemble you have used certain calculations, that you have included certain figures, that,

---

1 *Isographie des hommes celebres; ou, Collection de facsimile de lettres autographes et de signatures* (Paris: A. Mesnier, 1828–1830) *[Autographs of famous people; or, a collection of facsimiles of autograph letters and signatures].*

from my viewpoint, are not as precise as those found in the writings in question. That is why, sir, if you ever reprint this work, I urge you to pay attention to these calculations, relating to the distance between planets, etc., etc. I do not say to you . . .

The forger was apprehended during the preparation of this involved draft. The letter was not finished and it is not known who would have become the signer.

Library of St. Geneviève, Paris

II

Overview of the Collection of False Autographs Bought by M. Chasles

━━━━━━━━ ❯❮(❖)❯❮ ━━━━━━━━

*I*T IS A VERY SMALL PORTION of the mass of autographs bought by M. Chasles from the forger Vrain Lucas that passed, from 1867 to 1869, before the eyes of the Academy, and that it had printed in its *Weekly Proceedings*. The spurious autograph letters and pieces inserted, in part or in their entirety, in this collection, number 381. Now, M. Chasles declared to the Academy, on 13 September 1869 (*Proceedings*, p. 648), that he had bought more than twenty thousand (at a cost of about 150,000 francs), and in the examination that the experts made, without being perfectly certain that they had every item, they found 27,320 sent by 660 different people and addressed to hundreds of others, thus, ... 27,320

In addition, the false letters of Rotrou, Pascal, etc., given by M. Chasles to the library of the Institute of France, to the number of 25

Next, 74 authentic manuscripts of the 16th, 17th, and 18th centuries, worthless pieces, of which 22 were altered by fraudulent notes that the seller had added to them to create the impression that they had come from famous people, thus 22

In addition, one hundred five works, almost all of them printed, that he [Lucas] altered in the same way by false provenances and fake annotations . 105

Total 27,472

These last two categories deserve special mention. It will be informative to explain to what extent they deserve to be included in the same group as the false autographs.

When, in the course of the preliminary investigation, the accused was asked to acknowledge, which he did without any hesitation, the thousands of autographs he had produced, he expressed his great amazement not to see as well the authentic documents and the printed books that he had included among the false pieces in the dealings he had had with M. Chasles. "I recall among others," he said in a statement of the case that he drafted concerning this point, "an old parchment signed by Charlemagne, another of the same period, signed by Alcuin ..., a very old manuscript, on vellum, signed Gerbert, who later became pope under the name of Silvester II; two charters, on parchment, signed by the king Saint Louis; another parchment, signed by Blanche of Castile .... I considered that the money that M. Chasles gave me was not so much payment for my labors, but more a compensation for the true and genuine documents that I delivered to him at the same time as the extracts in the form of feigned letters. It was always M. Chasles who fixed the price of these objects after carefully considering and examining them. This was the manner of our dealings that his notes can verify. I would deliver to him a parcel of items; in this lot were to be found genuine documents, that sometimes would be worth 400 francs, more or less, in dealings of this sort of material, excluding the notes and the extracts, in the form of feigned letters that were intermingled with them, and that I used to deliver to him at the same time. When M. Chasles had examined these documents carefully, I would ask him what he would give me for the entire lot; he would sometimes tell me 100, 150, or 200 francs.... I would sometimes reply to him that he would have to give a bit more; then he would say to me again: 'I am going to give you 300 francs. But you will give me *into the bargain* one hundred or two hundred, or three hundred other pieces.' That would depend on the type. In certain cases, he would say to me: 'You will give me a hundred letters of Louis XIV, a hundred letters of Galileo, a hundred letters of Pascal, or of Newton, etc.' Now, I would agree, particularly since I knew that I was not cheating, because the authentic pieces that I was delivering were alone worth the amount he gave me, and sometimes even more."

When the accused begins the list of genuine pieces that he supposedly supplied with some documents signed by Charlemagne, by Alcuin, by Gerbert, by Saint Louis, by Blanche of Castile, he demonstrates to what extent even now he is unaware that such pieces could not even exist. As to the value of those [documents] that were authentic, the appraisal did not confirm Lucas' assertion, because it placed a value of 500 francs on the entirety of the genuine pieces given to M. Chasles for his 150,000 francs; but furthermore, it would be difficult to know how their price was set. While they were not actually paid for and were thrown in only as an afterthought as part of a lot, they were, according to all the evidence, without any kind of value, even in the opinion of M. Chasles, or at most when they had any value at all they were well paid for separately. The genuine pieces were not paid for at a price less exorbitant than were the spurious ones, since every piece of writing, every notebook, every printed book the value of which could be increased by some fraudulent reference was presented to M. Chasles only when decked out with such addition. The complete list of printed books purchased from Lucas by M. Chasles confirms this statement, since all carry false autographs of famous people.

Now, here is an example, probably an example extremely well done, but perfectly obvious, of the use made of these references added to a printed book. Before the eyes of the tribunal passed a little volume in octavo entitled: *Cento favole bellissime de'_più illustri antichi & moderni autori Greci, & Latini, da M. G. Mario Verdizotti* [One hundred most lovely stories by the most illustrious ancient and modern Greek and Latin authors, by Monsieur Giovanni Mario Verdizotti], Venice, 1613. This is a book without the half-title, without end-papers, stained, dirty, badly printed, filled with worn engravings and bound in the most commonplace calf. But it carries on the title-page: *Ex libris J. de La Fontaine*, and on the back of the cover, facing the title, these words written in the hand of one of the Monsieurs de Boisjourdain, an imaginary family [authors' note: Imaginary in this instance. But there actually existed a family de Boisjourdain, or more accurately de Boisjourdan, about which documents are preserved in the office of titles (Imperial Library)] behind which the forger hid himself[1] and with which we will soon have occasion to become better acquainted:

> "This book is extremely rare" (says Monsieur the Count de Boisjourdain); "only one copy is known in a library in Venice, and moreover, this present copy is unique because it belonged to the good-natured La Fontaine and inspired his delightful fables. Also I paid dearly for this volume at an auction. Monsieur the Duke de La Vallière having raised the bidding to 900 livres, I was forced to pay more. Later, monsieur the duke made me several offers in order to acquire the book and I never wanted to let go of it. Its engravings are exceedingly delicate.

This note, joined with the signature of La Fontaine on the title, had the effect of inducing M. Chasles to pay for this worthless old book the unbeliev-able price of *eight hundred francs*. But almost as soon as his seller left, the buyer

---

1 The Boisjourdain family was prominent in the religious wars that plagued France in the sixteenth century. According to a manuscript note in the copy of the translator, what prompted Lucas to choose this name was, however, a work entitled *Mélanges historiques, satiriques et anecdotiques de M. de B.[ois] Jourdain, ecuyer de la grand ecurie du roi (Louis XV); contenant des details ignores ou peu connus sur les evenements et les personnes marquantes de la fin du regne de Louis XIV, des pre-mieres années de celui de Louis XV, et de la regence* [historical, satirical, and anecdotal miscellany by M. de Bois Jordain, equerry to the Master of the Horse of the king (Louis XV), containing details unknown or little known concerning the prominent events and people from the end of the reign of Louis XIV, to the first years of that of Louis XV, and of the Regency]. The note adds that this work could have given Lucas the idea that the author was a collector of manuscript material.

had the idea, too late, to consult the *Manuel du libraire* [bookseller's guide] of [Jacques Charles] Brunet, to confirm the rarity of the work and its high price. Brunet gave him information very different from that he was seeking. A copy of the first edition (Venice, 1570), with engravings in mint condition and bound in blue morocco, was sold for 48 francs at the auction of La Vallière [1783]; in ordinary binding, the same edition was worth 15 to 24 francs; a copy of later editions (1577, 1599) generally was worth from 6 to 9 francs, and copies of the edition of 1613, the very one that was in the hands of M. Chasles, did not even have the distinction of a price noted in Brunet. M. Chasles, in his initial shock, could not stop himself from writing to Lucas to complain of such dealing, and the latter returned, in the name of his Monsieur de Boisjourdain, some sort of excuse and with the expression of the desire to offer to M. Chasles compensation for this matter; and he offered him [M. Chasles] in fact a dozen letters of Pascal, but under the condition that M. Chasles would add another one hundred francs. Thus the matter was resolved: this book worth 2 or 3 francs, and a dozen spurious letters of Pascal yielded the seller 900 francs ready money.

It is quite likely that this exorbitant dealing would have been undertaken more than once, because M. Chasles also possesses a small volume without value, printed in 1711 (*Nouveaux mémoires sur l'histoire du cartésianisme* [new dissertations on the history of Cartesian thought])[2] enriched with spurious notes given under double warranty, doubly false, of Newton and of the imaginary Count de Boisjourdain, who supposedly paid 1,200 francs in the year 1772. It must be added that it is true that the most insignificant books can suddenly receive considerable value if one transforms them into books containing either annotations, or complete letters, or small literary accounts, or mere signatures of people famous in history.

The lot of 27,472 pieces noted above, as the totality of the collection of M. Chasles, is incomplete in the sense that, if their author had fulfilled the promises he had made, he would have been obliged to deliver another 2,949. This is the exact number that comes from a piece seized in his possession and containing a settlement reached in complete agreement between M. Chasles and himself to repay the first of the sums that he had advanced to the seller. It must be that they were relying heavily on the famous collection of de Boisjourdain and [expecting] that it contained all imaginable treasures by way of autographs, since the two parties stipulated in advance, as obliged to be supplied by it, almost 3,000 letters or notes, among which one notes 36 pieces from King James, 110 from the poet Rotrou, 140 from Louis XIV, 80 from Montesquieu, 40 from Lorenzo de' Medici, 40 from the good [Jean] Dunois,

---

2 The actual title is *Nouveaux mémoires pour servir à l'histoire du Cartésianisme,* by Pierre-Daniel Huet (Paris: Raymond Mazieres, 1711)

63 from Louis XI, 274 (receipts) from Joan of Arc, 89 from Copernicus, 122 from Rabelais, 53 from Boethius, 22 from the geographer Ptolemy, 87 from Augurinus, the friend of Pliny [the Younger], etc.

What were, according to M. Chasles, or more precisely according to the statements of his supplier, the nature, the extent, the history of this imaginary collection? The bulk of the materials of which it was composed originated with the baronet Claude-François Blondeau de Charnage [authors' note: See M. Chasles, *Proceedings*, 12 August 1867, p. 271, and 14 October, p. 621], infantry officer and amateur genealogist, who in fact gathered, towards the middle of the eighteenth century, an important collection of titles of which he printed the inventory (5 volumes in duodecimo) in 1764 and in the years following. But the collection of Blondeau de Charnage was very badly chosen as the source of the autograph letters and papers of M. Chasles, because it was composed mainly of charters and title-deeds on parchment. In truth, it was claimed, that to Blondeau de Charnage's collection were joined many other diverse collections [authors' note: partially listed by M. Chasles, *Proceedings*, 28 October 1867, p. 690], and principally that of the papers of Desmaiseaux. The totality of these documents, forming a considerable body, supposedly had been, in the period of the [French] Revolution, the property of one Monsieur the Count de Boisjourdain, who supposedly immigrated to the United States in 1791 [authors' note: M. Chasles, *Proceedings*, 13 September 1869, p. 646] and supposedly took his collection there with him. Now it was still the property of the same family, that is to say of its last heir, a man very old and very attached to the precious documents he had inherited, who would part with them only with the greatest sorrow, and under the expressed condition that he read each piece before relinquishing it. The collection was, moreover, scattered without any order in the attic of a town-house, in Paris; it included, apart from the papers, a good number of printed books, and it was mingled with a quantity of other papers and other books. Vrain Lucas, who was only, he said, the representative, the agent of the *old man*, as he [Lucas] called him, not having permission to reveal his name, always had the task of searching for the items under the direction of the owner, to unearth them rather at random, and received for his total remuneration 25% [commission] on the sales he made. It was through this state of affairs that he explained the randomness of the communications that he provided to M. Chasles, bringing him, instead of complete files, scattered pieces appertaining to the most disparate people, or also, after having brought an important letter, finding afterwards one, two, and even three other copies of the same piece, all with variations, all in almost the same handwriting, such that it was impossible to say which of these pieces was the original, which the draft, which the copy. This confusion was very favorable for the projects of the forger.

Vrain Lucas never abandoned the modest role of agent that he gave himself; he did not at all seek to inflate his importance. He sometimes supplied autographs the signature of which appeared to him illegible, or signed by some person that was to him, he said, completely unknown; but he diffidently suggested to M. Chasles the idea of looking in the *Biographie universelle* [universal biography] for such or such a name, and the mystery was cleared up. Often, too, he asked M. Chasles to add to the price of these purchases, on which price he had only, he said, his commission, some bonus from which he [Lucas] alone would profit. These prices meanwhile were not low (although the inexhaustible quantity of the goods must necessarily have driven the prices lower), considering that M. Chasles paid 500 francs for the first letter of Molière that Lucas forged for him. And so great a desire for these autographs seized him that he enjoined the accused above all not to sell to anyone else, to the extent that having learned one day that four brief notes of Margaret of Alençon, Rabelais, Montaigne, and Rotrou had come into the possession of another person, M. Belley, who worked in the ministry of public works, he hastened to go to repurchase them for a price of 200 francs. Vrain Lucas was so certain of the infatuation of his buyer, that he came to speak with him [M. Chasles] of different renewals of reservations that were torturing the old man; the old man had a relative, almost as old as himself, a retired soldier: he had consulted him about the advisability of the sales allowed to M. Chasles, and the soldier had shown himself completely opposed and angry, such that M. de Boisjourdain begged M. Chasles to return the pieces and take back all his money, a proposition that the buyer totally rejected, as he who made it well expected. Finally, that which gave the final sign of the enthusiasm with which M. Chasles allowed himself to be carried away, was that declaration, many times repeated by him, that if he had this man arrested, it was not at all to have him punished for his fraud, but to prevent the sale to foreigners of the remainder of the Boisjourdain collection and so deprive France of it.

The great quantity of the pieces forged for M. Chasles was much less amazing than the very nature of some of these autographs. People quoted, during the trial of Libri [Guglielmo Libri (1802-1869) stole many manuscripts and books from various French libraries that he had been appointed to inspect. He also, like Lucas, manufactured provenances, adding "Di Dante Alighieri" to one fourteenth century manuscript. On 20 March 1848 the French government began legal proceedings against Libri, who had fled to England on 29 February. Libri was tried in absentia and convicted in June, 1850. When Chasles' documents were first suspected of being forgeries, some thought that Libri was responsible for these, or was at least the mastermind behind Lucas' efforts.], a witty song: *The Seller of Autographs*, aimed, twenty-five years ago, against the abuses of a trade subject to much fraud and about which the author certainly believed he was giving himself to exaggeration, to absurdity, in the lines where he said,

> I have brought from Astrakan
> The papers of Genghis Khan
> And from the convent at Mt. Tabor
> One of Nebuchadnezzar
> And then I am on the track
> Of an antique papyrus
> Shown by a hellenist to be
> An autograph of Cadmus

But the author of the little song would be today speaking the pure and simple truth. Among the autographs of M. Chasles, we have those of the sage Thales, of Pythagorus, of Anaximenes, of Sappho, who yield nothing to Nebuchadnezzar in antiquity, who greatly surpass him in literary attraction, and as to papyrus, it is completely beyond the scope of the house of Boisjourdain, all of whose forgeries, without a single exception, are executed on sheets of coarse laid paper borrowed from old record books. M. Chasles only feebly indicated the antiquity of part of his collection, when he made to the Academy, in the session of 13 September (p. 649), that confession that we have already recorded: "The collection extends to the earliest days of the Christian era and even beyond, because it includes some letters and many notes from Julius Caesar and the Roman emperors; from the apostles, chiefly from Saint Jerome, from Boethius, from Cassiodorus, from Gregory of Tours, from Saint Augustine, from several Merovingian kings; a large number from Charlemagne as well from Alcuin."

That which is not less surprising than the rest, is that all these pieces, supposedly ancient, are written in French, it is true in antiquated French, apparent in the old forms of words and affecting a spurious archaism, but too awkward for them to be presented as modern translations, against which moreover is opposed the nature of the script that aims, on its part, by its rudeness, if not by its accuracy, for an antique appearance. Thus the letters of Charlemagne, among others, are written entirely in elogated characters, evidently inspired by the look of official documents of the eighth and ninth centuries, the first line of which usually is set out in characters of this type, and the forgeries often end with an imitation of the imperial monogram. For this part of his work, as for the pieces relating to the history of seventeenth-century science, the art of the forger consisted in all likelihood of claiming nothing, of hiding, on the contrary, under his role of intermediary, and of allowing the curiosity, the joy, the passion of the buyer to create by themselves the sense of the age and the value of these pieces. That is what M. Chasles did, and what he expressed in the midst of the Academy (13 September), when, after having mentioned his autographs of the Roman emperors and the apostles, he sought to explain to himself this extraordinary occurrence, which was still very unclear to him, by adding, "Here, according to these documents, is the source of this treasure. The abbey of Tours was very rich in ancient documents. Alcuin, who was the abbot there, enriched it further by having searches made in Italy and in foreign lands by anyone he could meet from these places. Rabelais, who was a great lover of pieces of this sort, and who was encouraged in his quest by François I and Margaret d'Angoulême, knew of these archives of the abbey of Tours, and had a considerable number of copies and translations made. All these were found at his hermitage at Langey, an outlying building on the property of [Guillaume] du Bellay,[3] and supposedly passed into the collection of the manager [Nicolas Joseph] Foucault, who died, at the beginning of the last century, a member of the Academy of Inscriptions. [The Académie des Inscriptions et Belles-Lettres, 23 quai de Conti, Paris, concerns itself with orientalism, classical antiquity, and the Middle Ages.]

We place before the eyes of the reader copies of some of the pieces that, however strange they may be in the choice of their supposed authors, are no less so in the ideas and the style that have been lent them.

Thales to the most illustrious and most dreaded Prince Ambigat, king of the Gauls, greetings.

Most powerful prince you have requested of me some maxims that you know I have collected regarding the way to govern and conduct oneself well. Herewith you will find that I hold you in high regard, for to live well it is necessary first of all to abstain from anything that one finds reprehensible in others. Happiness of the body consists in health and that of the spirit in knowledge. According to my thinking water is the principle of all things despite its homogeneous nature; it is disposed to take all sorts of shapes, and to become a tree, metal, gold, blood, wine, wheat, etc.,

---

3 Rabelais was friendly with Guillaume du Bellay, seigneur de Langey (d.1543); in his will du Bellay even left Rabelais money. However, Rabelais probably spent his last years in Paris; he was buried in Saint-Paul's Cemetery in that city. Lucas may have mistaken the priory of Ligugé, where Rabelais lived in the 1520s, for Langey, or he may simply have used the friendship of Du Bellay and Rabelais to concoct his story. François I protected Rabelais from clerical critics, but the king did not urge Rabelais to collect and transcribe ancient manuscripts.

because vapor is the ordinary nourishment of the stars and the Ocean their cupbearer. As to the nature of astronomy about which you have asked me for some observations, my discoveries accompany this letter along with some designs of the globe that I have divided into five parallel circles; you will also find some of my observations touching the physical reasons of eclipses of the sun and of the moon, in all of which I will be happy if you are satisfied with this [information] that you request of me for the instruction of the princes your nephews . Yours truly this tenth of June in the year of Rome 155.

Thales

Archimedes to his dearly beloved Hieron, greetings.

My dearly beloved according to my thinking the languages that today are spread out among all the countries of the world must have been formed from the wreckage of the original language that appears to be the Celtic that appears to be the same language that Moses used whom one must consider as the most ancient author who presents himself to us in the course of time. This great man can be seen in two aspects, in the first as the voice and minister of the laws of the all powerful [i.e., God]. He is the leader of the chosen people, he is the creator of an admirable government which all rulers must have as their model, in the second aspect Moses is a sublime author, plain precise in his narration. As it is according to the degree of imagination that one must judge people, few people have had one as strong and as brilliant as Moses just as I will say in my other account, where this Moses will be considered not as a legislator but as a poet. Yours truly this twentieth of February.

Archimedes

King Alexander to his dearly beloved Aristotle greetings.

My friend I am not satisfied with what you have made public through your books that you must guard under the seal of secrecy, for you thus profane their worth. Now then I engage you to retrieve these from uninitiated hands and no more henceforth make them public without my consent. As to what you asked me about going to make a voyage to the land of the Gauls, in order to learn there the wisdom of the druids, of whom Pythagorus made so beautiful a panegyric, not only do I allow you, but I urge you to do so for the good of my people, because you are not unaware of the esteem I have for that nation that I consider as being that which has brought the light [of learning] into the world. Yours truly, this twentieth of the Kalends of May, in the year of the 105th Olympiad.

Alexander

Queen Cleopatra
to her dearly beloved Emperor Julius Caesar

My dearly beloved[,] our son Caesarion is doing well. I hope that soon, he will be in condition to endure the voyage from here to Marseilles where I intend to have him instructed both because of the good air that one breathes there and the fine things that are taught there. I ask you then to tell me how long you will remain in these provinces because I want to escort our son there myself and I beg on this occasion to tell you my dearly beloved the contentment that I feel when I find myself near you and while waiting for this I engage the gods to have you in mind. The eleventh of March, the year of Rome 709.

Cleopatra

Safe conduct of Trogue Pompey

I grant the return of the young Trogue Pompey to the Emperor Julius Caesar his master and order those to whom these letters come to allow him to pass freely and to help him in case of need.

This tenth of the Kalends of May . . . (date torn).

Vercingetorix

On the back.

This is the letter that Vercingetorix the leader of the Gauls gave to Troque Pompey who had come to bring him a letter from Julius Caesar, so that he could return freely to his master.

Lazarus the resurrected to St. Peter

My dearly beloved Peter you report to me that you have observed in the writings of Caesar and in those of Cicero that one of the principal parts of the religion of the druids used to be the sacrifice of savage people, that is true; they used to take in an erroneous sense the principle that a person cannot better acknowledge the life that God has given him than by offering to Him the life of a person. They continued this inhuman and bloody practice until the time of Cicero, that is why he says that they sully and profane their temple and their altars by offering human victims there, and here Cicero is right to revile a cult sufficiently barbarous in saying: a strange thing, in order to fulfill what they owe to their religion it is necessary beforehand that they disgrace it by some murder, they cannot be religious without being homicides, the infamy of this horrible maxim has reflected on all the Gauls even though it was practiced only in certain provinces, but the arms and the conquests of the Romans have put an end to this infamy and I do not believe that it is practiced anywhere now. So be it, this tenth of August 47.

Lazarus

Magdalene to her dearly beloved Lazarus.

My dearly beloved brother that which you have sent me regarding Peter the apostle of our gentle Jesus gives me hope that soon he will appear here and I am prepared to receive him well, our sister Martha rejoices at the prospect also. Her health is failing badly and I fear her death, that is why I recommend her to your good prayers. the good girls who have come to place themselves under our protection are wonderful to us and make much of us it is impossible to be nicer. it is as you say my dearly beloved brother that we are very fond of our sojourn in these provinces of Gaul, that we have no desire to leave it, just as some of our friends suggest to us. Do you not find that these Gauls, who we were told are barbarous peoples are not at all that way and to judge them as we have come to know them, it must be from there that the light of learning must come. I will say nothing more except that I have a great desire to see you and pray our Lord to hold you in grace this tenth of June 46.

Magdalene

The same to the king of the Burgundians.

Most exalted and most redoubtable Prince of the Burgundians greetings from me Magdalene, sister of Martha and of Lazarus, accept my respects and with them this casket. In it you will find the letter of which I spoke to you that was sent to me by Jesus of Nazareth a few days before his Passion. And this letter is accompanied by two maxims that are the bases of the religion of Christ. Therefore hold these precious objects in esteem and remember my instructions. Thus you will be happy and you will live in peace, which is what she who considers herself your most grateful servant wishes you. The year of the Lord, 46.

Magdalene

The general of the Franks to the duke of the Moors.

Moorish Duke, I have read your menacing letters but I little fear their contents. Gather if you can all the forces of Africa and come at their head to swoop down on my country. You will see me fly to meet them. I need only small armies to defeat large ones. A handful of Frenchmen suffices me to disperse a multitude. Do not hope therefore to see me betray those who have begged my protection; place if you wish a ransom price for your [female] prisoner and gold will be lavished on you, if not respect her as you should and I promise the same consideration for your *seraglio and your favorites. Whereupon I pray the Eternal to keep you in His care. This tenth of June 732.*

Charles Martel

Charlemagne to Alcuin.

Most learned and dearly beloved Alcuin, I rather think just as you told me that long ago the Celtic language, which appears to be the mother of all languages, was better known among all the people of the earth and that Pythagorus, Plato, Aristotle, etc., etc. not only knew it but also taught it this is what is evident from the various documents that you have sent me and that I return to you. These documents are letters from these same Pythagorus, Plato, Aristotle and also the king Alexander of Macedon and of learned travelers, geographers, and historians and also mathematicians who have taken together traversed the two ends of the world, some to the north and others to the south, I charge you to preserve these writings as precious objects and to make accurate copies for me.

This immense collection was destined to shine in its entirety or almost its entirety in the sun of publicity. Many times, in the course of the discussions maintained by M. Chasles at the Academy, those of his colleagues who supported him urged him to take this great means to reply to all the criticism, and many times he pledged himself to undertake this vast publication. It was already begun, in the sense that M. Chasles already had had a copy made of each piece. Moreover, some of them had nearly received or actually had received the honors of public notice. Thus, in 1865, at the request of M. de Lucca, a famous Neopolitan chemist, M. Chasles had sent to Florence one of his autographs of Dante to appear in the patriotic celebration that the Italians were observing that year in commemoration of the six-hundreth anniversary of the birth of their great poet. But the autograph was delayed en route and reached M. de Lucca only after the ceremony. M. Chasles also proposed giving to some public library in the region of Chartres the considerable collection that he possessed of autograph letters of Rotrou, a poet of that area, and he had agreed with the bookseller Garnier, of Chartres, on the outlines of a book of which these pieces would supply the substance.

In 1866, M. Chasles also generously offered to a foreign Academy with which he is associated, the Royal Academy of Belgium, two of his letters of the emperor Charles V (M. Chasles had fifteen of these) addressed to Rabelais. The permanent secretary of the Academy, M. [Lambert] Ad.[olphe Jacques] Quételet, presented them with the letter of transmission of M. Chasles at the session of 13 October (*Bulletin of the Academy*, 35th year, p.204); both were printed in the proceedings of the meeting (p. 206), and one of them was given in facsimile (p. 478). But it must be said that at the first sight of these two absurd pieces [authors' note: Here is the essence: "Master Rabelais, you who have a fine and subtle mind, would you be able to gratify me? I have promised 1,000 écus to the person who will find how to square the circle and no mathematician has been able to solve this problem. I have thought that you who are clever in all matters would gratify me, and if you do so you will receive great recompense for it. May God come to your assistance. The tenth of September 1542. Charles, To master François Rabelais, learned in all sciences and good letters."] the archivist of Belgium, M. [Louis Prosper] Gachard, protested forcefully against their authenticity (5 November, p. 343), and with more force still (p. 544) when he had seen the original that had been presented.

Two other letters from the collection of M. Chasles have the honor of appearing in a learned book published in 1867; they are by the historian of the diocese of Paris, the abbot [Jean] Lebeuf, and were included in the correspondence of this scholar, printed by Monsieurs [Maximilien] Quentin, archivist of [the department of] Yonne, and [Aimé-Alexandre] Cherest, a lawyer. It is true that these are not at all imaginary letters; they were only prepared by the forger of autographs: one, of 9 April 1735, from an original letter extant at the Imperial Library (Correspondence of the president [of the Parliament of Dijon, Jean] Bouhier, vol. IV, p. 319); the other, from the beginning and end of a letter of [Jean] Lebeuf inserted in the *Mercure de France* of the month of September 1742 (p. 1915).

Perhaps other unfortunate publications were made from the autographs in the Chasles collection; those that we have cited are the only ones about which we have known until now.

III

Other Possible Forgeries by Lucas

───═»《《◉》》═───

E HAVE SPOKEN UNTIL NOW only of the autographs provided to the collection of M. Chasles by the forger. The industry of this latter also betook itself elsewhere with success. At least in this regard we have found one glaring and public example in a small volume about which we are going to speak.

In 1865 there appeared at Versailles, under the imprint of Beau, printer-bookseller, a small volume in octavo, of 216 pages, entitled: *Glanes et Regains, récoltés dans les archives de la maison Du Prat, recueillis et réunis par le marquis Du Prat, membre correspondant de l'Académie de Clermont-Ferrand* [gleanings and aftermaths, harvested in the archives of the family Du Prat, collected and reunited by the marquis Antoine Théodore Du Prat, corresponding member of the Academy of Clermont-Ferrand]. One finds in this work fifty-two letters of the sixteenth and seventeenth centuries, of which fifteen are presented as having been copied from the originals preserved in the archives of the family [authors' note: Here are the titles of these letters: Letter from François I to Chancellor Du Prat, 20 July 1527: The beauty of His Holiness Leo X; Magnificence of the religious ceremonies; details of the Pragmatic Sanction [of Bourges, 1438, which limited papal power. It was replaced by the French concordat of 1516 between Pope Leo X and François I], p. 5.—Letter from the same to the same, 12 March: On certain rumors and scandals of the court, p. 6.—Letter from Charles V to King François I, regarding a mission to him [Charles V] the Chancellor Du Prat was charged with, p. 7—Letter from Margaret d'Angoulême, duchess of Alençon, to the Chancellor Du Prat. She congratulates him on the powers that her brother the king conferred upon him; she signs herself: "Your very humble servant Margaret," p. 15 and 16.—Letter from Margaret d'Angoulême, duchess of Alençon, to the Chancellor Du Prat. She reveals to him the clauses of the treaty imposed by the Emperor Charles V. January 1526; p. 18.—Letter from the same to the same. She asks him about the life of Chapelet Du Prat, 15 May 1526, p. 23.—Letter from the same to Antoine Le Maçon. She asks him for a copy of his translation of Boccaccio, 10 May 1538, p.23—Letter from François Rabelais to M. de Chastillon. He tells him by what ruse he obtained an audience with Chancellor Du Prat, 20 May 1549, p. 33.— Letter from Catherine de Medici to King Henry III. She informs him of the excellent qualities of Anne Du Prat, she recommends her to him, and urges him to reveal himself to her with complete confidence, p. 113.—Letter from Anne Du Prat to Sir Jehan d'Avost, officer of the queen. She sends him some manuscripts of Petrarch that she has from Queen Catherine de Medici, p. 114.— Letter from [Pierre de Bourdeilles] Brantosme to M. [Pierre] de L'estoile, on the death of Madame de Bourbon, wife of the High Constable. The Chancellor Du Prat urges the Duchess d'Angoulême to marry the prince who has become a widower, signed Bourdeille, seigneur de Brantosme, p. 148.—Letter from Montaigne to Antoine Du Prat, seigneur de Nantouillet, Provost of Paris, 24 August, p.152.—Letter from the same to the same, 22 November 1582, p. 153.— Letter from M. de Thou to M. de Harlay. He there discusses the journey of Montaigne to Nantouillet, the causes of the present troubles, and the assassination of Anne de Barbançon, wife of Antoine Du Prat, p. 164.—Letter from the same to Brantôme. He there discusses the love intrigue of the Count d'Angoulême regarding Mary of England, wife of King Louis XII, and the obstacle that Antoine Du Prat placed in the way of its growth, p. 165.], which, according to the editor, contained many others. The period when these pieces were deposited in the aforesaid archives could not be very ancient, because they were all forged by Lucas, as it is easy to assure oneself of the fact by comparing their text with that of the letters in the Chasles collection. There are the same turns of phrase, the same unrefined tone, the same blunders [authors' note: A letter from François I to Chancellor Du Prat begins thus: "You never are right, M. the chancellor, to be *charmed* by the distinguished look and by the *pretension* of sanctity of *Leo X*." The author does not know that the king would not say informally *Leo X*, especially in an official dispatch; that *pretension* would not have the sense of favorable turn of mind but that of condescension; that charming, in the sense of delighted, dates only from the seventeenth century; finally, that *oncques* [the opening word of the forged letter] means just the opposite of what he wants to express, and that in using the word the king says to his chancellor that he is completely wrong.—Another letter of the same to the same (p.6): "Come *this evening, after matins,* to attend on us." This is exactly as if he would say: come this evening, after daybreak; etc., etc.], the same misspellings and the same kind of banal ideas serving to construct a letter. Some observations will suffice to put the fact beyond doubt.

Margaret d'Angoulême asks Chancellor Du Prat, in a letter of 15 May 1526, whether he can give her any information about a person of his name who appears "in the work of Jean Boccaccio, Florentine poet, Master Chapelet Du

Prat, who after his death was called Saint Chapelet." [The first story of
Boccaccio's *Decameron* deals with Chapelet du Prat.] She wishes to know
whether he was in any way the chancellor's ancestor. Margaret apparently took
this question seriously to heart and was little satisfied with the reply of the
chancellor, because twelve years later, on 10 May 1538, she writes to Antoine Le
Maçon, translator of Boccaccio, in these terms:

> I pray you, Sir, to send me the translation of the first story found
> in the novel of Boccaccio the Florentine, *concerning Master Chapelet*
> *Du Prat, regarded in his life as an evil person, and who after his death*
> *was reputed holy, under the title of Saint Chapelet.* I need this transla-
> tion as soon as possible. I beg you therefore to attend to this matter
> as soon as you can and please me. Yours truly.
>
> Margaret

This letter, where the italicized words are borrowed from the very translation of Antoine Le Maçon, would suffice in itself to establish the falseness of
these documents very carefully preserved in the archives of the Du Prat family.
But what is truly odd, is that Vrain Lucas, with his pitiful autographs that reveal
forgery in every line, took in his net the author of *Causeries d'un curieux* [con-
versations of an inquiring person], the most experienced of collectors, he whom
the sellers of autographs have called, for the past twenty-five years: "Monsieur
Feuillet [Felix-Sébastien Feuillet de Conches], the premier of French auto-
graphiles."

One finds, in fact, in *Glanes et Regains*, two letters of Montaigne that, in
their style and spelling, do not in any way resemble the genuine letters that we
possess of the author of the *Essays*. One reads for example in one of these pieces
the word *aristogratic* for *aristocratic*, an error that betrays the hand of Lucas and
that so well calls again to mind that phrase of a memorandum addressed by him
to his judges: "I intentionally left indications that could reveal that these pieces
were fictional and *apogryphal*."

These two letters of Montaigne had already appeared the previous year
(1864) in the third volume of *Causeries d'un curieux*. They had been communicated to M. Feuillet de Conches by the Marquis Du Prat. M. Feuillet de
Conches, whose long experience would appear never to be at fault, when it
comes to autographs, printed these letters without expressing the slightest
doubt of their authenticity. Moreover he remarked that, contrary to his custom,
Montaigne, in these letters, took care in his writing and used periods, commas,
and accents that he hardly ever used except whimsically. Even the noun *doloir*
invented by the forger did not give him [Feuillet de Conches] pause. Here is
the text of the letter:

Montaigne to Antoine Du Prat

Monseigneur, you wish to know from me how the king should maintain the three reins by which absolute power is regulated. Here is my sentiment. And first regarding the three reins about which I have already spoken in my previous letter, by which the power of the prince and monarch that is called tyrannical when it is used contrary to reason is curbed and reduced to civility, and thus reputed just, bearable, and *aristogratic*, I say on authority that the king cannot do anything more agreeable, more pleasing, and more profitable to his subjects, and more honorable and laudable to himself than in maintaining the stated three things by which he acquires the name of good king, of most Christian, of father of the people and well beloved, and all other titles that a valiant and glorious prince can acquire. Such is my *doloir* and advice. Whereupon I pray God, monseigneur, to grant you good health and long life. This 24 November 1582. Your servant,

Montaigne.

"This word *doloir*," says M. Feuillet in a note, "does not afford a clear meaning, and one sees that Montaigne was right in confessing that he wrote his letters *hastily*. Borel, Lacombe, Roquefort, Duez [Pierre Borel, *Dictionnaire des termes du vieux françois*, 1750; François Lacombe, *Dictionnaire du vieux langage françois*, 1766-1767; Jean-Baptiste-Bonaventure Roquefort, *Dictionnaire étymologique de la langue françoise*, 1829; Nathanael Duez, author of various bilingual and multilingual dictionaries and of *Le Vrai et parfait guidon de la langue française*, 1669] cite *douloir* [to suffer, grieve, moan, lament] only as a verb, whereas it is used here as a noun; now, in giving the word the meaning of concern, if not of sorrow, what would be the application here? Did Montaigne wish, by this word, to express only the idea of an opinion, of an impression, in a prim manner? It is perhaps a Périgordian or Gascon word!" (vol. 3, p. 252).

As for the word "aristogratic", it also would have well deserved a philological commentary, but it appears to have escaped [the notice of] M. Feuillet.

IV

General Character of the Pieces
Forming the Collection of M. Chasles

———————⊶«(◉)»⊷———————

$\mathcal{T}$HESE PIECES, which the author acknowledged as having all been forged by his hand alone, all possess, in fact, a general similarity of appearance, of style, and in a manner of speaking, of complexion. They have the air of being sisters in every way, although displaying the pretension of emerging from the most diverse of pens [i.e., writers], countries, and eras; and that which is the main point, which is to say the handwriting, is there so careless or so daring, however one wishes to describe it, that the scholars who were to examine it, for example, in England those that were attributed to Newton, or in Italy those that were attributed to Galileo, manifested their surprise that these were forged by a scribe who appeared never to have seen the handwriting of either the one or the other of these great men. In sum, all the important processes of this forgery were most imperfect.

The least skillful of forgers know today how essential to them is the choice of paper. They must have old paper made at the time that they imagine their figures [to have lived], or a bit before, because lovers of autographs are on the alert for these details. Now, it is becoming very difficult to procure old paper, especially in great quantity. One may still find old registers to cut up, but this is a commodity more and more rare and expensive. The author of the autographs of M. Chasles had wide experience in this matter; he often used for letters of the seventeenth and eighteenth centuries coarse paper that was no longer in use for the correspondence of the period; he also did not hesitate to use paper colored on the edges, which declared itself by this fact, of primary evidence, as originating from old cut up registers. [According to a manuscript note in the copy of the translator, letters of the nobility in this period often were written on paper with colored edges, especially in the seventeenth century.] The vast majority of the counterfeit letters belonging to M. Chasles are written on one square of paper, that is to say on a single sheet. Thus among 182 letters, for example, from Galileo to Samuel Petit, among 243 from the same [author] to Rotrou, and 391 to Pascal father and son, there are only three letters on two sheets to the first, one to the second, and two to Pascal. In a very rare exception, the letters from Jacqueline Pascal and those from [Alain René] Lesage are generally written on two sheets. This strange scarcity was remarked upon during the debates of the Academy; and in fact, applied to a series of pieces, even of limited number, the economy of paper would alone suggest a forgery.

An even stronger reason [for suspecting forgery], the accused did not pay attention at all to watermarks, and there is a certain paper the watermark of which depicts a fleur de lis, that he uses indifferently and identically in the same way, for all countries and all periods, even in times when the fleur de lis was not yet invented [as a symbol]. He probably does not know that, in many countries, people are employed in carefully assembling the history of the paper industry and in making known the designs of all the watermarks, which is a great service rendered by the learned against forgers. It appears that his skill did not extend to imitating documents on parchment; at least there does not exist a single example of these among the pieces he forged that he sold to M. Chasles.

His autograph document once written, all means were acceptable to him to give to the piece an air of antiquity. Soiling it, soaking it in water, browning it with fire, blackening it in the smoke of a lamp, were his normal practices. It also appears that he sometimes smeared them with a bit of wax to complete their antique appearance. Sometimes the fire damaged them too much, such that they fall apart in small fragments that crumble under the fingers.

The first 1,200 or 1,500 pieces that the accused sold to M. Chasles were, says the latter, very damaged and often almost illegible after their immersion in water. The seller explained this circumstance by relating the history of the conveyance of the collection to America and of the shipwreck it suffered. A greater confidence on the part of M. Chasles in the authenticity of the autographs that were being sold to him even resulted from this account, because having entrusted some of the documents to his colleague at the Institute, M. Sainte-Claire Deville, to restore the faded writing, the learned chemist made them completely black, telling him that these pieces must have been moistened, because the sulfate of iron contained in the ink had spread throughout the page.

The adulteration of the ink is the area where the accused best succeeded. In the course of the discussion undertaken at the Academy by M. Chasles, a chemist, M. Carré, suggested a procedure that he believed infallible for recognizing whether a piece of writing was undertaken recently or long ago. Two other chemists, members of the Academy, had experience with this procedure based on the fact that "the alteration that organic substances undergo in contact with air" (*Proceedings of the Academy of Sciences*, [vol.] 69, p. 25 and following) "... allows the prediction that old ink will be more difficultly removed by acids than that which was more recently placed on the paper." To prove this argument, these gentlemen (M. [Antoine-Jérôme] Balard and M. [Jules-Célestine] Jamin) submerged for twenty-four hours, in acidulated water, on the one hand fifteen documents dated from 1577 to 1770, and on the other hand sixty documents dated from the years 1800 to 1867; the result of this immersion having confirmed the assertion of M. Carré, they submitted to the same treatment fragments of letters of M. Chasles that had been published in the *Proceedings*, and one of the two expressed their conclusion in these terms:

"Almost all (of the documents of M. Chasles submerged in a 10% hydrochloric acid solution) resisted the action of this agent even when it was continued for a very long time.... We hope that the Academy will conclude with us that it is extremely likely that the fraud, if there is one here, is of an ancient date. I do not say however that that is certain, since one could object that the forgers could have made use of special inks, acquiring more quickly the properties of age."

M. Chasles seized on the first part of this statement as proving the antiquity of his documents, even though the truth lay in the exception with which the declaration ends. The accused probably had the skill to adulterate his ink by some procedure that had the double advantage of giving it great stability, since it placed at fault the test made by the Academy, and at the same time to give it [the ink] a yellow tinge that very closely imitated age. It was only by going on, and by the great practice that the extensive forging to which he devoted himself gave him, that Vrain Lucas learned gradually to improve his procedures. The first 1,200 or 1,500 pieces that he delivered to M. Chasles, and that bore extensive signs of their stay underwater, were the product of a skill still imperfect, but that its inventor would come afterwards to perfect.

The most numerous part of the compositions of Vrain Lucas did not demand any great expenditure of imagination. This fact was demonstrated to the Academy by revealing the manner in which he used the treatises of [Alexandre] Savérien and of Father [Giacinto Sigismondo] Gerdil, for or against Newtonian science. He would take a treatise, cut it into an infinity of fragments or scraps, and each of these scraps, by means of a little transition at the beginning and at the end, easily would become a letter or, without any transition, a scientific note. Each letter, which contained more [material], or even each scientific note, which contained much less, would receive a signature and, therefore, a distinguishing feature.

How many other works, along with those of Savérien and Father Gerdil, were cut up like them by the same hand and the same procedure, to create so many thousands of false autographs? A considerable number certainly, but the search for which would be quite superfluous. We have come upon some articles from the great *Encyclopédie* of [Denis] Diderot and [Jean le Rond] d'Alembert thus transformed into letters of Pascal. We have also verified that a complete series of counterfeit letters from Lesage to [François Antoine] Jolly, editor of Molière, letters including opinions on almost all the works of the great comic writer, are nothing but the word-for-word copy of the memoirs of [Jean Louis Ignace de] La Serre inserted at the beginning of the edition entitled *Oeuvres de Molière. Nouvelle édition précédée d'un avertissement* (by Jolly, editor) *et de Mèmoires sur la vie et les ouvrages de Molière* (by de La Serre) [the works of Molière. A new edition preceded by a foreword … and by memoirs of the life and work of Molière]; Paris, Pierre Prault; 1734, six volumes in quarto. One may believe that Lucas used this edition because it is less common than that produced by [Antoine] Bret in 1773 [Paris: Companie des libraires associés].

Similarly, [Jean de] La Bruyère wrote so sparingly that only twenty of his letters are known today to have survived. Yet he is represented by seven hundred thirty-nine [pieces] in the collection of M. Chasles. For this extensive forgery the items were drawn from various works, such as the *Mercure galant*, the prefaces to the *Oeuvres posthumes de La Fontaine* [posthumous works of Jean de La Fontaine] by Madame Ulrich (Paris, 1696), and chiefly from the works of La Bruyère himself, cut up and arranged in the standard fashion of the forger.

Let us take two more examples, relating to ancient authors, to show very clearly the process of composing the fake pieces that had a certain authentic appearance and by means of which one could produce them in as great a number as one wished, without giving oneself any other trouble than that of transcribing them.

It is known that there remains to us of [Jean, Sire de] Joinville only his history of Saint Louis, his *Credo,* a letter to Philip the Bold, and a certain number of charters given by reason of his agreements with his vassals, charters that have recently been published by M. Nat.[alis] de Wailly [*Receuil de chartes originales de Joinville*, Paris: A. Lainé et J. Havard, 1868— collection of original charters of Joinville].

In the Chasles collection, the Joinville file is composed of many letters addressed to the king Saint Louis and to William of Chartres, confessor to the king; also, of a certain number of poems, most titled "sirventes" [a form of Provençal lay]. One is even more surprised to find these last under the name of Joinville, since one knows that the faithful companion of Saint Louis was more accustomed to handling the sword than the pen, and that he dictated, but did not at all write his history of Saint Louis. Moreover, the text of his letters to William of Chartres was borrowed by Lucas from the accounts of the confessor of Queen Margaret printed in volume twenty of the historians of France. We will restrict ourselves to a few examples.

The letter "Sir and dearly beloved you will say how much the blessed king ... " is a slightly modified copy of a passage of this chronicler, p. 100, D. "Sir and dearly beloved, I returned yesterday with the king." A copy of another passage of the same chronicler, p. 78, C. "Sir, yesterday I was with the king our lord." A copy of the same chronicler, p. 102 D.

The poems, all signed Jehan de Joinville, have been drawn from well known works. Thus the lay that begins,

> But in France there was some consternation
> Because the barons were in disagreement

has been transcribed in the rhymed chronicle of Philippe Monsket. *[Recueil des]Histor.[iens des Gaules et] de France* [collection of historians of the Gauls and of France, 1738-1904], vol. 22, p. 46, verse 27946.

The following was drawn from the same chronicle, verse 27953.

> Philip the Count of Boulogne
> Undertook that task with much care.

The letter in verse, beginning, "Lord my greatly beloved,"

> It is my desire to tell that
> To which I have given thought,

was copied in the works of Hugues de la Ferté, memoirs of France 844, folio 97 recto.

The "Departure of King Louis for the Crusade," signed Joinville,

> In the year 1248
> Lord [Saint in the original] Louis and the others
> Who previously had gone crusading
> Set out from the kingdom of France, etc.

was copied in the *Branche des royaux lignages* [division of royal lineages] of Guillaume Guiart, etc. [published in *Collection des chroniques nationales françaises ...* by J. A. Buchon, Paris: Verdiere, 1828, 8:28]

Gregory of Tours furnished the text of a dozen false letters: some composed using his writings, such as a letter to his enemy Felix, bishop of Nantes, which is nothing but the reproduction of a passage from the History of the Franks, in which the pious bishop of Tours mocks and scoffs at his colleague (book 5); the others are merely inspired by Gregory, such as a note to Fortunatus, drawn from the complaints contained in the preface of the History of the Franks on the decay of the Latin language. But here is a very characteristic example of the manner in which Lucas would adulterate and render foolish an ancient text to transform it into a spurious letter. It is the history so well known of the vessel of Soissons. We place on one side the account of Gregory and facing it the wording of Vrain Lucas in the form of a letter addressed by the bishop to Saint Radegonde [Here Gregory's account appears first, followed by Lucas' version]:

Certain soldiers stole from a church a vessel of astonishing splendor and beauty. The bishop of this church sent messengers to Clovis, asking him that if he could not secure the recovery of the other vessels that [particular] one at least might be returned to him. The king, having heard these words, says to the messenger: "I am [going] all the way to Soissons, because it is there that the spoils of war will be divided, and when in the division of the spoils I will be given this vessel, I will do what the pontiff asks." The king and his soldiers having arrived at Soissons, all the booty is placed in the middle of the town square, and the king says: "I beg of you, my brave warriors, willingly to grant me, in addition to my share [of the booty], this vessel that is here." The wisest reply to the words of the king: "Glorious king, all that we see is yours: even we ourselves are subject to your power. Do therefore that which pleases you, because no one can resist your might." When they had thus spoken, a presumptuous warrior, envious and hot-headed, raised his Frankish battle axe and struck the vessel with it, exclaiming, "You will receive from all that is here nothing but what the division of the spoils actually gives you." At these words, all remain aghast. The king hid his resentment of this outrage under an air of patience. He gives to the bishop's messenger the vessel that had fallen to his share, keeping at the bottom of his heart a hidden anger. A year having passed, Clovis ordered all his warriors to come to the Field of Mars, dressed in their arms, to see whether they were polished and in good condition. As he was examining all the soldiers by passing before them, he arrived beside the man who had struck the vessel and says to him, "No one has weapons as badly maintained as yours, for neither your spear, nor your sword, nor your axe is in good condition," and snatching from him his axe the king threw it to the ground. The soldier having bent down a little to recover it, the king raising his Frankish battle axe brought it down on the soldier's head while saying to him: "That is what you did to the vessel of Soissons." The soldier dead, the king ordered the others to retire. This action inspired great fear in the others. (*Histoire des Francs*, by Gregory of Tours, vol. 2, p. 27, translated by François Pierre Guillaume Guizot.)

[Lucas' version:]
To the blessed Queen Radegonde.

Blessed queen

You have asked me for some details concerning history, wishing, you have told me, to teach them to the young women who have come to your monastery to live there in the shadow of your virtues. This request does me great honor; also, I do not want to fall short of your request. Today I will tell you some things about King Clovis, the first Christian king. There was a law among the Franks to divide all the spoils of war among the fighters, but this king, although at that time idolatrous, one time asked following a battle that he be given in addition a sacred vessel seized in a church to give it to Bishop Remi of Reims who had asked him for it. But an insolent soldier opposed him saying that he wanted to have it for his share. And since the king insisted, this soldier gave a blow to the vessel with his axe and broke it [the vessel]. The king hid his anger for the time because such was the law; but some time later it fell out that in a general review the king noticed this same soldier whose weapons were not in proper condition, and since for this offense the soldier found himself liable to the punishment of death, the king split his head with his axe while saying: You thus struck the sacred vessel. It is thus that this king knew how to render justice. I tell you nothing more, but another time I will tell you other adventures. I pray God to hold you in his good graces. This tenth of June 585.

Gregory bishop of Tours.

It is thus truly little here that the forger borrows from Gregory. Another step further and he draws all from his own imagination. This he often did. He was particularly obliged to do so for the many correspondences he created to inspire belief in the [existence of a] hoard of papers [that had been] scrupulously preserved, [papers] in which the scholars of all times particularly concerned themselves (although it is Lucas himself who makes them express that concern) and that were carefully transmitted from hand to hand. Vrain Lucas, afraid of nothing, dared to create two letters from Newton to Voltaire. What did he imagine that these two great geniuses could say to one another, the one as brilliant as the other [was] profound? He lends them the customary preoccupations of Vrain Lucas, and transforms them into two seekers of autographs.

To M. Voltaire. This 3 July

I told you, sir, that I would put you in contact with the possessor of the writing of [Pierre] Bayle if you so wish. I spoke with him recently about this matter and he told me that he would be most flattered thereby. He possesses not only a rich collection of historical and literary documents formed by this important scholar, but also a good number of other documents of all sorts. It is enough to tell you that if you come here you will find [material] to gather. It is enough to tell you that I urge you to make this voyage. I will tell you nothing more. I am, sir, your most humble and most affectionate servant.

Is. Newton

This was enough banality to lend to the great Newton. But it is truly from his own funds that the forger drew it.

CHARTRES. *The city where Vrain Lucas is belived to have sold his first forgeries.*

V

The Man Behind the Forgeries

—————⏃⸨⦿⸩⏃—————

*U*RAIN-DENIS LUCAS received only the first rudiments of a literary education, and M. Chasles would appear to have exactly represented him in saying before the Academy that one would not suspect as a forger of pieces and of so great a number of pieces a man not knowing among other things either Latin, or Italian, or any branch of mathematics; and to this one could have added: only poorly knowing even French.

But if he lacked basic formal education, he made up for this deficiency in part by reading, by solitary effort, and he had received some natural gifts that he was able to put to good use. The son of a day laborer in the fields, he probably began life in the same occupation; this is at least what an old passport found in his possession and in which he is described as a domestic servant seems to indicate. But if he really was in this humble station, it was only for a very short time. The memories he left at Châteaudun are very different.

Lucas began as a lawyer's clerk in nearby Chartres and was employed by the law-court. In 1847 he entered as clerk of the board of mortgages, and remained there for five years. He was considered then as a hard worker and an indefatigable reader, especially fond of old documents. The loan register of the public library of Châteaudun records the kind of serious withdrawals he used to make (1848-1851): *Histoire de l'Académie* [History of the Academy];— *Mémoire signifié à M. Léon de Montmorency* [Memoir Relating to M. Léon de Montmorency];—*Défense de M. Libri* [Defense of M. Libri];— *Rapport de M. Lenormant à l'Académie des Inscriptions et Belles Lettres* [Report of M. Lenormant to the Academy of Inscriptions and Belles-Lettres];—*Bibliothèque historique et critique* [*Bibliothèque historique, et critique du Poitou*, by Jean François Druex de Radier, Paris: Chez Ganeau, 1754; Historical and Critical Library of Poitou (France). I have not been able to identify the other titles.];— *Notice sur la bibliothèque Mazarine* [Account of the Mazarine Library];— *Bibliothèque des auteurs qui ont écrit l'histoire* [Library of Authors Who Have Written History];—*Mémoires de l'Académie* [Memoirs of the Academy];— *Receuil du procès de M. de Chevreuse* [Account of the Trial of M. de Chevreuse].

And at the bottom of this page of the register of loans, one of the librarians, the abbot Sonazay, a respectable churchman, now deceased, wrote this note: "*The industrious M. Lucas is going to live in Paris. He deserves to succeed. A self-made young man from Lanneray. 18 February 1852.*"

Lucas also had a taste for poetry. At his house was found a notebook containing fifteen pieces of verse, most of which bear dates from 1848 to 1850, and each routinely followed by the signature of the author. These are: *The Garland of Flora* or *The Melodies of Nature*; *The Bride*; *What I Like To See* [authors' note: How I like to see the new-born verdure,/That in the spring proclaims fair days!/ How I like to see the brook that murmurs/Over the gravel, pursuing its way …]; *The Divinity*; a patriotic ode; some epigrams. *The Garland of Flora* begins with a preface, in which the author paints his portrait:

> You then would like on Pegasus
> You, poor and without a stay,
> To climb up Mount Parnassus?
> A friend said to me one day.
> I, no; I am more modest!
> And in order so to attest
> I very much wish to tell you
> (Although this state I spurn)
> That I am quite unlearned;
> By habit I rhyme,
> For fun and to pass time.
> I swear by all that's holy
> Reader, that in my infancy
> No one, such was my destiny,
> Taught me either Greek or Latin,
> Important matters these
> If one would rhyme with ease,
> And then see his work in print!
> I give my heart in pledge,
> At school in the village,
> To my lesson I applied,,
> Apollo was my guide, etc.

Like so many others, Lucas came to Paris expecting to find a position. He first tried to secure one at the great library on the rue Richelieu [i.e., the Imperial Library, later the Bibliothèque Nationale, on Richelieu Street], by means of recommendations he had to the chief administrator of this establishment, but he was unable to succeed because he did not have a bachelor of letters [degree]. A professor at the college of Chartres, and a lover of autographs, the late M. Roux, who acted as his patron, tried to place him in a profitable establishment of a Parisian bookseller, the establishment of Auguste Durand, on rue des Grés [street of pleasures]; M. Durand, although a close friend of M. Roux, refused to hire him, arguing that he did not know Latin.

Meanwhile Vrain Lucas came into contact with the owner of a genealogical collection, the Letellier collection, that had formerly been the Courtois collection and no longer exists, the remainder having been sold en bloc a dozen years ago. This was for Lucas a bad relationship and a fatal school. These genealogical collections have as a commercial purpose, not only to resell to families originals or copies of documents that they buy or have copied, but also to draw up for them reports and genealogies. In such an operation, the false and the true tend incessantly to get mixed up by an irresistible attraction; and the Courtois-Letellier collection, in particular, was noted from the moment of the establishment of the room of the Crusades in the Palace of Versailles, some twenty-five years ago, as a dispensary from which emerged a mass of false documents forged with amazing skill. Lucas was employed in this establishment as clerk or agent, that is to say, that he went about offering to families the services of the collection, and that he received a commission for the business he would procure. According to what he has said, his efforts supposedly brought into the coffers of the collection a sum of fifty or sixty thousand francs. No doubt he was working at the same time for himself, in the same way. But this is a point about which information is lacking.

To conclude matters concerning the literary abilities of this curious author, we add that in 1856, on the nomination of M. Roux, he was named corresponding member of the Archeological Society of the department of Eure-et-Loir. He remained a member of this organization until it removed his name last October; but he never gave them any trouble and does not appear to have ever published anything either there or elsewhere. In 1865 he was proposed to draw up the inventory of the archives of the alms-house of Châteaudun, which are very rich, and this was agreed to by the administration. However, he delayed from month to month to apply himself to the task, which was undoubtedly beyond his abilities because many of the documents in this depository are Latin charters. At the end of eighteen months, the administrators of the alms-house, tired of this futile waiting, gladly transferred the responsibility of this task to the archivist of the department, M. Lucien Merlet.

It appears to us that these pieces of information present well the scope of what the accused was capable of doing, literarily speaking, and that this scope corresponds exactly to what we see he did for M. Chasles.

This is a man without competent education, who has a natural bent for historical research, for the organizing of ideas, for a sense of order, and for stage-craft; who, therefore, is able to imagine a story and manage it, but within the limits of what he knows. We have had occasion to show, regarding a spurious letter of François I, (p. 38) the little mistakes that he made; one would be able to show almost as many of these in every piece. He produces Cornelia *widow of Pompey* and Catherine Baro [i.e., Bora] *widow of Luther*. He calls Julius Caesar *emperor* at the time of his Gallic wars. He addresses letters to the *blessed* Radegonde, abbess of Sainte-Croix of Poitiers, and to the *blessed* Saint Vincent de Paul, as if one were canonized while living; Madame de Maintenon writes to *monseigneur* Massillon; almost all the people of the past two centuries write to each other as one would today, but as one never would have done then: sir *and dear such a one*. All the correspondents of the astronomer Ismaël Boulliau write to him *M. the abbot* Boulliau, and *my reverend father*, even though this scholar, who died, it is true, at the abbey of Saint-Victor in Paris, but without having entered into orders, left forty volumes of authentic correspondence (at the Imperial Library) where he is not addressed thus a single time. In the correspondence of the author of *Portraits*, which he always signed Delabruyère (and not de Labruyère or Labruyere), the archbishop of Cambray, director of the convent of the New Converts, Fenelon, is taken for a journalist and the *New Converts* for a journal. These continual slips [authors' note: In addition we cite as a bit thick those that he committed in the printed books that he embellished with false *ex libris*, among which he did not hesistate to write: *Ex libris Franciscus Rabelais; ex libris Rabelesius; ex libris Rabelasius; ex libris J. Keplerus; ex libris Newtonius* and the signature still more extraordinary: "Henrietta-Maria of France, *ex-queen of the English.*"] are inherent to Vrain Lucas, just like the platitude and vulgarity of phrase; and also like the little care that he took to research the authentic handwritings of his characters and to make a faithful copy of them. But it is less easy to fault him on the actual substance of his stories. We have counted a thousand people figuring in the correspondence sold to M. Chasles. This mass of people move and speak together in an ordinary manner, each with his contemporaries, and in mentioning hundreds of other people, without one's detecting many obvious errors and anachronisms in the whole collection. There are indeed some letters of Strabo to Juvenal, although the latter was born ninety-two years after the former, and a famous safe-conduct pass delivered by Vercingetorix to the historian Trogue Pompey, even though the latter died at least sixty-one years after the Gallic hero; there are also letters of the Venable Bede to Alcuin, even though Alcuin was only nine years old when Bede died, in 735. This is a small number of errors for so great a quantity of people, and one is obliged to add that in fact among the errors of this kind in the letters that M. Chasles showed the Academy of Sciences, one can point out only that consisting of making the mother of Newton sign herself using her maiden name (sessions of 29 July and 12 August, p. 187 and 262).

VI

Did the Forger Have Accomplices?

URING THE ENTIRE COURSE of the debates held at the Academy of Sciences, those who believed in the authenticity of the pieces produced relied chiefly on the extraordinary number of these pieces and on the excellent style of some of them. "One cannot allow," M. Chasles would say, "that one person alone would have been able to compose such a great mass of writings and of correspondences between the most eminent people in the sciences, in literature, in philosophical, theological matters, etc. What fertility of imagination, what skill would not such a task presuppose?" (*Proceedings*, 1867, p. 442).—"Without speaking of the prodigious activity and the knowledge to which it would testify, would it not suffice for me to call upon this style of two centuries ago, this style imprinted with the genius of Pascal in all phases of his scientific or literary life, that the forger supposedly knew how to reproduce? Where would he be found, this forger?" (p. 685).

Another scholar, M. the abbot [François Napoléan Marie] Moigno, wrote in his magazine *Les Mondes* [the worlds] (vol. 15, p. 508; 21 November 1867): "The letters read today by M. Chasles are astounding, overwhelming, one no longer knows where one is, and the forger becomes absolutely impossible. He would be more than a demi-god. A certain number of the 2,000 letters in the possession of M. Chasles are dated from a place, with a year, with a month, with a day. When one consults the history or the memoirs of the period, one will confirm that at the period designated, the person who wrote or who was written to was indeed at the place indicated. How could the forger know the actual place of residence of so many correspondents? It would be more than a miracle." M. Faugère himself, hard-pressed by this argument, conceded that it was "not impossible that these documents, *written in the same hand*, had been composed by several people" (*Proceedings*, 1867, p. 442).

It is very easy now to condemn the error in reasoning by which people allowed themselves to be seduced. It was assumed that the pieces were composed while they were only copied and slightly altered. Thus, neither the great number of documents, nor an accidental appropriateness of style would be at all surprising; a single scribe, even but slightly educated, provided he had a certain skill at forging and a ready hand, would have been capable of executing this feat.

The examples that we have given herein above of the methods of work which this copyist used establish this fact, that he worked completely alone and without assistance, beyond any kind of doubt regarding the purely historical or literary pieces before the sixteenth century. Certainly if he had been able to borrow the ear of some kindly counselor, if he had been inclined to receive advice, we do not say from a learned person, but from an ordinary collaborator possessing the slightest notion of history, such a person would have rescued him from the absurdity and from the danger of putting into circulation Carolingian, Merovingian, [and] early Christian pieces and even pieces earlier by ten centuries than our most ancient manuscripts.

As to the letters and notes that deal with pure mathematics, and that disturbed the Academy of Sciences for more than two years, Lucas demonstrated these considerations: (1) a dominant and persistent desire to exploit false patriotism inspired by the idea of the glory of France usurped and fraudulently hoarded by foreign countries; (2) a certain tact in the choice and arrangement of his extracts. Through the following piece we can put our finger on the manner in which Lucas knew to compose scientific letters favoring Pascal. The basis of this piece is part of an article inserted by M. [Louis] de Jaucourt in the great *Encyclopédie* of Diderot (vol. 12, p. 444, under the heading "Gravity" *[pesanteur])*; the complete text is placed within brackets, but the forger completely distorted this fragment by adding to it that which we place outside the brackets, that is to say the formulas of the beginning and the end, and above all in substituting for the words *he found*, that M. de Jaucourt applied to Galileo, and *thus Galileo concluded* the words *I find* and *Now I conclude with Galileo* that Lucas compelled his Pascal to use.

This 23 November

Sir,

As I have already told you [Galileo who has given us the true law of gravity, first opposed the error of Aristotle who believed that different bodies will fall in the same medium with a speed proportional to their mass. Galileo dared to take a firm stand against the authority of Aristotle that the resistance of the media in which bodies fall was the sole cause of the differences that are found in the time of their fall towards the earth. . . .~~He found~~] I found [that the differences of their respective falls in different media correspond closely to the density of these media and not to the mass of the bodies. ~~Thus Galileo concluded~~*] Now, I conclude with Galileo that [the resistance of the media and the size and sharpness of the surface of the different bodies are the sole causes that render the fall of some bodies faster than that of others.] By repeating these same experiments you can assure yourself of these facts. I am, Sir*

Your most humble and most affectionate servant, Pascal.

The tact consisted of not unduly mistaking in copying the authors of the eighteenth century by attributing their phrases to those of the seventeenth; however, it is precisely there that the forger fell short, since it is in taking from Savérien the numbers expressing the masses of the sun, of Jupiter, of Saturn, and of the Earth (1, 1/1067, 1/3021, 1/169282), according to Newton, to attribute them to Pascal, that he clumsily went astray, in that Newton himself, in the first edition of his work, published a long time after the death of Pascal, had given numbers far inferior in exactitude to those cited. A mathematician would not have fallen into this mistake; a mathematician would not have dared to speak of Newton and against Newton or to meddle with his immortal book the *Principia* without attaching importance to it; he would rather have instinctively distanced himself from so elevated a subject about which a member of the Academy of Sciences [Jean Baptiste Biot], who lived some years ago, said, "Among the contemporaries of Newton only three or four were capable of understanding his treatise the *Principia*: Huyghens only partially adopted his ideas; Leibnitz and Jean Bernouli opposed him; [Bernard le Bovier de] Fontenelle himself, this judge so shrewd, did not believe he was compromising himself in expressing little more than doubts about gravity; in fact more than fifteen years passed before the great truth demonstrated by Newton was, I do not say followed up and expanded, but merely understood by the majority of scholars." (Biot, *Biographie universelle* ["Notice Historique sur la vie et les oeuvres de Newton," *Biographie universelle* (Paris: Michaud frères, 1811-1862), 31: 27-194]).

A mathematician probably also would not have committed the other numerous errors pointed out by M. Le Verrier in his thesis. But how was this learned thesis necessary, one will say to oneself. How could this discussion have lasted two years? How did the *Proceedings* of the Academy bestow on it more than 400 pages of print in quarto, and accept 381 spurious pieces?

It is the consequence of surprise. It is the consequence of the confidence inspired by the eminent glory of M. Chasles as a geometrician and of the respect commanded by his character. Moreover there were, from the first moment, academicians, like Messieurs Duhamel, Le Verrier, Brewster, whom surprise did not affect and who did not hesitate to protest quickly against these new documents, just as outside [the Academy] M. Bernard, M. Faugère, and many others [objected]. Far from attesting to a knowledge of mathematics, the fables of Vrain Lucas could only have been attempted, we think, by a man who drew boldness from his very ignorance, and who hoped, against all expectation, that a catastrophe did not necessarily lie at the end of his undertaking.

It is unbelievable, one thinks, that, not knowing mathematics, he did not make more and more glaring blunders. But one must keep in mind that one is speaking about what was presented to the Academy and was published in the *Proceedings*; now the Academy did not see or know of all that he had executed in this field, moreover it did not know of his Roman and Greek letters. The Academy had only that which M. Chasles showed it, and M. Chasles, naturally imbued with the desire to prove a thesis, saw only that which agreed with his argument. He produced eighty letters or notes of Pascal, twenty-nine of Newton, twenty of Galileo; but in his collection there were 1,745 of Pascal, 622 of Newton, more than 3,000 of Galileo.

One may also say: but Lucas never took part in the Monday [sessions] of the Academy of Sciences; he never set foot there and did not mix with the mass of listeners, of scholars, of journalists who overcrowd these weekly meetings. Now since it is incontestable today that he forged part of these false autograph documents as they were needed for the discussion, he must have had one or more accomplices who kept him up to date and who assisted him with their instructions, in this prolonged hoaxing of the Academy.—Not at all. We do not need to believe in the existence of guilt of this sort, which would be even more odious than the guilt of the forger, because Lucas had access to the most informed, the most passionate, of all "accomplices," one who was most certainly [his partner] without having the least suspicion that he was [acting] in this way or that there was any deception in this affair. It is M. Chasles himself who aided and directed him without knowing that he [Chasles] was doing so. One sees sufficiently in the *Proceedings* of the Academy the unshakable faith of M. Chasles in the authenticity of his documents; there is only too much proof of this [fact]; there is only too much evidence of the anxiety, the agitated state in which the debates of the Academy placed him, his excessive desire to have pieces to support his pronouncements, his insistence on having Lucas find, in this inexhaustible Boisjourdain collection where he was finding so many things, the documents that he needed. Vrain Lucas, ardently sought by his customer, in the course of these two years of scientific agitation, very often called at the house of M. Chasles to bring him that which he called his discoveries and which in truth were only his productions. He particularly would arrive on

Mondays while M. Chasles was still attending the academy's meeting, and he awaited M. Chasles' return. Whether during this period of waiting, since it would sometimes be an hour, or in the very presence of M. Chasles, it would not be hard for Vrain Lucas to slip new pieces into the files; or indeed, something even easier, he could place them in the very hands of M. Chasles, while presenting them as new discoveries made at the house of M. de Boisjourdain. M. Chasles, arriving from the session extremely excited, completely preoccupied with the objections that had been made to him and to which he had been unable to respond, naturally would pour out his feelings in a carefree manner without the least suspicion in the presence of Lucas, would urge him to see whether, by chance, such a letter of Newton proving his connection with Pascal might not be found, such a letter of Galileo proving that he had not been blind, such a letter of Huyghens proving that he had had notice of the observation of Galileo on the subject of Saturn. Chance would agree almost always to bring it [the desired result] about, fortunate for the argument maintained by M. Chasles, and all the more profitable for the supplier. The honesty of the former was so great, that he went so far as to give to the other, as was shown above, lists of pieces to find in the fantastic treasure of Boisjourdain, lists that immediately became syllabi of false documents to make.

"Are you not," Vrain Lucas, once in prison, wrote to M. Chasles on 7 October 1869, "Are you not he who introduced me to the handwriting of Newton? Who pointed out to me and made me see how he made his *e*, his *h*, his *l*, his *t*, and how, above all, he signed his name? For Galileo, is it not the same: is it not you who observed to me how he always made the *G* of his name, how he never would forget the dots over the *i*, and many other remarks? And this letter of 5 November 1639, corrected many times, was it not [made] according to your instructions? Is it not you who pointed out to me that the first word of this letter, which had first had been written *aurei,* should have been written *haurei;* and afterwards did you not tell me, following the observations that you received from Italy, that this word should be written *hauerei?* Is it not you again who made me notice how the signature of father Boulliau was made, how he used to make his *y,* his *p,* his *q?* Is it not you also who remarked to me that Maupertuis never crossed his *t?* Is it not you once more who introduced me to a letter of Cardinal Gerdil, and who even conveyed to me a *facsimile* of his handwriting? And then, an infinite number of other particulars and remarks that you made to me ..."

He wrote this letter with the evident aim of sheltering his guilt behind the too trusting man he had deceived; but the details that it contains, if not the interpretation that he wished to draw from them, have the stamp of truth.

It is boasting inordinately that he undertook, as Vrain Lucas bragged in several letters or statements written by him during his imprisonment on suspicion, to forge 10,000 autographed documents a year, which was making thirty of them each day; but we firmly believe that he spoke truth when he affirmed to have forged by himself all that he delivered to M. Chasles. This statement agrees with the preliminary investigation, that did not reveal any indication of any complicity whatever. And above all, the family likeness, the homogeneity, the perfect similarity of form, of ink, of paper, of damage, even of handwritings, despite the futile effort in these last to attain variety, prove that the 27,000 pieces are by the same hand, as the similarity of thought, of language, of method of working, and of errors, testifies that they emanate from the same mind.

A true scholar probably would not have dared to chance a similar undertaking, while half-formed knowledge easily faces dangers it has not weighed. Happily, audacity has its correctives. Considering that Montaigne was useful like so many others for the hoax that we are here to recount, and provided for his part six hundred pieces to the collection, the hoaxer must know this statement of the philosopher (1:24):

Knowledge is a good drug; but no drug is sufficiently powerful to preserve itself without alteration and corruption, according to the defect of the vessel in which it is placed. ["Of Pedantry"]

Court of Summary Jurisdiction of Paris— Sixth Chamber

———)((O))(———

M. [Joseph-Mathieu] Brunet Presiding

Session of 17 February 1870

*U*RAIN-DENIS LUCAS IS A FIFTY-TWO YEAR OLD MAN, of short stature; he has no fixed occupation. {authors' note: The substance of this account is borrowed from the *Gazette des Tribunaux* [gazette of the tribunals] but [it has been here] corrected and completed by the editors.} He received little formal education, but he has complemented it, he says, by extensive reading. It is in the midst of old books, of old manuscripts, of autographs from all periods that he spends his life. The question for the tribunal to determine is to know whether, by using fraudulent schemes, Lucas has swindled all or part of another's wealth.

EXAMINATION OF THE ACCUSED

PRESIDING JUDGE: "You have abused in the most brazen manner the passion of an old man, of a scholar, his passion as a collector and his love for his country, in order to deceive him shamefully. In the course of six or seven years, you have sold him spurious autograph documents, emanating from the most illustrious people of all times, of all places. For these pieces, which he believed authentic, historical, to the number of more than 27,000, he has paid you the enormous price of 140,000 francs, and upon examination, it turns out that all these pieces, if one excepts one or two hundred of them, which have no value, were counterfeit pieces, forged by you. You have done an even greater wrong to M. Chasles, if that is possible; you have caused him bitter disappointment. Among the autograph letters that you have sold him, there were two signed Blaise Pascal. M. Chasles produced these letters before the Academy of Sciences of which he is a member, and during protracted sessions, these letters were debated, letters that must have, if they had been genuine, stripped Newton of the credit of the discovery of the laws of gravity.

59

"The debate had lasted two years, when M. Chasles learns that these letters are counterfeit, and that he is obliged to make a humiliating confession that he has been deceived.

"In order to trick him, you made up a story: you told him that a comte de Boisjourdain, who became a political exile in 1791, had left France, taking [with him] a rich collection of autograph documents of all periods; that in taking them to America, he had suffered shipwreck; that a certain number of pieces had been damaged by sea-water, but that the greatest number of them had remained in good condition. You added that a great person had become the owner of this collection rescued from shipwreck, that you were his authorized agent, charged with selling to scholars the many pieces of this rich collection, and in support of your story, you showed to M. Chasles some of the documents that had escaped the shipwreck. The better to deceive him you had recourse to other schemes; you wrapped the autographs in folders that you said came from an eighteenth-century collector. All these schemes succeeded, and M. Chasles resolved to deal with you. You sold him a counterfeit letter from Molière for 500 francs, and you presented to him as far as books go, a [volume supposedly belonging to] La Fontaine, with annotations by M. the comte de Boisjourdain, and you made him pay 900 francs for it. Do you acknowledge as true this summary of the actions attributed to you?"

Our Mr. Lucas.—"In part, but not completely."

Examiner:—"Do you mean to say that among the many counterfeit pieces that you sold at ransom price, there are some that are authentic?"

Respondent:—"Yes, sir, I sold more than 30,000 pieces to M. Chasles, and he has introduced only 27,000 of them; there are therefore three or four thousand of them that M. Chasles has not shown and that are authentic."

Examiner:—"Still, there are at least 27,000 pieces that you supposedly forged?"

Respondent:—"Yes, sir."

Examiner:—"In these extensive deceptions that you practiced, you displayed great ability, very great, and that one would not expect from a man who received only a mediocre education. It is unfortunate that a man of your age, so well endowed, should use such good qualifications for evil.

"Besides the offense of swindling with which you are charged, the indictment further charges you with a breach of trust to the detriment of M. Chasles: he would lend you books, and you would sell them for your own gain?"

Respondent:—"We traded."

Examiner:—"Yes, you traded, but apart from trades, you kept borrowed books?"

RESPONDENT:—"I shall explain all of that in a brief memorandum that I have written and which I ask your permission to read."

PRESIDING JUDGE:—"Later, when the time comes to present your defense."

EXAMINATION OF THE WITNESSES

The first witness called to the bar is M. Michel Chasles, aged seventy-six years, member of the Academy of Sciences; a seat was prepared for the venerable academician, but M. Chasles expresses the desire to speak standing; he deposes:

"A long time ago now, more than eight years, M. Lucas appeared at my house; he said he was from Châteaudun; since I am from Chartres, we being almost from the same locality, I welcomed him. He tells me that he was entrusted to sell, on behalf of a collector, a large quantity of manuscripts and books of great value, and most especially, autograph letters. The first piece that he brought me was a letter from Molière for which he made me pay dearly, 500 francs; then one from Rabelais, one from Racine, at 200 francs each. This collection, he told me, had been formed by M. the count de Boisjourdain, who, emigrating in 1791 and going to America, had suffered shipwreck and had died, but his collection had been saved; one part only had been damaged by the water, but it could still be sold.

"After these first purchases, I refused nothing that he brought me, and I always paid him for the items; when I would not pay him, we would make trades in which I would always lose, because in return for the genuine works that I would give him, he supplied me only with pieces later recognized as counterfeit.

"In eight years, I gave him more than 140,000 francs, of which he used to tell me that the owner of the collection would give him 25%. Apart from this sum of 140,000 francs, I also gave him tips or gifts, or agreed to give him loans. Often he would bring me autographed letters by the hundreds; among them there would be duplicates, triplicates, quadruplicates; he would tell me that these were copies of those that he presented to me as being the original. It was all the same to me to have copies; from the moment that I accepted the original, it was very easy to allow that copies of it had been made. It is thus that I had several copies of a letter from Marie de' Medici, to whose intercession, if one believes the letter, was due the kindness accorded to Galileo by the pope. In all these letters there was a good deal of agreement. With the greatest sincerity, I invited my colleagues of the Academy of Sciences to examine a large quantity of these letters, and I also showed the letters to all foreign scholars who came my way.

"M. Lucas told me one day that Louis XVI, who also used to be a collector, no longer having time to busy himself with his collection, had sent to the great collector M. the count de Boisjourdain five or six thousand very uncommon pieces. You know what happened because of the two letters of Pascal communicated by me to the Academy. After the deception of which M. Lucas thus made me the victim, I willingly undertook the unpleasant task of writing all about the hoax of which I had been the object, so that others would not be fooled after me; I did more, I circulated a large number of photographic copies of these letters, and yet the idea of finding fault with M. Lucas did not yet occur to me. It is because he did not give to me three thousand pieces that he owed me, and for which I had paid him, that I feared he would send them out of the country, and that I threatened him; his replies not having satisfied me, I had him watched, and I became certain that he had shamefully tricked me."

PRESIDING JUDGE:—"Was he not already followed to the Library of Saint-Geneviève, where he often used to go, and where he was suspected of certain appropriations of fragments of books or of manuscripts by means of scissors?"

M. CHASLES:—"So I have heard."

PRESIDING JUDGE:—"You gave him gifts and loans, you say, to what extent?"

M. CHASLES:—"Yes, Mr. President. I shall not speak of the gifts made in the form of tips; but I made many loans to him. One time, I lent him 400 francs; another time, he came to tell me that his furniture was going to be sold, that he needed 1,800 francs; I lent them to him; I had great trust in him; we were from the same locality, I believed him incapable of deceiving me. Finally, one day, I wished to settle accounts with him, and he gave me an I.O.U. for 3,880 francs.

"Apart from loans of money, I also lent him books and manuscripts, including a valuable manuscript from the fifteenth century, containing forty miniatures. He sold it."

PRESIDING JUDGE:—"For how much?"

Our MR. LUCAS:—"100 francs."

PRESIDING JUDGE:—"What! Such a manuscript, with twenty [sic] miniatures!"

M. CHASLES:—He told me that M. Fontaine, the bookseller in the thoroughfare of Panoramas, would give 1,500 francs for it, and I believe him, because he charges 300 francs for volumes less valuable that have only three or four miniatures. I also entrusted to him an illustrated La Fontaine that he never returned to me. At a certain point, in the course of our transactions, I found that he was being very slow in delivering to me items for which I had paid him. Among other subterfuges, with which he often deceived me, he told me that the collector, of whom he was the authorized agent, parted with them reluctantly, that he wished to read them before surrendering them. One day, I was angry, and I went so far as to call him a rogue; but he, with a composure that surprises me even more now that I know the man, answered me soberly and gravely: 'If you are not satisfied with me, return to me my pieces, and I shall return to you your 150,000 francs.' That had the effect that he expected; from that time, at any price, I would not have wanted to give back my pieces."

PRESIDING JUDGE to Lucas:—"You have heard M. Chasles. His story, equally plain and dispassionate, leaves you without excuse; you have shamefully deceived a man who had the most blind confidence in you; we see no excuse for your conduct."

Our MR. LUCAS:—"I have admitted my wrong-doings, but if I delivered counterfeit documents, I also delivered authentic ones, and the authentic [pieces] I gave are well worth the money that he gave me."

PRESIDING JUDGE:—"You gave this reply in the preliminary examination, even after the experts had declared that all that are authentic among the sales that you made are not worth more than 500 francs. In summary, you have collected from M. Chasles a sum of nearly 150,000 francs; what became of this money?"

RESPONDENT:—"I bought very expensive books and manuscripts."

EXAMINER:—"One may doubt it when one knows that a book that you bought for 25 sous, you sold for 800 francs to M. Chasles. You did not squander these 150,000 francs on amusements, because, to forge your autographed documents, you were obliged to work like a Benedictine monk; how much of this money do you still have?"

RESPONDENT:—"I have suffered misfortunes."

EXAMINER:—"That is not a proper reply; one more time, do you still have some of this money and how much of it do you still have?"

RESPONDENT (*Our Mr. Lucas, under his breath and as if desiring to hold back his words*):—"2 or 3,000 francs."

EXAMINER:—"Where are they?"

RESPONDENT:—"They are objects of little value."

EXAMINER:—"But still, in holding on to this sum, you assume the worst attitude. You are about to have a good impulse; have the courage to go through [with it] to the end. What are these objects of little value?"

RESPONDENT:—"Some books slightly damaged throughout."

M. Mabille, librarian of the Imperial Library, one of the two experts who have examined the autographed documents, declares that, except for about a hundred authentic pieces, all the documents, to the number of 27,000, sold by the accused to M. Chasles, are counterfeit, and that those that appear authentic are without value.

PRESIDING JUDGE:—"Have you not appraised the value of the authentic documents at a sum of 500 francs?"

THE WITNESS:—"At most."

PRESIDING JUDGE:—"The counterfeits, were they not executed with skill?"

THE WITNESS:—"Most certainly, and the first concern of the forger was to prepare an ink that would have the color of ink used long ago. He had some knowledge of old books and old manuscripts; he was always in libraries, where his actions led the employees to watch him."

PRESIDING JUDGE:—"He was even suspected of having damaged books at the Saint-Geneviève Library?"

THE WITNESS:—"It is possible. I am not aware of the fact."

M. HENRI BORDIER, man of letters:—"I was charged, at the same time as M. Mabille, with examining the 27,000 and some hundreds of pieces purchased by M. Chasles. We found only about a hundred authentic books, and about as many [authentic] manuscripts, most of them worthless, despite the markings of the great people to whom they supposedly had belonged."

PRESIDING JUDGE:—"Have you any knowledge [as to] whether he sold any of these to others besides M. Chasles?"

THE WITNESS:—We found two examples of this: M. the marquis Du Prat and an employee of a ministry that I no longer recall.

PRESIDING JUDGE:—"Tell us whether you find in him [Lucas] the capacity to have made all the forgeries that he is accused of and to have acted completely alone?"

THE WITNESS:—"I reply affirmatively to the two questions. His initial studies were not extended very far, but he complemented his studies by reading and by great assiduousness in his work; I do not believe that he [had] accomplices. His chief stratagem was to assume an imaginary collection, assembled by a great person, at once rich and scholarly. With the calm and composure that you know he has, he simply told his story, and allowed the buyer to excite himself on his own: the result was thus to enhance the value of the treasures that he said he possessed. After the discovery of an ink that is unique to him, we think that his principal method consisted in browning the paper with a lamp to give it an air of antiquity. We have tried his methods, but we are obliged to confess that we have not succeeded so well as he."

The accused, called upon regarding the methods he used, replies with a certain air of satisfaction that the gentlemen experts determined well enough he manner of proceeding, but he adds that he did not always succeed, and that he often had to try again several times.

The presiding judge congratulates the experts on the manner in which they discharged their task, and on the drafting of the report that was asked of them.

The list of witnesses being exhausted, the prosecuting magistrate is called upon to speak :

The imperial counsel FOURCHY expressed himself in these terms:

Gentlemen,

Lucas, who appears before you, is the author of counterfeit autograph documents by Pascal, by Newton, by Galileo that were presented to the Academy of Sciences by M. Chasles, and that gave rise to debates the echo of which has resounded throughout the scholarly world. The discussion lasted two years. From the beginning, many members of the Academy pointed out the deception; but the hoax was prepared and executed with so much skill, it found such powerful support in the complete sincerity of M. Chasles, that the counterfeit nature of the pieces presented in 1867 could be demonstrated and conceded by all only in 1869.

The forging of these counterfeit autograph documents was certainly the most skillful work of Lucas, but it represents only a small part of the colossal effort of this singular individual. In the course of eight years, Lucas devoted all his time to the completion of a fraud the success of which is unparalleled. He succeeded, by means of schemes that I shall make known to you, in being given by M. Chasles sums of money the total of which exceeds 140,000 francs.

Exploiting the passion of this scholar, he made him accept as authentic more than 27,000 counterfeit pieces[,] all of which he forged. It is because of this fraud that he is now prosecuted. He has acknowledged himself the author and the sole author of the collection that he sold to M. Chasles, and it seems that in the face of his confessions an account of his actions must become unnecessary. I have believed nonetheless that it was essential to present you with some details, the results of the preliminary investigation that has shed light on this shadowy affair. It is essential that you should know the seriousness of the swindle, that you should be convinced that Lucas falls under the application of the penal law that is claimed against him, and finally that you should be enlightened as to the ethical standards of the man whom you are about to judge.

I hope that the interest that attaches itself to this affair will excuse the extent of the treatment of the subject that will occupy my address to the court.

Almost all the questions that I am about to consider are treated in a most remarkable document that is the basis of the entire trial;

I mean the report of the two experts whom the examining magistrate charged with investigating the enormous mass of pieces forged by Lucas. If the duration of your session had allowed me, I would have read to you the report of Monsieurs Mabille and Bordier, and you would have been able thereby to appreciate its excellence. Monsieurs Mabille and Bordier have applied their knowledge to the exposure of everything, and they have presented with perfect taste the principal aspects of the considerable task that they undertook. They preserved towards Lucas an objectivity that I must praise. For these men whose whole life is devoted to the search of historical truth, a forger, like the accused, is the evil genius, and I should have forgiven these experts if I should have found in their report the expression of indignation as fierce as they felt; but they understood that the accused, solely by the fact that he is before the court, has the right to some consideration. I hasten to add that Lucas gave them no credit for their moderation. In a note that he drafted after having becoming aware of the report, he addresses to them a most unexpected reproach. He accuses them of bias, of bad faith. Lucas, whose vanity is immense, was deeply wounded by the criticisms of ignorance that the experts directed at him. He did not want his learning to be questioned; he lived for a long time with scholars of past centuries whose work he would copy, but he proved that he knew poorly the scholars of his own era; if he had studied them better, he would have known that a charge of bad faith brought against men like Monsieurs Mabille and Bordier could only be taken as a joke in very bad taste, and he would have spared himself the recriminations that can only injure himself.

I shall draw from the complete and conscientious work of the two experts almost all the arguments that I shall present to you to establish how the swindle was prepared and completed. I shall distinguish, in the entirety of the counterfeit documents sold by Lucas, between on the one hand those that remain buried in the portfolios of M. Chasles, and on the other hand those that were given by him to the Academy of Sciences. You will thus be able to appreciate at once the productivity and daring of the accused, and then his subtlety, his skill, and his sense of managing matters.

[The editors feel themselves obliged to omit from the indictment of the counsel's speech, as too long, all the sections that are only the presentation of facts already known to the reader through the preceding sections. They regret this necessary mutilation.]

. . . .

Lucas' imagination was fertile in stratagems, and he quickly carried out his ideas, but the arguments of all kinds that beset M. Charles in the course of two years were too powerful for him not to yield to the evidence.

On 13 September 1869 he solemnly acknowledged his error before the Academy.

Lucas had been arrested four days earlier.

In the course of this long discussion, the opponents of M. Chasles all thought that he was the victim of a hoax, but they would have been most surprised if they had learned that the man who alone had imagined, who had executed this audacious enterprise, was an obscure forger having no idea of the exact sciences.

Did Lucas, in acknowledging himself the sole author of the swindle, tell the truth? Did he not yield to the desire to make himself greater in the eyes of the public and to conceal his accomplices?

The experts reply without hesitation that all the autograph documents, without exception, are the work of Lucas. But could Lucas perhaps be only the workman used by an unknown person? No, gentlemen, there can remain no doubt on this point, perhaps the most interesting of all those that you have to investigate. Lucas has alone, and without other resources than the rudiments that he drew from the public libraries, dealt with all the scientific questions that were debated before the Academy of Sciences. I go so far as to say that, in all his work, the scientific part is that which is handled best. That is because in these matters Lucas used only borrowed knowledge. All these spurious letters from Pascal, from Galileo, from Gassendi were forged with the aid of fragments excerpted in specialized treatises. Lucas was only a copyist, but he was a very skilled copyist. He is not the only one who succeeded in deceiving through similar means. Every day we encounter relaters of anecdotes who have no other learning than that provided them by the *Dictionnaire de la Conversation* [dictionary of conversation. Several works appeared with this title, including *Dictionnaire de la conversation et de la lecture*—dictionary of conversation and reading (Paris: Belin-Mondar, 1833–1851) and *Nouveau dictionnaire de la conversation* (Brussells: Librarie-Historique-Artistique, 1842–1845)], or of charming conversationalists who each morning renew their stock of wit in *Figaro* or *Gaulois*. Their learning and their wit are no more genuine than that of Lucas, and nevertheless they know how to make themselves listened to, as long as they know to use their borrowings with tact. Their success explains the success of Lucas. The idea was crude; it was executed with consummate art.

. . . .

M. Chasles was the dupe of a deception that caught others unawares and deceived others besides him. One of the most famous members of the Institute himself also believed in the authenticity of the letters from Pascal, from Newton, and from Galileo.

Here is what I read, under the date of 1 June 1868, in a publication undertaken by M. [Armand Prosper] Faugère in defense of Pascal:

> The printing of this memorial *[Défense de B. Pascal etc. contre les faux documents présentés par M. Chasles*—defense of Blaise Pascal etc. against the counterfeit documents presented by M. Chasles—Paris: L. Hachette et cie, 1868] was nearly finished, says M. Faugère, when an unexpected circumstance occurred to give a new importance to grounds that urged me to publish it. I learned that one of the most important members of the Institute, belonging at once to the Académie française and to that of Moral Sciences and Politics, openly declared himself in favor of the thesis supported by M. Chasles, and that he accepted as authentic the writings attributed to Pascal. The famous historian of the Consulat et de l'Empire *[Histoire du consulat et de l'empire*—history of the consulate and the empire—an account of Napoleanic France, by (Louis) Adolphe Thiers], whom I have the deep regret of seeing lending the authority of his name to a cause that could not aspire to such an honor, very much wished to explain to me his point of view. As I believed I understood that he would wish to wait for the opportunity to publish himself the considerations on which he bases his opinion, I believe myself obliged to refrain from summarizing it here; it will suffice for me to say that they are connected with the works of Pascal on the force of gravity of the mass of the atmosphere. As a result ingeniously derived from this set of facts, M. Thiers arrives at this conclusion, that Pascal must have naturally been drawn to the threshold of the great discovery of sidereal attraction, and his divining intuition would have accomplished the rest....
>
> In thanking M. Thiers for the intention with which he was about to favor me, I challenged his opinion in person, and he promised me to examine carefully the considerations developed in my memoir. I should know to have no doubt as to the result of this examination; but if the spurious documents attributed to Pascal were able to deceive a man of universal knowledge and also of such unusual intelligence, does it not become advisable and necessary to demonstrate before the world their complete falsehood?

What then is this Lucas who held the world of scholars in check for so long? I am going to give you the particulars about him that the legal proceedings provided us.

Lucas is the son of a day laborer from Lanneray, near Châteaudun. His childhood was spent in his village, and he had no other teacher than the instructor of the elementary school. He worked in Châteaudun in the chambers of an attorney, as a clerk of the record office of the court and as registrar of mortgages. He was very industrious, and sought to educate himself. He assiduously frequented the library of the town of Châteaudun, and one finds in 1852, in the loan register, the following note in the hand of one of the librarians:

"The industrious M. Lucas is going to live in Paris. He deserves to succeed. A young man from Lanneray, self-made. 18 February 1852."

This loan register shows that Lucas was interested in historical research; but one sees appearing there one book the title of which is significant: *La Défense de M. Libri* [the defense of M. Libri. I am not certain which title this is, though several people wrote works taking Libri's side. For Libri, see ante pp. 7–8, 28.].

Upon his arrival in Paris, Lucas futilely sought employment in a library and in a bookshop. At this moment, an unfortunate chance placed him in contact with the director of a genealogical collection of ill fame, the Letellier collection, formerly the Courtois collection. It is there, apparently, that Lucas was lost and that he became what he is now.

He frequented the libraries of Saint-Geneviève, of the Arsenal, the Mazarine, and the Imperial Library. He was expelled from the Saint-Geneviève library as the result of a serious incident. A keeper [of the books] surprised him near some shelves where the books are [kept], carrying a very sharp intrument that could have been used to remove leaves. One assumes that he was seeking to detach the end-papers from volumes to procure old paper for himself.

Seized in one of his former residences:

1 A large number of letters that had been addressed to him by the people to whom he made offers of genealogical pieces;
2 Papers relating to Galileo, Rabelais, Copernicus, etc.;
3 A large quantity of autographed pieces taken from the *Isographie*, and a certain number of facsimile signatures;
4 Old paper;
5 Volumes of Moreri [Louis Moreri, *Le grand dictionaire historique*—the great historical dictionary—first published in Lyon in 1674 and frequently reprinted and translated] and of the *Mercure de France,* the end-papers of which were torn out.

Lucas was arrested on 9 September, in Saint-Georges Street, in the house he occupied together with his mistress. Previously, for a month, he was the object of police surveillance. Here is what his life was like each day:

He would leave his house at eleven o'clock and lunched, sometimes at the café Riche when he had money, sometimes at the small restaurant when money was lacking. All day he would work at the Imperial Library, and at night he would return to his house after having dined. He would not speak to anyone, and he went only to the house of M. Chasles.

He led, one sees, the most laborious life, and except for some short-lived over-indulgences, the most modest. One may ask oneself how he used these 140,000 francs that he received from M. Chasles. At one sharp question from the presiding judge, he was at the point of revealing the whole truth. He admitted having placed in reserve 4,000 or 5,000 francs, then he reconsidered his confession. This man, of humble origin and hardworking, apparently had only one goal, to amass a small fortune, and it is hard to acknowledge that he did not succeed therein.

Monsieur the imperial counsel maintained that the facts established against Lucas constitute the offense of swindling, and he concludes in these words:

Gentlemen, I have discussed from the point of view of the law the guilt of the accused because I was loyally warned by his defense lawyer that he would attack this sort of ideas. Lucas, in a series of notes that he drafted in the course of the preliminary investigation, rested his defense on other grounds.

He intended from the beginning not to cause any injury to M. Chasles. He supposedly sold to M. Chasles a certain number of authentic pieces the value of which exceeded the sums he received.

The experts made an inventory and an appraisal of these pieces, and arrived with great difficulty at a figure of 500 francs. Lucas replied to them that M. Chasles intentionally hid a certain number of pieces, and he described some of these pieces. Here is the response of the experts:

"When the accused begins the enumeration of the authentic pieces that he supposedly provided with documents of Charlemagne, of Alcuin, of Gerbert, of Saint Louis, of Blanche of Castile, he shows to what point he is unaware that such pieces cannot even exist."

Finally, gentlemen, Lucas invokes in his favor his sincerity; yes, gentlemen, his sincerity! Listen to this passage taken from one of his justificative reports:

In the end, whatever may be said and whatever may be done, my conscience is easy; I am convinced that I have not done harm to anyone. If to arrive at my goal I have not proceeded with all possible wisdom, if I have taken a roundabout way, if I have used artifice to gain attention and to pique public interest, it was in order to remind [people] of historical facts forgotten and even unknown by the majority of scholars....

I taught while amusing. The proof is that during the entire time that the discussion at the Academy of Sciences lasted, many people paid attention to the sessions and became interested in what was going to be read there. Here is testimony that the reading of these documents interested the public as much as and perhaps more than certain reports and figures that are usually read there. Never has M. Chasles been more heeded.

... Yes, whatever happens to me, I shall always be conscious of having acted, if not with wisdom, at least with rectitude and patriotism.

Such is, gentlemen, the language that he uses towards the man whom he has so shamefully abused, from whom he has many times begged bountiful assistance, and whom he jeers today after having robbed him. I demand against the accused a most rigorous application of article 405 of the Penal Code.

The defense is called upon to speak.

Reading room of the Imperial Library where Vrain Lucas created many of his forgeries.

Session of 24 February

—————>·(())·<—————

M. Horace Helbronner, named to the post of counsel for the defense for Vrain Lucas, read out the following pleas:

"Regarding what concerns the statute of limitations:

"Considering that relations between M. Chasles and the accused go back about ten years;

"That from the beginning there took place sales of authentic or spurious autograph documents to M. Chasles, and the handing over of books or manuscripts by him to the accused;

"Considering that the investigation of the experts extended to the totality of the acquisitions and that the prosecution has not in any way specified what objects were supposedly sold to M. Chasles or given away by him, since less than three years before the beginning of the lawsuit;

"That in the absence of any precise enumeration of facts on the part of the public prosecutor, the accused has the right to invoke the statute of limitations decreed by article 638 of the penal code, and to demand from this right his acquittal.

"In addition and in case the court should not declare the prosecution ended;

"Regarding that which concerns the prevention of abuse of trust:

"Considering that M. Chasles gave to the accused books in exchange for autographs, that there was established between them a kind of running account; that in disposing of the books or manuscripts that were given to him [Lucas], if it was done within three years, a fact which has not been established, the accused would not have committed any infraction of the penal code, and especially would not be rendered guilty of the offense dealt with and punished by article 408 of the penal code.

"Regarding what concerns the prevention of fraud:

"Considering that fraud has for a constitutive and essential component fraudulent schemes;

"That the existence of these schemes cannot result from mere deceitful or exaggerated claims, morally reprehensible, but not punished by the penal code;

"That the law requires, for recognizing fraudulent schemes as part of the offense of fraud, that there must have been material or external actions, the intervention of a third party or of a group of plotters organized to support the false claims;

"That it is thus that the law is interpreted by one decision, henceforth established, by the Supreme Court of Appeal;

"That in granting, against all possibility, that distinctive fraudulent schemes could be found in the case, that would not be, for that alone, an offense of fraud, given, in fact, that they would not have been used to persuade [anyone of] the existence of spurious ventures, of an imaginary ability or credit, or to give birth to the hope or fear of success, of an accident or any other chimerical event;

"For these reasons,

"Acquit the defendant, without costs."

Gentlemen, before presenting the plea that I have the honor to set down before your court, I feel the need to make a preliminary observation; I am charged by the president of the French bar with ·the defense of Vrain Lucas, a delicate task, because it involves examining to what point a scholar could be led astray by his illusions, a task even more delicate since it involves M. Chasles, whose respectability, honesty, and goodness everyone, in this affair, warrants. I do not know whether the ardor of the defense and my inexperience will lead me beyond my intentions, but what I am eager to declare, so that there should be no false interpretation of the words that I may pronounce, is that careful study of this affair has convinced me that in all its stages the honesty, the sincerity of M. Chasles have been above all suspicion.

This having been said, I must begin the discussion of the points indicated by my plea.

The lawyer here presents the arguments that he draws from the statute of limitations, and he argues against the indictment of breach of trust.

I arrive at the most important point of this defense, the indictment for fraud, and here all my discussion is going to hinge on article 405 of the penal code, the text of which I have the honor to set before you. {authors' note: Whosoever, says article 405, whether by making use of false names or false titles, or by employing fraudulent schemes to persuade [anyone of] the existence of spurious ventures, of imaginary capability or credit, or to give birth to the hope or fear of success, of an accident or any other chimerical event, shall cause to be paid or delivered any funds, and will have, by these means, swindled or attempted to swindle the whole or part of the wealth of another, shall be punished with imprisonment of one year at least and of five years at most, and of a fine of 50 francs at least, and of 3,000 francs at most.} It is faced with this article that I arrived at the conclusions set down. They were communicated to the prosecutor, who believed he summarized the approach that I am going to take, in telling you: The defense sees in the entirety of the actions charged to the accused deeds morally reprehensible, but not punishable by our laws.—The prosecutor is deceived; such is not the approach of the defense: my role is simple, I must take the articles referred to by the written and oral indictment, and to ask myself whether they apply to the facts charged. From article 405 may be deduced the definition of fraud: this article enumerates its [fraud's] indispensable constitutive elements. Along with the intention to defraud must be the use of false names, of false qualifications [e.g. authority or title], or fraudulent schemes. There is nothing to say regarding the false name or regarding false qualifications, because the indictment focuses entirely on fraudulent schemes. I then must consider whether the arguments of the accused used in fraudulent schemes of a particular kind tend to create fear or hope of a future event, which article 405 of the Penal Code has had as an object to prevent.

To simplify the discussion, one can reduce into four distinct categories the actions noted in the indictment of Vrain Lucas that remain to be examined: 1. Procedures of forgery; 2. Annotations in the books; 3. False claims relating to the Boisjourdain collection; 4. Grouping and linking of the documents.

Before inquiring whether one can find in the processes of forgery undertaken by Vrain Lucas the elements of a fraudulent scheme, I ask the court for permission to say to it some words regarding autograph collections and the trade [therein] to which the infatuation of the public has given rise.

The presiding judge spoke in the previous session of the manual of [Jacques-Charles] Brunet [*Manuel du libraire*]; there exists for autographs an analogous work, a work by one of the experts [appointed by the court to examine the forgeries of Vrain Lucas], *Dictionnaire des autographes volés au dépôts publics* [*Dictionnaire de pièces autographes volées aux bibliothèques publiques de France, précedé d'observations sur le commerce des autographes* [Paris: Panckoucke, 1851][1]—dictionary of autograph documents stolen from the public libraries of France, preceded by observations concerning the business of autographs] by MM. [Henri] Bordier and [Ludovic] Lalanne. I there found a large quantity of information about this business, that dates from only some years past.

---

1 This work discussed the thefts by Guglielmo Libri and others.

There were in the last century private collections, rich in all sorts of documents, but it is only about 1820 that the first important sales took place. The public acquired a taste for these; the sales rapidly followed each other; demand brought forth supply; soon documents were lacking, and the appetite of the lovers [of autograph documents] being sharpened, forgery was known to satisfy it. Is it not thus for all these industries in which the opportunities for success are great? Which of us has not learned this to our cost? And it is not from yesterday that these forgeries in the area of objets d'art and curios date; I shall not speak of this matter, related by Vrain Lucas himself in the statements attached to the file [of the case], of Michelangelo hiding in the gardens of the cardinal of San Giorgio, the Sleeping Cupid, that he later caused to be discovered as an antique. ["But our artist, knowing that he was losing time at Bologna, returned to Florence, where he executed a San Giovanni in marble for Lorenzo di Pier Francesco de' Medici; after which he commenced a Sleeping Cupid, also in marble and the size of life. This being finished was shown as a fine work, by means of Baldassare del Milanese to Pier-Francesco, who having declared it beautiful, Baldassare then said to Michelangelo, 'I am certain that, if you bury this statue for a time, and then send it to Rome so treated, that it may look old, you may get much more for it than could be obtained here'; and this Michelangelo is said to have done, as indeed he very easily could, that or more, but others declare it was Milanese who, having taken this Cupid to Rome, there buried it, and afterwards sold it as an antique to the Cardinal San Giorgio for two hundred crowns. Others again affirm that the one sold to San Giorgio was made by Michelangelo for Milanese, who wrote to beg that Pier-Francesco would give Michelangelo thirty crowns, declaring that sum to be all he had obtained for it, thus deceiving both him and Michelangelo."— Giorgio Vasari, *Lives of the Most Eminent Painters*, trans. Mrs. Jonathan Foster (New York: Heritage Press, 1967), 2:114. The Cupid, generally regarded now as lost, was executed in 1496. It was sold to Cardinal Raffaello Riario of Rome as an antique. He discovered the fraud and returned the statuette, but this contretemps led to Michelangelo's first visit to Rome.] I take an example that touches us more closely; some years ago an Italian offered to M. [Alfred-Amilien O'Hara] the count de Nieuwerkerke [sculptor, collector, and museum director; from 1863 to 1870 he was Superintendant des Beaux Arts, a post created specifically for him] a bust of Bianca Capello; it was the work of Benvenuto Cellini; it cost 30,000 francs; the seller, paid, returned to Italy; it was then learned, but a little too late, that he was the creator of the bust. He returned to France, he revealed [the fraud]; the Superintendent of Fine Arts, far from prosecuting him in the court of summary jurisdiction, appreciating his talent at its proper value, bore him, as they say, as his [the superintendent's] cross; I do not ask the same treatment for Vrain Lucas. I concede an objection, which is that in these transactions the deceived purchaser found consolation in the intrinsic artistic value of the object that remained with him. But there are precedents almost identical to the actions that you must judge. Vrain Lucas has a professional ancestor of whom posterity has preserved the name with that sympathy that [the images of] youth and death always inspire when they are met with in a person of genius; it is [Thomas] Chatterton, who killed himself at the age of nineteen [actually seventeen]. At the age of thirteen he sold to a Bristol [England] editor spurious poems of the thirteenth [actually fifteenth] century, that for sixty years divided the literary critics in England. [Chatterton's first published forgery, a prose piece on the opening of the bridge in Bristol, England, in 1247, supposedly translated by Thomas Rowley, appeared on 1 October 1768 in *Felix Farley's Bristol Journal*, shortly before Chatterton's sixteenth birthday.]

Do you desire more recent examples? In 1865 the abbot [Emmanuel-Henri-Dieudonné] Domenech published a book entitled: *Histoire des antiquités mexicaines.* This was following a scientific mission with which the Minister of Public Instruction had entrusted him at that time. Almost as soon as it was advertised, censure seized upon it, and a learned German professor had no trouble demonstrating that the manuscript, the basis of the work of the abbot Domenech, was all or mostly the product of the indecent imagination of an ill-mannered schoolboy. [In 1860 Domenech published *Manuscrit pictographique américan* (Paris: Gide). Among its attackers were Julius Petzholdt and J. P. Meissner, who argued that the manuscript was the work of a seventeenth-century German schoolboy.] The minister of the imperial household, who had subsidized the work, contented himself with buying back the edition. [Under Louis-Napolean the Minister of State was also responsible for the imperial household in the 1850s. On 24 November 1860 the two posts were separated.]

More recently still, a gentleman who worshiped the memory of Marie Antoinette, M. [Louis Marie Paul Vogt, comte] d'Hunolstein, wished to published one last edition of his work; he applied to the person whom the experts have named the premier French autographile, M. Feuillet de Conches, who sold him twenty-five letters of the unfortunate princess. M. d'Arndt, curator of the imperial library of Vienna, immediately demonstrated their forgery. These facts were

known, known above all in the scholarly world, in the world of collectors to which M. Chasles belonged, he could not have been
unaware of them, and he most certainly would not have been able to
complain if, instead of obtaining them from Vrain Lucas, he had
bought in the salesroom or at the salle Sylvestre [a prominent site of
book auctions at the time] this collection that cost him so much
money, and that today causes him so much annoyance.

I insist on this point, the processes themselves would not be
regarded as constituting fraudulent schemes. You cannot indict for
the inks that defied analysis, or the browning of the papers, or the
artificial means that made the documents seem older than they were.
If there had been only these, I think that there would not have been
a case. This injurious skill, which has been spoken of, might constitute another offense, but it could not be regarded as fraud. What if
an imprudent buyer, a passer-by, had acquired these autograph documents at a second-hand bookstall, would the Department of the
Public Prosecutor regard , in the art applied to their forgery, the constitutive elements of fraud? This could not happen; if it could, the
negligence of the public prosecutor and his deputies would be truly
blameworthy, because there is not in this Paris avid for curios and
unusual objects one boutique of this type that is not full of ivories,
of armor, of earthenware, of sideboards and of chests, disguised to be
mistaken for antique, and that leave the hands of the workman still
warm. The display and the sale of these objects, free of any scheme,
could not be regarded as constituting fraud.

There is then another matter: yes, there remain three series of
actions for me to pursue; the indictment presents them as constitutive elements of fraudulent schemes. But here, gentlemen, you must
ask yourselves how are fraudulent schemes recognized? Is it by examining by whom and upon whom they have been practiced? I shall not
paint for you a portrait of the accused, but these debates have exaggerated Lucas too much; they have made of him I don't know what
evil genius who, in the course of three years, supposedly held at bay
the scholars of Europe. Even though I am his lawyer, even though his
self-esteem may suffer thereby, I must restore to him his true character: this is only a compiler gifted with imagination. Here again is how
the experts regarded him:

"He has a natural bent for historical research, for the organizing
of ideas, for a sense of order, and for stage-craft; he is, therefore, able
to imagine a story and to manage it within the limits *of what he
knows.*"

If one is surprised that the Academy should devote its attention to
these documents for so long, one must not forget that they [i. e., the

documents] borrowed from the scientific environment from which they emerged and from the well-founded influence of M. Chasles a portion of their authority.

Nothing there [in the documents] bears witness to any experience and any ability that the early education of Lucas would not be able to account for. The prosecutor has shown him to you, educated at the school in his village, devouring the library of his priest, then that of the village of Châteaudun; he did not show you Lucas employed in Paris, fleeing from his desk to go to the Sorbonne, not to the course of lectures of MM. [François Pierre Guillaume] Guizot, [Jules] Michelet, [Victor] Cousin, who drew at that time the youth to the foot of their rostrum, but to the lectures, certainly instructive, perhaps tedious, of MM. [Jean Philibert] Damiron, [Charles] Lenormand, and [Eugène] Gérusez. He returned to his province, there held several jobs; but he could not free himself from this need to read and to inspect books and documents; he was impatient to return to Paris; he returned there in 1852.

His ambition was to join the imperial library; he was a born bibliomaniac, as certain others are born consummate horseback riders. Access to this career [of librarian] was closed to him because he lacked a bachelor's degree; he could not enter a bookseller's establishment because he did not know Latin. He consumed the little savings gathered by his wife, but every day he went to work at the library. There he met the marquis du Pins, an old bibliophile, who introduced him to M. Letellier. The public prosecutor's charge has painted a sufficiently vivid picture of the practice of M. Letellier, who had succeeded the genealogist Courtois.

He spoke to you of the trickeries practiced by families eager for illustrious ancestors. You will recall that all this is foreign to Vrain Lucas, who entered the establishment of M. Letellier only in 1853. This latter [Letellier] then considered liquidating his business. He used Lucas as an agent, to offer to collectors the documents relating to their families. The greatest names in France did not disdain to become Letellier's customers.

In the files were found autograph documents that sometimes Letellier handed over to Lucas, that sometimes the families refused to purchase; it is thus that Lucas began his small collection, that contained some parchments of the Valois from the Renaissance, and that, in his eyes, were priceless. It is in the course of these transactions that Vrain Lucas was put in contact with M. de Menou, an old collector well known in Paris. They made certain transactions, certain exchanges; M. de Menou, who, you will not forget, was a refugee, spent time in America, returned from there with a highly regarded collection, even gave Lucas a group of documents. The accused believed that he [Lucas] received from him [M. de Menou] manuscripts of immense value; you know about the mistakes of a connoisseur like M. Chasles, you cannot have two weights and two measures, and you will agree that this man could deceive himself regarding what he received from M. de Menou.

In this remote past, I see nothing in the conduct of Lucas that would not be worthy of praise, and I am surprised that the prosecutor should reproach him for having read in 1846 and 1847 the proceedings of the Academy of Sciences and the defense of M. Libri. Did he do so in the expectation of a return to Paris for which he no longer dared to hope? Did he do so in anticipation of dealings with MM. de Menou and Chasles that he could not suspect? It would be unjust to blame in the past those actions that in no way relate to the indictment, in a past above all honorable through the efforts that this man made to cultivate his mind and to raise himself without help, without advice, without means beyond the situation in which the chance of his birth had placed him.

There is the man of assiduous reading, who, through praiseworthy desire and indomitable energy, was torn away from an inferior position; he knew a little about everything; but not having had a guide in his labors, his knowledge was not organized, it formed in his head a disorderly encyclopedia. He presented himself to M. Chasles, whose praise in my mouth, and after the facts that you know, would be a bitter irony; it will suffice for me to remind you that he is the foremost geometrician in France if not in the world and that he has received, in this regard, a prize as greatly coveted by, as it is rarely granted to, foreigners, the great medal of honor from the Royal Society of London.[2] It is not this calculator only, living among abstract ideas, who is described for you, it is the historian of geometry who has grown old in intimate dealings with scholars of all ages and all countries. Finally, he is an experienced collector, whose treasures formerly rivaled those of M. Feuillet de Conches and enjoyed a reputation and esteem that these debates perhaps diminished. There is the man on whom Vrain Lucas did not practice fraudulent schemes, but towards whom it was sufficient for him to exercise a little imagination to create the illusions you know, so true is it that passion blinds those whom it seduces.

The defense attorney here summarizes the facts regarding the annotations of the printed books. He cites particularly the endorsement: *Ex libris Franciscus Rabelais*, a solecism that would expose [the ignorance of] a student

---

2 In 1865 Chasles received the Copley Medal from the Royal Society.

in the second form of lower school; then, grappling with the third set of actions, the deceits relating to the collection of Boisjourdain, he recalls the connections that Lucas had with M. de Menou, collector and refugee, and he explains how, in the transactions between Lucas and M. Chasles, Lucas could have intended [to refer to] M. de Menou, whereas, through the association of ideas rising from the examination of the pieces and the accounts of Lucas, M. Chasles referred to M. de Boisjourdain; he [the defense attorney] insists that Lucas never indicated M. de Boisjourdain by name; and he cites in evidence a passage in the deposition of M. Chasles before the examining magistrate.

> There remains, gentlemen, resumes the defense attorney, one last element raised by the prosecution, which is the linking, the arrangement of these 27,000 pieces that stand completely without gaps, from mythological Greece to the French Revolution. I say that this linking is not a fraudulent scheme, is not a proof of the ability of the accused, that it is on the contrary a blunder that must have led inevitably to the discovery of the deception. How, for Galileo, from whom M. Chasles had more than 3,000 autograph letters and documents, could the *collector*, the *old man*, have succeeded in recovering, in England, in Holland, in Portugal, in Sweden, the letters that the immortal persecuted man wrote. Granting that they escaped the injuries of time, accidents of all sorts, what prodigious activity must he have displayed to retrieve these letters! Granted, I admit that a fanatical admirer of Galileo would be able to do this by consecrating his whole life to the task, but this was done for many illustrious people in the collection of M. Chasles; I err, for all, yes, for all; M. Chasles did not consider either the innumerable causes of loss or of destruction, or the difficulties of reuniting these correspondences scattered for two or three centuries to the four corners of Europe. Nothing stopped him; he must have believed, in fact, that until then history had not been written. In witness thereto I cite at random the documents pointed out by the experts.
>
> M. the duc de Noailles, descendant of Mme. de Maintenon, published her history; one or two letters could have escaped him; M. Chasles owns 89 unpublished letters of the second wife of Louis XIV [Mme. de Maintenon]. It is as if MM. Hachette hardly completed the monument that they raised to Mme. de Sévigné. [Between 1862 and 1868 the firm of Hachette et cie published fourteen volumes of the letters of Mme. de Sévigné.] Two colleagues of M. Chasles at the Institute [Adolphe Regnier and Louis-Jean-Nicholas Monmequé] studied her life day by day, and they supposedly ignored 424 letters of the mother of Mme. [Françoise Marguerite de Sévigné, comtesse] de Grignan! The revolutions in our country explain the dispersal of

family archives, and I shall go so far as to admit the possibility that certain documents might have escaped the investigations of historians. But in England, where the nobility preserve with jealous care all that relates to their lineage, how can one explain the absence of so many documents from these private repositories? Another colleague of M. Chasles, Sir David Brewster, dedicated part of his life to the writing of the biography of Newton; for this purpose he secured from M. the Earl of Portsmouth, who among his ancestors numbers two very different illustrious people—Mlle. de Quérouailles [Louise Keroual or Quérouaille, Duchess of Portland and mistress of Charles II of England] and Sir Isaac Newton—the communication of all that the mathematician of whom England is proud left to him by way of documents. In these papers, there was not a single trace of connections between Pascal and Newton. That did not prevent M. Chasles from having 542 letters to Pascal and 175 from Pascal to Newton. The collection explains itself too easily regarding all this, and especially thanks to the correspondence of Voltaire, of Montesquieu, and of Desmaiseaux, that the experts have pointed out to you, consistent with the debates at the Academy.

In truth, gentlemen, I would believe I was making up a tedious tale if I did not have before my eyes the report of the experts. Charlemagne, writing to Alcuin, refers to letters of Aristotle, of Archimedes, and of Alexander; they are all in the collection. Seven centuries later, François I refers to them in writing to Rabelais; in this perfect chain not a link is missing, and this connection, this absence of gaps that appears to the public prosecutor a fraudulent scheme, has been the means thanks to which the truth has come out.

I do not desire any proof other than the debates of the Academy, and particularly the communication of M. Breton de Champs relating to the passages taken from the *Histoire des philosophes modernes* [history of modern philosophers], by the engineer Savérien.

This connection and this linking could then not be understood to constitute fraudulent schemes, and they can serve only to testify to the incompetence of Vrain Lucas.

I have run through the four categories into which I grouped the facts raised by the indictment, but there remains for me to examine them in my turn, to ask myself what actually happened between these two men, and what portion of responsibility must devolve on Lucas. To do so, I must return to an earlier time, to the period when he was a broker of documents for M. Letellier; he met at that time the marquis Duprat, an old man infatuated with pedigrees, and especially of his own; his desire, his ambition, his dream was to count the chancellor Duprat among his ancestors. He requested any autographs or documents from this figure; Letellier did not have any. He [Duprat] desperately wanted them; he insisted, he begged to such good purpose that yielding most imprudently to the solicitations of this old man, Lucas forged various letters, and particularly two letters from Montaigne, that M. Feuillet de Conches inserted in his third volume of *Causeries d'un curieux*, satisfying himself with remarking that the style of Montaigne was a bit careless in those letters.

The court will understand what must have been the surprise of Lucas, in the face of a success that surpassed his wildest hopes; a new horizon was open before him; he saw in this forgery the means to make his controlling idea triumph, because as the presiding judge remarked, Vrain Lucas, too, has his obsession, his passion; to restore to France the glories that have been snatched from it. It is not only in the documents relating to the debates about Pascal and Newton that this idea is found: Thales gives to Ambigat, king of the Gauls, advice on how to govern his people; Alexander delivers a panegyric on Gaul and on the Gauls to Aristotle; Cleopatra sends Caesarion to Marseilles for him to be taught there, both because of the good air that one breathes there and because of the fine things that one learns there. Lazarus, after his resurrection, and Mary Magdalene in her letters to Saint Peter, find no subject more interesting than the druids and the Gauls.

It is by accident that one of these documents became known to M. Chasles; he wanted to keep it, Lucas did not know how to resist his solicitations and his offers, and thus began these transactions that brought to the study of M. Chasles the collection of which the prosecutor has given you such a striking picture. It appears to me impossible to admit that M. Chasles could have attached any value whatever to documents in French and on paper, the signatures of which belong to a period prior to the Christian era. He could not give credence to I do not know what story of a collection established by Charlemagne in an abbey close to Tours. How could he have believed in the existence of the originals of letters from Cicero to Atticus, from Pontius Pilate to Tiberius, and from a French physician Castor to Jesus Christ. These documents are beneath all refutation; they were accepted undoubtedly in the parcels [of documents]; M. Chasles bought all of them for what they were worth, hoping, like the Latin poet, to find some pearls in the dunghill of Ennius. [I have been unable to trace this allusion.]

It seem to me equally impossible that M. Chasles could have acquired as authentic the items that extended from the [beginning of the] Christian era to the Renaissance; he had only to look at these pieces in the light to see in the love letters from Abelard and from Heloïse, and in the official correspondence of Frédégonde to

Chilpéric, the watermark of the fleur-de-lis of the first paper mill of Angoulême. He had only to read his 197 letters from Charlemagne to be informed about their authenticity; some were signed with the royal monogram, but the others bore *Carlo Magno*, like *Ludovico Magno* over the door of Saint-Denis. These documents could not have existed, but they were not even bad copies of manuscripts of the period. I regret the very considerable losses of M. Chasles, but I cannot refrain from affirming that, in his relations with M. Chasles, Lucas did not need to employ deceit; M. Chasles granted him, one may reproach him for it, too much trust, too much opportunity, I shall say the word, too much credulity.

There remains the third category of pieces bearing autographs of the sixteenth, seventeenth, and eighteenth centuries. Here, certainly, it was necessary to display more effort, more imagination, more intelligence; doubt was possible. Nevertheless, in the book of M. Bordier, which is the Bible of collectors, the letters of Kepler, of [Daniel] Elzevir, of Rabelais, are designated as unique pieces. Cast your eyes on the inventory prepared by the experts, and see whether, in the *number*, there was not already matter for reflection. I am not speaking of obvious improbabilities such as the use of the French language by the scholars of the sixteenth century [who corresponded in Latin], or of the anachronisms that abound in these writings, but I beg you to observe the Rabelais section, which includes 1,367 pieces. M. Faugère has too fully defended Pascal for me to venture on this territory; the public prosecutor has spoken of his work in which he proved that nothing, in the 2,316 autograph documents that M. Chasles owns, calls to mind the thought, the manner, or even the handwriting of the author of the *Pensées* and the [*Lettres*] *Provinciales*. Expert reports were necessary to remove the scales from people's eyes regarding the authenticity of 3,663 pieces by *Galileo*; these reports were most unnecessary; in these pieces [themselves] were found, in my opinion, undeniable proof of their falsehood. There was an operetta: *Le déluge!* An extremely superficial examination revealed to me all these improbabilities. If the Academy could have had at its disposal, as M. Le Verrier asked from the very beginning, the entire collection, five minutes would have sufficed for it to inform itself of the collection's worth. But the Academy had only the cream of the crop, the documents copied in learned authors, and its error was so great, that I could give myself the malicious pleasure of reading to you the judgment the permanent secretary of the Academy pronounced on these letters [ante, p. 16].

You have been told of M. Thiers; I am not about to defend the illustrious historian of the Consulate and of the Empire, but I wish to interpret prudently the note drawn from the work of M. Faugère, *La défense de Pascal,* a note from which the prosecutor must have borrowed this part of his indictment in saying to you: that carried away by his patriotic ardor and by the knowledge of the works of Pascal, and not from the autograph documents of Vrain Lucas, M. Thiers said that "Pascal must have been led naturally to the threshold of the great discovery of sidereal gravity, and that his divining intuition did the rest."

I have thus finished with the facts: What must you retain from this discussion regarding the responsibility of the accused? The penal code, when it has spoken of offense and of fraud, must have put forward a standard, and this standard the Romans took in the matter of violence from the most courageous man (Gaius, L.5, Dig.[est], *quod natus causâ.*) . The French legislator did not think he needed to take so exalted a standard. He stopped short, in criminal matters as in civil matters, at the idea of a mean. Fraud exists only in so far as it is able to engender false impressions in the person of ordinary intelligence. Writers and court decisions have declared that fraudulent schemes can only be indicted if they are of a nature to influence a person of ordinary prudence. (Supreme Court of Appeal, 7 March 1817.)

Now, gentlemen, putting aside that which the judges must not consider, the fuss, the glare, the wounded pride, in weighing this affair does your conscience allow you to affirm that M. Chasles behaved with ordinary prudence, the most ordinary, with that prudence of which the legislator and the statute law speak?

You will recall that it was not with a view to the public debates that the documents of Newton and of Pascal were forged, that without the communication prompted by the Academy of Sciences the collection would still have rested on the shelves of M. Chasles. What must be remembered is that the first communication [by M. Chasles to the Academy] raised, in the course of a week, a general outcry of indignation, that M. Chasles was warned, and that from all sides the falsity of the documents was pointed out to him; I do not wish to return again to that discussion so brilliantly recounted by the prosecutor; but there is one fact that has not yet been pointed out to you: within the committee named by the Academy at the request of M. Faugère, M. Le Verrier asked M. Chasles: 1. The provenance of these items; 2. The depositing of the entire collection at the Academy. M. Chasles absolutely refused to do so; nevertheless, he declared that this collection consisted of about 3,000 pieces; it is therefore since the communication and the debates that the communication raised that he acquired the remainder.

You will recall that, from this time, M. Chasles was not left to himself and to his illusions; in Paris, MM. Faugère, Breton de

Champs, Bénard; abroad, Sir David Brewster, the academies of Utrecht and of Florence; at the Institute, his colleagues, finally the entire scientific press of England and France demonstrated to him daily the spurious nature of his collection, and still he stopped his ears, recalling those idols of the Psalms who have ears to hear not and eyes to see not. [Psalm 135.15-17: (15) The idols of the heathen are silver and gold, the work of men's hands. (16) They have mouths, but they speak not; eyes have they, but they see not; (17) They have ears, but they hear not; neither is there any breath in their mouths.]

That which strengthened the blind faith of M. Chasles, he himself said to the examining magistrate, were the experiments in which he indulged with the help of solutions that M. Sainte-Claire Deville provided him. Then came the battle, M. Chasles had to protect his endangered pride; to the objections that disconcerted him he had to reply with new documents; he could not stop himself from demanding of Lucas the sale of all the documents that the *old man* could have, and it is thus that, without suspecting it, he became, if not the instigator of the offense, at least an accessory at once the most innocent and the most dangerous, and at this sensitive part of my speech, I call upon the experts to speak. (Report above.)

In summary, gentlemen, I believe that I have established that, by themselves, the processes of forgery, however skillful they be, are not at all punishable by law. What remains then with which to charge the accused? Of lies, nothing more, of lies of merchants wishing to sell their merchandise, and to make the most of it with this cunning, this trick that is inherent in transactions of this nature, but that could not be regarded as constituting fraud. Of lies, I repeat it, because the material facts are extraneous to the purpose of Vrain Lucas, they proceed from M. Chasles, from his colleagues, from circumstances impossible to foresee, to create, or to plot.

The democratic leader Faure (*Exposé des motifs du code pénal* [report on the bases of the penal code, Paris: A. Galland, 1810]), MM. Faustin-Hélie and Chauveau Adolphe (vol. 5, p. 1993 and following). agree in certifying that there is actually a fraudulent scheme only when the intervention of a third party or collection of intrigues comes to confirm, to support the false allegations of the material facts. Three judgments by the Court of Appeals of 11 July 1861, 20 November 1862, and 18 June 1863, have confirmed this doctrine, henceforth unassailable. It was applied in a case almost identical to this one, in a decision of the court of Douai of 5 May 1846 (D.[écret] P.[arlementaire—parliamentary enactment] 1846, 4-270). There must then be something else besides lies for it to be fraud, and this

other thing you would look for in vain in the dealings of Lucas with
M. Chasles.

But even if you should find the presence of fraudulent schemes,
you would still not be able to apply to Vrain Lucas article 405 of the
penal code. The schemes that this text forbids are of a very special
type. They must tend to persuade [someone] of the existence of spurious business concerns, with imaginary capacity or credit, or to give
rise to hope or fear of success or of any other chimerical outcome.
This case presents nothing of the kind, nothing relating to the future,
unless the public prosecutor be prepared to maintain that Lucas
promised to M. Chasles the glory of success in the Academy, five
years before one could have imagined that the documents would be
presented in that environment.

One last word, gentlemen, and I am finished. I have spoken to
jurists and to judges; I am going now to speak to men. In judging
those who are brought before you, you must, like all jurors, examine
with the most scrupulous attention all the circumstances of a case; I
believe that I can tell you, independent of any legal issues, there are
in this affair grave reasons to hesitate before pronouncing judgment.
The legislator has asked of all citizens what he can ask of them; he
has not enjoined on them either stoicism or heroism; he could not
do so; these more elevated morals have the sanction only of the court
of the conscience. Without wishing to digress into considerations
that would be distracting, I ask you to reflect on the irresistible temptation that was offered to Vrain Lucas through the ease with which
M. Chasles bought all that he [M. Chasles] was able to buy.

Lucas should have told him the first day: this piece is forged; he
should have resisted from the first time the allure of such easy profit, in considering the never-failing benevolence of this aged scholar;
but when he [Lucas] had deceived him [Chasles] the first time ten
years ago, when the contest in the Academy had begun, and the ardor
of that struggle had seized upon M. Chasles and him [Lucas], it
would have required a superhuman strength to stop on the down-
ward slope, to repulse the temptation continuously renewed, and
presenting itself as ever more easy and more profitable; if you should
find in our Penal Code a statute for punishing Vrain Lucas, you
should not forget, you must not forget this article so just, so far-
sighted, thanks to which the legislator has allowed you to judge
humanely of human affairs.

Judgement

———————⸻⟪◉⟫⸻———————

*A*FTER AN HOUR'S RECESS, the court returns to session and pronounces sentence of which these are the terms:

THE COURT,

Considering that from the preliminary investigation and the trial the proof emerges that, within the past three years, in Paris, the accused sold to M. Chasles, an important group of manuscripts composed, in part, of autographs of various very famous people, and, in part, of very old copies of writings proceeding from these people, that, in their entirety, were forged by him, and that for these he was paid by M. Chasles more than 140,000 francs;

Considering that this misrepresentation does not constitute simply the offense of deceit relating to the nature of goods sold and that it presents all the elements of the offense of fraud;

Considering, as a matter of fact, that Lucas claimed that these pieces, to the number of several thousands, had belonged to an eighteenth-century collector; that, transported to America, they nearly perished in a shipwreck; that they remained in the ocean for several days; that, later, they returned to France, in the possession of a descendant of this supposed collector, and that their true owner, wishing to sell them off, entrusted him with carrying out the sale;

Considering that Lucas thus assumed the bogus title of agent of an imaginary owner of this rich collection of autograph documents;

That in fact, this bogus title does not appear to be the circumstance that caused M. Chasles to pay him [Lucas] the sums of money of which he has been robbed, and that it would not in itself suffice to cause the actions charged to Lucas to be styled as fraud; but it is essential to keep it in mind, because the story of a spurious collection, of a sea voyage, of a shipwreck, assumes an important place in the whole of the fraudulent schemes employed by the accused to obtain the confidence of M. Chasles by insidious means;

That the first of these incidents consisted of the procedures used in forging spurious pieces, in the choice of old paper, in the imitation of ancient handwritings, in the effort of immersing the paper for a longer or shorter time in water, of browning it in the smoke of a lamp, etc., etc., in the employment of substances that changed the ink used and that gave it the appearance of very old ink;

Considering that at the very time when he used these various fraudulent procedures, Lucas had in mind the sales that he was going to propose to M. Chasles, and that it was directly against M. Chasles, and with the purpose of more assuredly deceiving him, that he undertook these schemes;

That as a matter of fact, they produced the result that their author intended, and that some of them most particularly gained the trust of M. Chasles in coming to the support of the lies of Lucas;

Considering that this happened particularly in regard to the fraudulent scheme that consisted of soaking the writings in water, and in regard to that which consisted in using, for the ink, certain procedures of adulteration;

That thus, M. Chasles having requested one of his colleagues at the Institute to secure for him a liquid capable of restoring the writing of certain pieces, the use of this liquid gave to the entire surface of the paper a blackish hue, from which it was concluded that the fact of the shipwreck was true, and that the remaining in the sea had produced this result, such that the iron of the ink was spread throughout the sheet of paper;

That on another occasion, and while certain pieces forged by Lucas were, at the Academy of Sciences, the object of lively discussions, some members of this institution thought that with the assistance of a procedure reputed heretofore infallible, they could determine the antiquity of the ink, and declared, after this experiment, that most certainly the pieces brought forth by M. Chasles had been written a long time ago, when in fact they were the very recent work of the accused;

That thus, the adulteration of the ink defeated a method of testing and verification and yielded a result that must have increased the confidence of M. Chasles in the authenticity of the documents that were sold to him by Lucas;

Considering that one fraudulent scheme practiced most directly against M. Chasles consisted of presenting to him each group of pieces in such wrappers as collectors are accustomed to use, and bearing the annotations that they [collectors] customarily write on them;

That this scheme tended to strengthen M. Chasles in the belief that by means of these successive purchases, he was becoming the owner of the rich collection of a person of the eighteenth century who, at first, was not named, and whom, later, Lucas claimed to be M. the comte de Boisjourdain;

Considering that with the manuscript pieces of which the number exceeds twenty-seven thousand, Lucas, in addition, sold to M. Chasles a certain number of books of no value, for which he obtained exorbitant prices, after having decked them out with spurious signatures of famous people to whom these books were reputed to have belonged;

That to this first scheme, consisting of affixing spurious signatures to these books, Lucas added another, more directly employed against M. Chasles, that consisted of inscribing on the end papers of each volume annotations by which the imaginary eighteenth century collector made known in what circumstances he was able to secure this extremely rare volume, what price he was obliged to pay, what seductive offers he rejected after he had become the fortunate owner;

That thus, and by the use of fraudulent schemes, the sales of books constitute, as well as the sales of the manuscript pieces, the crime of swindling;

Considering that all these schemes tended to raise in the mind of M. Chasles the hope of a chimerical event, that is to say the hope that through the concluding of the dealings that were proposed to him, he was going to own ancient, rare, precious pieces, and [pieces] of undoubted authenticity;

That thus they certainly fall under the terms of article 405 of the Penal Code;

Considering, as to the statute of limitations, that it is true that the sales of spurious autographs go back to the year 1861, it is equally certain that they continued, without interruption, until the month of September, 1869, until the very eve of the arrest of Lucas, and that thus a large number of these sales go back to less than three years before the beginning of the prosecution;

Considering, with regard to that which relates to the offense of breach of trust, that M. Chasles has specified two facts; the first sufficiently serious, going back more than three years before the prosecution, and thus rendered immaterial by the statute of limitations; the second, unimportant, and concerning which one can, within limits, concede the good faith of the accused;

That in fact, it has been stated by M. Chasles that certain manuscripts were delivered to him in the form of exchange for books from his library, and that it is not impossible that Lucas believed, just as he claims, that the three volumes upon which rested the breach of trust not rendered immaterial by the statute of limitation were given to him in the form of exchange and not in trust:

For these reasons,

The court acquits Lucas of the count of the indictment that relates to the crime of breach of trust;

It declares him guilty in fact and in law of causing himself, within three years before the beginning of the prosecution, in Paris, by engaging in fraudulent schemes to give rise to the hope of a chimerical event, to be paid by M. Chasles various sums of money, and to have thus swindled part of the fortune of the other;

And, applying to him article 405 of the penal code,

It sentences him to two years in prison and a 500 franc fine.

It sets at two months the term of his imprisonment for debt, provided he has a place to exercise, for payment of the fine.

It orders him, moreover, to pay the costs of the trial.

FACSIMILES

━━━━━━━━━►((◐))◄━━━━━

We give under this heading, on the following pages, the text of the plates where we have reproduced some samples of the false autographs executed by Vrain Lucas (numbers I to XI), to which we have added, for purposes of comparison, three fragments of authentic writing (numbers IX(a), X(a), and XI(a).)

1.—Fragment of letter from Sappho to Phaon
[Compare Ovid's "Sappho to Phaon" in his Heroïdes]

Sappho to her most beloved Phaon, greetings.
My dearly beloved near these charming shores where the sight looks in wonder while losing itself in a vast expanse, where the depths of the sea and the arch of the skies seem to blend in the distance, not far from this same shore is a bed of verdure that a thick elm shades and a pure wave waters. It was there if you recall my dearly beloved that embraced by love you gave me the first kiss and urged me to return it. It was there dear Phaon that trusting in your caress, I blushingly confessed, alas, my affection and also my weakness. How would I have been able to resist your ardor, since in your eyes was portrayed the candor of your soul, sweet brilliance of love made your charms glow. Oh dear Phaon some beautiful day, I hope I will again see your tender eyes that will fill with tears. Oh do you remember how to your tender Sappho you appeared consumed in passion[?] I thought I saw the gods who seduced your heart, return to me, return because without you I cannot live. Farewell.
Sappho

No 2

2.—Challenge of Julius Caesar to Vercingetorix

Julius Caesar to the leader of the Gauls.
I am sending to you a friend of mine who will tell you the
purpose of my voyage; I wish to cover with my soldiers the
land where you were born. It is pointless for you to wish to
prevent me. You are brave, I know, but I will be so as well
if the gods wish, so surrender to me your arms or prepare your-
self for combat. This VI of the Kalends of July.

Julius Caesar

On the back.

This is the challenge that Julius Caesar sent to
Vercingetorix, leader of the Gauls.

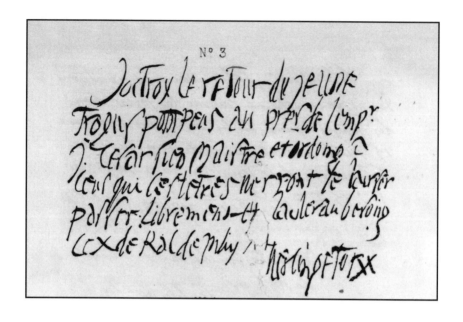

3.—Safe conduct pass of Trogue Pompey

Safe conduct of Trogue Pompey

I grant the return of the young Trogue Pompey to the Emperor Julius Caesar his master and order those to whom these letters come to allow him to pass freely and to help him in case of need.

This tenth of the Kalends of May . . . (date torn).

Vercingetorix

On the back.

This is the letter that Vercingetorix the leader of the Gauls gave to Trogue Pompey who had come to bring him a letter from Julius Caesar, so that he could return freely to his master.

4.—*Letter from Dagobert to Saint Eloi*

My very dear and most beloved Eloi that which you urge me to do for the remembrance of the blessed Dionysius who was the first to come to the Gauls to preach there the faith of Jesus Christ has been undertaken as you know by the most illustrious Geneviève of Nanterre [patron saint of Paris], despite which, I will follow your advice and [your] desire to have built near this church a monastery bearing this name [i.e., Saint-Denis] where my Oriflamme [banner of the French kings] will be. Therefore come to see me and we will devise the plan for this together. This XX of May 629.

Dagobert King

No. 5

Tres doste et tres ame alcuin au nombre des escrits
les authorites que nous auons. pour estre enseignee aux.
enfans et test-uons mon tres ame a qui se donne ce som. adieu
ce 20 aoust 802   carlemaigne Rex.

5.—Letter from Charlemagne to Alcuin

Most learned and most beloved Alcuin in the number of writings that you have sent me I have told you that there were some that give proof to me of the stay of Hercules among the Gauls and that he there married Galatea, daughter of King Celtus, what reason could anyone have not to believe in this union and that I should believe rather in that of Alexander with Roxanne. After all why must we have less regard for the Gauls our ancestors than for the nations that are foreign to us. Whence comes it that I should believe that a Ninus and a Semiramus reigned in Babylon and that I should refuse to believe that there were also at that time kings among the Gauls and for what reason of the same authorities that certify to me these two facts one should be believed and not the other. This can only be the effect of a faulty education that from our infancy teaches us foreign history that we are told about and that one neglects to instruct us in that of our country, there is an (evil) which I understand must be remedied in the education of the young; therefore after having closely reflected on this matter I desire and intend that a work of history be made in the best manner based on the authorities that we have to be taught to the children and it is you my dearly beloved to whom I give this task. Farewell.

This 20 August 802.

Charlemagne, King

Nº 6

Mon doulx amy. Je vois que je n'estois pas
née pour estre heureuse je viens d'enfuire
le preuve. de l'estat le plus brillant ou je tous
je tombe tout a coup.......... Heloïsse .

a mon doulx amy mon amé Abaillard

6.—*Fragment of letter from Heloise to Abelard*

*My gentle friend I see that I was not born to be happy I
am about to prove this [fact]. From the most splendid state I fall
suddenly into the greatest torments following the horrible tortures
that you have been made to endure. Ah! How cruel people are
my gentle friend, you have been forced to bear such sufferings if
you cannot survive them neither will I be able to survive them.
Moreover and for me I wish to die, yes to die to this pitiless
world. My resolution is well-fixed just as I have told you. I am
entering a convent never to leave, because a misfortune so sudden,
so unexpected removes from me all hope of happiness. It is not the
wealth that my uncle has taken from me that I miss, of this you
must be convinced, but must I not complain against the destiny
that takes from me not only a lover, but a husband before God
whom I love so tenderly since to believe that your love will survive
the test of such a blow would be too much to imagine. Alas! What
a weak resource are inclinations when one no longer has anything
to satisfy them: there still remains to me enough money for me to
go to plunge myself into a cloister in the deplorable [authors:
state?] in which I find myself it is the only course that I have to
take. I will mourn my misfortunes, I will mourn my gentle
friend, happy if I can succeed in recovering a repose that will be
henceforth the object of my desires. Do not forget me my gentle
friend, if courage does not desert you write to me often, let me share
your thoughts. This will be for me great consolation. Farewell,
farewell, may the Lord and the blessed Virgin Mary his mother keep you in their good graces. This X June.
       Heloise.   To my gentle and well-beloved Abelard.*

7.—Letter from Joan of Arc to the Parisians

Jesus + Mary

Brave Parisians be and remain at rest. The army of your king has arrived before Paris and is camped here between the village of La Chapelle and Saint-Honoré gate. I myself am going to approach the knoll of the mills. Paris is ours, tomorrow we will sleep there, this is true as [this is] the same day [8 September] that the mother of God was born. God be praised. This seventh day of September.

Joan

To the Parisians from Joan called La Pucelle [the maid].

8.—*Letter from Rabelais to Luther*

This X June 1544

Master Luther, I have told you many times and moreover for a long while that I do not at all wish to involve myself in matters of religion or of controversy, but since you have nevertheless condescended to send me your pamphlet entitled Adversus papalum Romae a satanum fundatum etc. [against the Roman papacy established by Satan] I promise you to read this said manuscript and to tell you my opinion of it. Meanwhile I beg you to accept my greetings.
I am sir your most humble servant.

F. Rabelais
To Master Martin Luther.

9.—*Letter from Galileo to Pascal.*

Saturday.

Sir, according to your observations distances varying directly with forces in equal time and bodies traveling fifteen feet per second because of the force of gravity of the earth one will have 41083200 1 :: 15 x = 15/41083200=7/2738880' and this will be the distance traveled in a second by one of the planets towards the other supposedly fixed. Now in thirty days there are 2592000 seconds so this movement remaining constant one will have 1.2592000::2/2738880x = 2592000/2738880 x 2 this will not amount to two feet, particularly if one considers friction, which is a third of the mass or equivalent to 41083200/3 and therefore immense in comparison to the tendency towards the planet. One will see that the most polished spheres placed on the most level plane cannot approach each

other in the least in the longest period of time, for the same reason, light bodies that fly towards our most massive buildings,
will be so little attracted by these masses in comparison with
their weight or tendency towards the earth that the diagonal
that they must describe to satisfy these two forces, will differ from
the radical only by an immeasurable amount. Whereupon I
am, Sir, your most humble and most obedient servant.

Galileo Galilei
For Monsieur Pascal.

N° 9ᵇⁱˢ   (Authentique)

*9(a).—Fragment of an authentic letter of Galileo
taken from Isography*

. . . Waiting, an order to serve you in agreement to that;
and meanwhile to you and to your Francesco your son with
all my affection I kiss your hands, and I pray for your most
serene highness' happiness. From Padua 24 August 1607.
From your serene highness' most obliged servant.

Galileo Galilei

10.—Letter from Pascal to Galileo

Sir I have just received your dialogues as I have expressed to you the desire to have them and I thank you most sincerely for the willingness you have shown to satisfy me I will be eternally grateful to you for that, I intend sir to reread from the beginning and at my leisure this interesting product of your genius, and I will return the French translation as you ask me as soon as I have compared them, which is to say to you sir that I plan to attend to this matter immediately. I will put you in possession of this translation through Monsieur Diodati who has assured me [that he will] soon make a new voyage to Italy before he settles here, I will say nothing fur-

ther in this letter, except to join with my thanks, the assurance
of my affection and my esteem *[.]* happy to be sir
    Your most humble, most devoted and most obedient ser-
vant,

Pascal.
To Monsieur Galileo.

N⁰ 10ᵇⁱˢ   (Authentique)

10(a).—Fragment taken from the original manuscript of
Pascal's Pensées, preserved at the Imperial Library

    It is unfair that one become devoted to me even though
one should do so with pleasure and voluntarily, I should mis-
lead those in whom I have awakened desire, because I am not
the ultimate end of anyone and do not have the means to satisfy
them [Pensée 15].

Pascal.

11.—*Letter from Louis XIV to M. de Tracy.*

Monsieur [Alexandre de Prouville, Marquis] de Tracy [governor of Canada, 1663-1667] I have seen with complete satisfaction all that you have written here to inform me of what is happening in the area of your responsibility and although I have ordered Sieur [Jean Baptiste] Colbert to respond to it by a fuller dispatch on which I rely[,] Your conduct is so consistent with my intentions and so beneficial to my undertakings that I cannot stop myself from testifying to you through these lines how grateful I am to you for it, waiting for the occasion to give you better signs of my gratitude[,] I pray God to hold you Monsieur de Tracy in his good graces. At Saint-Germain 18 October 1666.

Louis.

To M. de Tracy my lieutenant in America.

N° 11ᵇⁱˢ (Authentique)

11(a).—Authentic letter from Louis XIV.
Imperial Library F.[onds] Fr.[ançais—French archives] 10261 p. 45

You have too good an opinion of me to give me the glory of the taking of Besançon my troops had a great part there and moreover I must acknowledge that it is principally owing to God, but I cannot fail to feel the affection that you convey in expressing yourself as you do. Things that come from such a cause cannot fail to be agreeable.

Louis.

On the back:

To my cousin the wife of field marshal [Philippe] de La Mothe[-Houdancourt].

Inventory of Autographs Forged by Vrain Lucas, and Sold by Him to M. Michel Chasles, of the Academy of Sciences

———⟫«(●)»⟪———

ABACO (PAOLO DALL'), 1 letter to Boccaccio. — Abelard (Peter), 1 letter to Heloise; 2 letters to the Pope; 1 letter to William of Champeaux; 1 letter to the abbot of Fleuri sur Loire; 3 pieces of poetry, of which one is entitled: *L'Amant infortuné* (the unfortunate lover). — Abbon, Abbot of Fleuri, 1 letter to Pope Gregory V. — Abd-er Rahman, 1 letter to the general of the Franks. — Adalberon, Archbishop of Rheims, 2 letters to Gerbert. — Adam de Nevers, 1 piece of poetry. — Adrian, emperor, 4 letters. — Aetius, Roman general, 1 letter to Epiphanus. — Agnes Sorel, 8 letters to King Charles VII; 14 letters to Jacques Coeur; 3 letters to Madame de Villequier; 1 letter to Poton de Xaintrailles; 1 letter to the Count de Dunois; 2 letters without the name of recipient. — Aiguillon (Duchess of), 2 letters to Galileo. — Alamanni (Luigi), 1 letter to Rabelais; 3 pieces of poetry. — [Guilio] Alberoni, 2 letters to Montesquieu; 1 letter to Father Mersenne. — Albert, bishop of Ratisbonne, 3 letters to Jean de Meung. — Alcibiades, 5 letters to Pericles; 2 moral precepts. — Alcuin, 1 *Chronicon regum Francorum* (chronicle of the kings of the Franks); 1 *Regulae Abaci* (rules for abbots); 50 pieces of poetry, maxims, etc., most drawn from Boethius; 2 letters to Einhard; 5 letters to Bede; 4 letters to Queen Gisele, at Argenteuil; 1 letter to Cuthbert; 116 letters to Charlemagne; 1 transcript of the letter of Saint Remi to Clovis. — Aldus Manutius, 2 letters to Grolier; 1 letter to Frédéric Morel; 1 letter without the name of the recipient. — Alexander the Great, 1 letter to Aristotle. — Alexander VI, pope, 3 letters, of which one is to Christopher Columbus. — Alembert (d'), 12 letters to Voltaire, Fontenelle, La Beaumelle, Borda, Montesquieu, etc. — Alfonzo d'Este, 2 letters to [Philippe] Desportes. — Anacreon, 2 letters to Pythagoras; 2 notes. — Anastasius, pope, 1 letter to Clovis. — Ambigat, king of the Gauls, 1 letter to Thales. — Amerigo Vespucci, 8 letters to Rabelais, 7 letters to René de Vaudemont; 1 letter to Comines; 2 letters in Latin to his father and to the duke of Lorraine. — Anaximander, 1 letter to Thales. — Anaximenes, 2 letters to Anaximander. — Angennes (Julie d'), 2 letters to Jacqueline Pascal; 4 letters without the name of the recipient. — Anne of Brittany, 8 letters to the king, to the lord of Guemené, etc. — Anne, queen of England, 7 letters to the king of France; 2 letters to Fontenelle. — Anselm of Canterbury, 2 letters to the prior of Canterbury. — Antonius (Titus), 2 letters to Augurinus. — Apollinarius (Sidonius), 2 letters to Eubulides. — Apuleius, 3 letters. — Arcesilaus, 1 letter to Euclid. — Aratus, 1 letter to Antigonus. — Archytas, 4 letters to Plato. — Aretino (Pietro), 1 piece of poetry; 3 letters to Rabelais; 26 sonnets; 34 quatrains. — Ariosto, 2 letters to Rabelais; 2 pieces of poetry. — Aristarchus, 1 letter to Crates. — Aristotle, 4 letters to Euthymenes. — Arius, 1 letter to Eusebius. — Arnaud de Villeneuve, 5 letters to Raymond Lulle. — Arnaud d'Andilly, 1 letter without the name of the recipient. — [Francis] Atterbury, bishop of Rochester, 3 letters to Newton. — Atilla, 1 letter to the general of the Franks. — Aubrey (John), 2 letters to Pascal; 2 letters to [Charles de Marguetel de Saint-Denis de] Saint-Evremond; 1 life of Abraham Cowley. — Augurinus, 12 letters to Pliny; 10 letters to Pomponius Mela; 3 letters to Tacitus; 3 letters to Florus; 2 letters to Suetonius; 15 miscellaneous notes. — Augustus, emperor, 1 letter to Virgil; 1 letter to Varus; 2 letters to Trogue Pompey; 2 letters to Montanus. — Saint Augustine, 1 letter to Epiphanus; 3 letters to Ausonius. — Aventin, archdeacon of Chartres, 1 letter to his parents. — Avienus (Festus), 1 letter to Ausonius. — Avitus, 1 letter without address. — Avitus, abbot of Micy, 1 letter without name of recipient.

[FRANÇOIS LE COIGNEUX DE] BACHAUMONT, 3 letters or reports. — Bacon (Francis), 3 letters to Montaigne; 3 letters to Mademoiselle [Marie le Jars] de Gournay; 1 letter to [François de] Malherbe; 5 letters to various people. — Bacon (Roger), 2 letters to Sire de Joinville; 3 letters to Jean de Meung; 1 letter to the pope. — [Jean Antoine de] Baïf, 3 pieces of poetry. — [Jean Sylvain de] Bailly, mayor of Paris, 2 letters, of which one is to the king. — Balzac (Guez de), 18 letters to Salmasius, Corneille, etc.; 3 pieces of poetry. — Barberino (Francesco), 5 pieces of poetry. — Barberini (Maffeo), 5 letters to Galileo, in Italian; 12 pieces of poetry. — [Johan van Olden] Barneveldt, 12 letters, one of which is to the king and another to Mademoiselle de Gournay. — Baro [for Bora] (Catherine), widow of Luther, 1 letter to the king of Denmark. — Baron (Michel), 2 letters to Jean Baptiste Rousseau. — [François, Baron de] Bassompierre, 2 letters to Galileo. — [Pierre du Terrail] Bayard, 4 letters to Rabelais; 2 to the king; 1 song to his sweetheart. — [Pierre] Bayle, 3 letters to [Adrien] Baillet. — Bede, 6 letters to Alcuin. — Beauxoncles (R. de), 1 letter to Clément Marot. — Belisarius, 2 letters to Cassiodorus. — Belleau (Rémy), 2 pieces of verse. — Bellini (Gentile), 1 letter on optics. — Bembo (Pietro), cardinal, 4 letters to Rabelais; 1 letter to the king; 1 letter to Clément Marot. — [Isaac de] Benserade, 3 letters to Molière; 2 letters to La Bruyère; 2

letters to La Fontaine; 11 letters to [Jean François] Regnard; 3 letters to [Charles Rivière] Dufresny; 3 letters to [Charles] Perrault; 2 letters to Galileo; 12 letters to [Jean Donneau] de Vizé and others. — [Cornelio] Bentivoglio (the cardinal), 2 letters to Pascal; 17 letters to the king of France; 6 letters to Balzac; 3 letters to Mademoiselle de Gournay; 2 letters to [Anthony] Van Dyck; 1 letter to Madame [Jeanne Françoise Fremiot] de Chantal; 2 letters to the *blessed* Vincent de Paul; 1 letter to Boulliau; 1 defense of the most illustrious Galileo. — Bernard, abbot of Clairvaux, 4 letters to Suger; 1 letter to Abelard. — Bergman, 1 letter to the abbot of Saint-Léger. — [Matthäus] Bernegger, 1 letter to Galileo. — [Giovanni Lorenzo] Bernini (the cavalier), 2 letters. — [Christophe] Bernouli, 5 letters to Voltaire; 8 letters to [Pierre Louis Moreau de] Maupertuis; 3 letters to [Guillaume François Antoine de] L'Hôpital; 12 letters to [Willem Jacob van] 'SGravesande; 5 letters to [Pierre] Desmaiseaux; 25 letters to [Bernard le Bovier de] Fontenelle; 1 letter to [Jean le Rond] d'Alembert; 3 letters to [Charles Louis de Secondat, Baron de] Montesquieu; 3 letters to the Marquise [Gabrielle Emilie le Tonnelier de Breteuil] du Chastellet [Voltaire's mistress]; 1 letter to Newton; 2 letters to [Carlo] Sigonio; 4 letters to Cartaud de La Vilate; 3 letters to the king; 5 letters without indications of recipients. — Bertha, daughter of Caribert, 2 letters to the pope. — [John] Bessarion (the cardinal), 1 letter to Comines. — Beza (Theodore de), 1 letter to Rabelais; 2 letters to Montgomery; 1 piece of poetry. — [Jean Paul] Bignon (the abbot), 2 letters to [Joseph Pitton de] Tournefort; 2 letters to Newton. — Blanche of Castile, 3 letters to Sire de Joinville; 4 letters to her son Saint Louis; 2 letters to Thibaud [II], Count of Champagne; 3 songs. — Boethius, 12 letters to Victorinus, Gregory of Tours, etc.; 6 letters to Simplicius; 6 letters to the bishop of Bourges; 4 letters to Cassiodorus; 2 letters to Sidonius Apollinarius; 6 letters to Ennodius; 18 notes or comments. — Boccaccio (Giovanni), 23 letters to Petrarch; 2 letters to Nicolas Flamel; 1 letter to Pierre Bercheure; 1 biography of Petrarch; two pieces of poetry. — Boëtie ([Etienne] de la), 6 letters to Montaigne, to the queen, to the Duke of Guise; to Du Bellay, etc.; 52 sonnets. — [Robert] Boyle, 3 letters, of which one is to the king. — [Nicolas] Boileau, 2 letters to [Claude] Brossette; 2 letters to Racine; 1 letter to [François de] Maucroix; 2 letters to Desmaiseaux; 3 letters to various people. — Boisjourdain (de), 2 letters. — Boisrobert, [François de] Metel, 2 pieces of poetry. — [Henry St. John, Viscount] Bolingbroke, 1 letter to Voltaire; 1 letter to the king; 2 letters to [Françoise d'Aubigné] Madame de Maintenon; 3 letters to various others. — Bonaventure (brother), 1 letter to the Reverend Father Alexander of Hales. — Boniface VIII, 1 letter to Charles of Valois. — [Jean Charles] Borda, 2 letters. — [Carlo Federigo] Borromeo (the cardinal), 5 letters to the king of France; 5 letters to Montaigne; 1 letter to Jean d'Auton; 1 letter to Philippe

Desportes; 3 letters to Christopher Columbus; 2 letters to the Duc [Louis de Gonzague] de Nevers. — [Jacques Bénigne] Bossuet, 12 short treatises addressed to J.[ean] Hamon; 2 letters to Madame Perrier; 4 letters to various others. — [Ismaël] Boulliau, 12 letters to M. [John] Flamsteed; 16 letters to Huygens; 9 letters to Pascal; 18 letters to the king; 3 letters to Newton; 4 letters to the abbot [Jean Paul] Bignon; 4 letters to Pierre Petit; 8 letters to [Vincenzo] Viviani; 3 letters to [Edme] Mariotte; 1 letter to Father Mersenne; 1 letter to [Thomas] Hobbes; 2 letters to Doctor [Isaac] Barrow; 3 letters to Bernouli; 2 letters to Desmaiseaux; 1 letter to [Giles Personne] Roberval; 1 letter to [Evangelista] Torricelli; 6 letters to various others; 9 extracts of other letters. — Bourbon (Armand de), 16 letters to Molière. — Bourbon (Charles, Cardinal of), 3 letters to the king. — [Louis] Bourdaloue, 2 letters. — Burgundy (Philip, Duke of), 1 letter to Comines. — [Edme] Boursault, 1 letter to [Nicolas] Malebranche; 2 letters to Boileau; 1 piece of poetry. — [Pierre de Bordeilles] Brantôme, 26 letters to various people; 2 letters to Galileo. — Brégy (comtesse de), 4 letters. — Breteuil du Chastellet (Madame de), 8 letters to Desmaiseaux; 3 letters to Voltaire; 2 letters to [Pierre Louis Moreau de] Maupertuis; 2 letters to [Jean] Bouhier; 1 letter to the Duke de Richelieu. — [Pierre Jacques] Brillon, 1 letter. — Brunetto Latini, 1 letter to Sire de Joinville; 1 letter to the Duke of Anjou. — [George Villiers, first Duke of] Buckingham, 1 letter to Galileo. — Budé (Guillaume), 5 letters to Rabelais; 1 letter to Erasmus. — [Georges Louis Leclerc, Comte de] Buffon, 3 letters to various people. — [Roger] Bussy-Rabutin, 4 letters to various people.

CALIGULA, 1 letter to the prefect of the Praetorium at Lyon. — Callot (Jacques), 1 letter to Galileo; 3 letters, one of them to the king; 6 descriptions of tapestries. — [Augustine] Calmet (Dom), 1 letter to [Laurent Josse] Leclerc, Doctor of the Sorbonne. — [John] Calvin, 3 letters to Rabelais; 9 letters to Theodore de Beza. — [Tommaso] Campanella, 4 letters to Galileo; 3 letters to [Nicolas Claude Fabri de] Peiresc. — [Jean Galbert de] Campistron, 5 letters to [Jean] Racine and to [Luigi] Riccoboni. — [Jerome] Cardan, 11 letters to Rabelais; 10 pieces on numbers, mathematical problems, etc. — Carausius, emperor, 2 letters to Diocletian. — [Ugo or Girolamo] da Carpi, 1 letter to Rabelais. — Caracci, 1 letter to Pierre Charron. — [Giovanni Domenico or Jacques] Cassini, 7 letters to the king; 8 letters to Newton; 6 letters to the abbot Boulliau. — Cassiodorus, 1 letter to Belisarius; 2 letters to Avitus; 3 letters to the bishop of Bourges; 8 letters to Boethius; 4 letters to Simplicius; 5 letters to Fortunatus. — Castor (Antonius), Gallic [actually Roman or Greek] physician, 1 letter to Tiberius; 1 letter to Jesus Christ. — Catherine de Medici, 4 letters to Charles IX; 3 letters to Montaigne; 9 letters to various others. — Catherine of Russia, 3 letters to d'Alembert. — Catherine of Navarre, 5 letters to

[Philippe] Desportes, Mademoiselle de Gournay, etc. — Catullus, 2 pieces of poetry. — Caus (Salomon de), 1 letter. — Celestine I, pope, 1 letter to the dean of Bayeux. — Cervantes, Miguel de, 5 letters to Montaigne; 30 letters to Mademoiselle de Gournay; 105 mottoes, moral proverbs in quatrains, etc. — Julius Caesar, 1 challenge to Vercingetorix; 6 letters to Trogue Pompey; 2 letters to Divitiacus; 2 letters to [C. Lutorius] Priscus; 1 letter to Valerius Procillus; 182 historical notes, reflections, etc. — Chabiau (Laura), 18 letters to Petrarch; 18 pieces of poetry. — Chabot (Philippe), 4 letters to Rabelais. — [Sébastien Roch Nicolas] Chamfort, 4 letters to the Duke de la Vallière. — Champagne (Philippe de), 10 letters to Nicolas Poussin; 4 letters to [Pierre] Puget; 3 letters to the king; 4 letters to Galileo. — Chandon (the abbot), 1 letter. — [Jean] Chapelain, 3 letters to Galileo; 6 letters to [John] Milton; 2 letters to [Johann Friedrich] Gronovius. — [Claude Emmanuel Luillier] Chapelle, 5 letters to Molière; 2 letters to [Michel] Baron; 2 letters to [Jacques] Rohault; 20 letters to Ninon de L'Enclos; 2 letters to Mademoiselle [Marie Émilie de Joly de] Choin; 7 letters to various others; 17 pieces of poetry. — Charlemagne, 135 letters to Alcuin; 43 notes, essays, quatrains, octets, poems to his beloved, etc.; 18 notes on numbers and Pythagoras; 1 imitation of Boethius (*On the Consolation of Philosophy*). — Charles Martel, 3 letters to the Duke of Aquitaine. — Charles the Bald, 1 letter. — Charles V [of France], 16 letters to King John, to Petrarch, etc.; 2 letters to Nicolas Flamel. — Charles VI, 6 letters the Count of Angoulême. — Charles VII, 13 letters to Agnes Sorel; 3 letters to Poton de Xaintrailles; 8 letters to various others. — Charles VIII, 1 letter to the Duc d'Orléans; 3 to Phillipe Desportes. — Charles IX, 2 letters to Ronsard; 3 letters to Phillipe Desportes; 2 pieces of poetry. — Charles V [Emperor of Germany], 7 letters to Rabelais; 2 letters to Copernicus; 4 letters to the king of France; 1 letter to the Grand Duke of Tuscany; 1 letter to Albrecht Dürer; 2 letters to Madame d'Angoulême, regent. — Charles the Bold [of Burgundy], 6 letters to Philippe de Comines; 2 letters to the king of France. — Charles IV of Lorraine, 1 letter to Galileo. — Charles I of England, 5 letters to Galileo; 4 letters to the queen of France. — [Geoffrey] Chaucer, 2 letters to [Giovanni] Boccaccio. — [Guillaume Amfrey de] Chaulieu (the abbot), 2 letters. — Christine of Savoy, 1 letter. — Childebert, 1 letter to Antharic. — Childebrand, 1 letter to Fredegarius. — Childeric, 1 letter. — Christian (king of Denmark), 1 letter to Madame the widow of Luther. — Christina, queen of Sweden, 3 letters to [Antoine] Godeau; 5 letters to the king of France; 3 letters to Boulliau; 2 letters to Viviani; 1 letter to Gassendi; 12 letters without indication of recipient. — El Cid, 2 letters to the king of Navarre. — Cino da Pistoia, 3 pieces of poetry in Italian. — Cicero, 2 letters to Trogue Pompey; 3 letters to Varro; 1 letter to Atticus. — Cyrano (de Bergerac), 2 letters to Molière. —

[Henri Coiffier de Ruzé, marquis de] Cinq-Mars, 1 letter. — Claude (the queen), 2 letters to Master [Guillaume] Gouffier [Bonnivet, the admiral]; 2 pieces of poetry. — Claudian, 1 letter to the emperor Honorius. — Clémence Isaure, 4 letters to Laura Chabiau; 4 pieces of poetry in French. — Clement VII, pope, 1 letter to Rabelais. — Clement of Alexandria, 4 letters. — Clément (Jacques), 1 letter to his father. — Cleopatra, 1 letter to Cato; 1 letter to Castor, Gallic physician; 1 letter to Caesar; 1 letter to Pompey. — Clodion, 1 letter to his son. — Clodomir, 2 letters to his mother; 1 letter to Saint Avitus, abbot of Micy. — Clotilda (the queen), 2 letters to Aurelian. — Clovis, 3 letters, of which one [was written] before the Battle of Tolbiac [in 496, against the Alemanni. Losing, Clovis promised to convert to Christianity if he defeated the Alemanni. He won the battle and later converted.] — Coeur (Jacques), 4 letters to Agnes Sorel; 2 letters to the king, 2 letters to Jean Chartier. — [Guillaume] Colletet, 10 letters or pieces of poetry. — Columbus (Christopher), 35 letters or narratives addressed to Rabelais. — Colonna (Edigio), 2 letters to the king. — Comines, 27 letters to the king and others; 76 narratives or notes. — [Marie Jean Antoine Nicolas de Caritat, marquis de] Condorcet, 3 letters to [Antoine Laurent] Lavoisier. — Condé ([Louis Henri Joseph] the Prince de), 5 letters to Galileo. — [Valentin] Conrart, 5 letters to [André] Félibien and others. — Copernicus, 23 letters to Rabelais; 1 letter to Comines; 1 letter to the pope; 12 miscellaneous notes. — Constantine, emperor, 2 letters to Eusebius; 1 edict. — [Pierre] Corneille, 1 letter to the king; 12 letters to Madame de Maintenon; 3 letters to Galileo. — Cornelia, widow of Pompey, 2 letters to Julius Caesar. — Cornelius Gallus, 1 letter to Lucan; 4 pieces of poetry. — Coulanges ([Philippe Emanuel, marquis] de), 2 letters. — Cousin (Jean), 2 letters to [Pierre de] Ronsard; 1 letter to Philibert Delorme. — [Prosper Jolyot de] Crébillon, 16 letters to Desmaiseaux; 2 letters to others. — [Oliver] Cromwell, 32 letters to [Cardinal Jules] Mazarin and to Richelieu; 2 letters to Queen Christine in Paris. — [Jacques] Cujas, 1 letter to [Etienne de] La Boëtie.

DACIER ([ANNE] LEFEVRE), 3 letters. — Dagobert, 3 letters, of which one is to Saint Eloi. — Damon, daughter [sic] of Pythagoras, 2 letters to Pythagoras. — [Philippe or Louis] Dangeau, 4 letters to [Paul de Beauvillier] the duc de Saint-Aignan. — Dante Alighieri, 33 letters to Jean de Meung; 1 letter to Philip the Fair; 1 letter to Master Sigeher; 75 pieces of poetry, songs, etc.; 9 letters lacking names of addressees. — Dorat, 3 letters or pieces of poetry. — [Joost van den] Vondel, 1 letter to Galileo. — Saint Dionysius, 1 letter to Tertullien. — Dionysius of Halicarnassus, 1 letter to Strabo. — Descartes, 85 letters to [Evangelista] Torricelli, to the Reverend Father Ignatius, to Johann Kepler, to [Gerard] Vossius, to Galileo, to [Claude] Clerselier, to Father

Mersenne, to [Blaise] Pascal, to [Pierre] Chanut, etc.; 33 notes, experiments, mathematical problems, etc. — [Antoinette de Ligier de la Garde] Deshoulières (Madame), 3 letters to Molière. — Desmaiseaux, 19 letters to Fontenelle; 3 letters to Raymond [or perhaps Raimondi]; 3 letters to Bernouli; 1 letter to [Richard] Mead; 2 letters to Maupertuis; 2 letters to 'SGravesande; 6 letters to Voltaire; 5 letters to M. [Louis] de Jaucourt; 3 letters to [Anthony] Hamilton; 2 letters to Dom [Jean] Liron; 3 letters to Madame Perrier; 14 letters to the Marquise du Chastellet and others; 7 letters to the abbot [Joseph Thoulier] d'Olivet, etc. — Desportes (Philippe), 10 letters; 9 pieces of poetry. — [Nicolas Boileau] Despréaux, 2 letters to [François de] Maucroix. — Desvignes (Pierre), 1 letter to Diane de Poitiers; 1 letter to the Duke of Lorraine; 3 letters to the king; 5 letters to [Claude] the Duke of Aumale; 2 letters to the Constable [Anne, duc] de Montmorency. — Van Dyck, 5 letters to Galileo; 5 letters to [Pierre] Mignard; 3 pieces of poetry. — Diocletian, 1 letter to Alectus. — [John] Diodati, 1 letter to [Pierre] Gassendi. — Diodorus Siculus, 1 letter to Trogue Pompey. — Diogenes Laertius, 6 letters, — Divitiacus, 3 letters to Julius Caesar, — Dolet (Etienne) 14 letters to Rabelais, 19 letters to various others. — [Louis Biancolelli] Dominique (harlequin), 1 letter to De Vizé. — Dominis (Marcantonio de), 1 letter to Father Mersenne. — [Marie-Anne Legendre] Doublet (Madame), 1 letter to Bachaumont. — [Guillaume de Salluste] Du Bartas, 1 letter. — Du Bellay (the cardinal), 14 letters to Ronsard, to Baïf, to the king, etc.; 1 account of what Rabelais did in Rome the first time he was there; 10 pieces of poetry; 3 letters to Rabelais. — [Charles François] Dubos (the abbot), 1 letter to [Joseph Thoulier] abbé d'Olivet. — Dudley, 1 letter. — Dufresnoy, 1 letter to Mignard. — Duguesclin (Bertrand), 1 letter to the king. — Dürer (Albrecht), 3 letters to Rabelais; 1 letter to King François I; 1 letter to Pietro Aretino. — Duverdier (Antoine), 2 letters to Montaigne. — Dungal, 1 note.

EINHARD, 6 letters to Alcuin and others. — Elzevier (Daniel), 3 letters. — Ennodius, 1 letter to Boethius. — Erasmus, 43 letters to Rabelais; 3 letters to Cardinal Du Bellay. — Estrées (Gabrielle d'), 5 letters, of which 3 are to Henri IV. — Euclid, 3 letters to Ptolemy; 2 letters to Eratosthenes; 1 to Plato. — Elizabeth (the queen), 1 letter to Ronsard. — Entragues (Henriette d'), 1 letter to Brother Hillary. — Aeschylus, 1 letter to Pythagoras. — Eudoxus, 1 letter to Pytheas. — Eubolides, 1 letter to Plato. — Eusebius, 3 letters to Ausonius; 2 letters to Aurelius Victor; 2 letters to Arius. — Euthymenes, 3 letters to Pytheas.

FAYDIT (GANCELM), 2 plaintive ballads. — [François de Salignac de la Mothe] Fénelon, 6 letters to Father Querini, Benedictine; 2 letters to [Jean or Claude] Santeul; 3 letters to the abbot Dubois; 4 letters to various others. —

Fernel (Jean), 1 letter to Copernicus. — Feronnière (the Fair), 1 letter to Clément Marot. — Ferdinand, king of Hungary, 4 letters to Rabelais; 2 letters to Galileo. — Flamel (Nicolas), 12 letters to Boccaccio and others. — Flavia Gilia, 1 letter to Sir Hugh, known as Guyot of Provence. — Flavius, bishop of Chartres, 1 letter. — Flavius Josephus, 2 notes; 8 letters to Pomponius Mela; 25 letters to Pliny; 20 historical notes. — Florus, 2 letters to the emperor Adrian. — [Bernard le Bovier] Fontenelle, 7 letters to various people; 1 poem on the love of Louis XIV for literature; 2 letters to the king; 6 letters to Maupertuis; 2 letters to Desmaiseaux; 1 letter to Montesquieu; 1 letter to 'SGravesande. — [Johann Heinrich Samuel] Formey, 1 letter to the Count de Boisjourdain. — Fortunatus, 3 letters to [Pope] John [V] of Antioch. — [Nicolas Joseph] Foucault, 1 letter. — Foucher, 1 letter to Ives of Chartres. — François I, 13 letters to [Emperor] Charles V; 2 letters to Magellan; 3 letters to Copernicus; 2 letters to Erasmus; 1 letter to [Petrus] Ramus; 1 letter to [Pierre de Terrail] Bayard; 27 letters to Rabelais; 1 letter to [Philip] Melanchthon; 15 letters to his sister Margaret of Navarre; 2 letters to Leonardo da Vinci; 6 letters to his son in the form of instructions; 19 letters to various people; 12 historical notes. — Francis of Assisi, 2 letters, of which one is to the king; 4 pieces of poetry. — [Saint] Francis de Sales, 2 letters to Mademoiselle de Gournay; 1 letter to the pope. — Fredegunda, 2 letters to Gregory of Tours. — Fredegarius, 4 letters to Childebrand, Duke of Burgundy. — Frederick II [i.e., Frederick the Great], 28 letters to Condorcet, d'Alembert, etc. — Fremiot de Chantal, 1 letter to Galileo; 1 letter to the pope; 3 letters to various others. — Froissart, 1 letter to the king. — Fulbert, bishop of Chartres, 2 letters to Odilon [de Mercoeur], Abbot of Cluny; 4 other pieces. — [Antoine] Furetière, 4 pieces of poetry. — Furius Bibaculus, 2 letters to Valerius Cato.

GALILEO, 99 letters to Bacon; 49 letters to [Jean-Louis Guez de] Balzac; 2 letters to Barneveldt; 1 letter to Bassompierre; 8 letters to Beaugrand; 1 letter to Benserade; 8 letters to Bernegger; 47 letters to Boulliau; 17 letters to Brantôme; 14 letters to Salomon de Caus; 1 letter to [Jean] Chapelain; 3 letters to Charles I; 116 letters to [Marin Cureau] de la Chambre; 3 letters to [Miguel de] Cervantes; 3 letters to Philip of Champagne; 3 letters to Corneille; 1 letter to the marquise de Combalet; 2 letters to [Louis II de Bourbon] the Prince de Condé; 2 letters to [Jeanne Françoise Fremiot] Madame de Chantal; 117 letters to Descartes; 14 notes for Descartes; 3 letters to Desportes; 18 letters to Diodati; 6 letters to Kenelm Digby; 2 letters to Elzevier (Daniel); 42 letters to Gassendi; 289 letters to Mademoiselle de Gournay; 1 letter to [Antoine] Godeau; 4 letters to Gustavus Adolphus; 3 letters to [Hugo] Grotius; 5 letters to Hanze; 4 letters to [Thomas] Harriot; 8 letters to Hobbes; 5 letters to Huygens; 5 letters to Father [Athanasius] Kircher; 3 letters to Ninon de

L'Enclos; 3 letters to Lesueur; 2 letters to the Duchess of Lorraine; 14 letters to Louis XIII; 7 letters to Malherbe; 1 letter to Margaret of Valois; 9 letters to Marie de' Medici; 2 letters to [François] Maynard; 10 letters to Mignard; 219 letters to Father [Marin] Mersenne; 1 letter to Midorge; 27 letters to Milton; 1 letter to Molière; 19 letters to [Gabriel] Naudé; 3 letters to [Richard] Norwood; 90 letters to the Comte de Noailles; 10 letters to [William] Oughtred; 5 letters to [Axel, Count] Oxenstiern; 1 letter to the Cardinal [Arnaud] d'Ossat; 36 letters to Pascal; 391 letters to Pascal, father and son; 197 letters to Samuel Petit; 19 letters to Peiresc; 16 letters to Poussin; 9 letters to [Pierre?] Puget; 14 letters to Mathurin Regnier; 8 letters to Roberval; 1 letter to Jean Rey; 7 letters to Mademoiselle [Catherine de Vivonne] de Rambouillet; 89 letters to Cardinal [Armand Jean du Plessis] Richelieu; 12 letters to Alphonse de Richelieu; 243 letters to Rotrou; 3 letters to [Peter Paul] Rubens; 1 letter to Saint Francis de Sales; 44 letters to M. [Joseph de] Saint-Gery; 3 letters to [Paul] Scarron; 1 letter to [Louis] Savot; 2 letters to the abbot [Kaspar] Schott; 1 letter to François de Sermet; 9 letters to Shakespeare; 2 letters to [Willebrod] Snell; 3 letters to Stella; 2 letters to [Henri de la Tour d'Auvergne] Turenne; 2 letters to [Honoré] D'Urfey; 3 letters to [François] Viète; 92 letters to [Vincent] Voiture; 14 letters to Vondel (Joost); 1 letter to Vincent de Paul; 1 letter to Van Dyck; 3 letters to Simon Vouet; 2 letters to [John] Wallis; 1 letter to Luke Wadding; 1 letter to the pope; 495 letters without name of recipient; 11 notes about mathematics; 1 treatise on Petrarch; 8 short treatises on light; 96 short treatises on mechanics; 43 on the regeneration of colors; 8 on music; 18 on astronomical harmony; 41 French translations, some of them of the poetry of Dante, of Petrarch, etc.; 1 *Le Déluge* [the flood], operetta; 1 episode of Ugolino, translated from Dante; 1 [account of] science before the Flood; 1 theory of colors; 1 state of astronomical science before the Copernican system; 14 letters, of which one is to his beloved; 44 pages of studies on [Nicola Gabrini] Rienzi [dictator of Rome]; 15 translations of sonnets of Shakespeare; 101 brief annotations, all signed, consisting of corrections of *Orlando Furioso*; 1 *Les Supplices* [the torments], fragment of a libretto of an opera; 16 pieces of poetry in Italian; 188 notes about science, of which the foremost is the retraction of Galileo on the subject of the rotation of the earth; 6 various pieces about Galileo; 6 notebooks in quarto. — Garnier (R.[obert]), 1 letter to Philippe Desportes; 1 piece of poetry. — Gassendi, 1 letter to Cardinal Richelieu; 3 letters to Galileo; Gautier Garguille, 3 letters or songs. — Saint Geneviève, 2 letters to Saint Germain. — Gennadius, 1 letter to Sulpicius Severus. — Geoffrey Tory, 1 letter to Rabelais. — George of Trebizand, 1 letter. — Gerbert, 5 letters to Abbo; 2 letters to Adalberon; 4 letters to Fulbert; 1 letter to Gerauld d'Aurillac, 1 letter to Remi de Trèves [Trier]; 1 letter to Rainard; 16 letters to Richer; 11 letters to various people; 1 envoy from the treatise *De nummorum divisione* [on the classification of numbers] by Bede; 10 questions about morality; 19 pieces on numbers. — [Giacinto Sigismondo] Gerdil, 2 letters to the Count de Boisjourdain; 2 letters to the marquise de Pompadour; 5 letters to [Joseph Jérôme Lefrançais] Lalande; 4 letters to Maupertuis; 2 letters to Savérien; 2 letters to La Beaumelle; 1 letter to [Pierre Louis] Ginguené. — [Thomas] Germain, goldsmith to the king, 1 letter to M. [Antoine] de la Roque. — Gerson (Jean), 5 drafts of letters to Thomas à Kempis. — [Pierre Louis] Ginguené, 4 letters to [Marie Charles Joseph] Pougens. — Gisele (the queen), 4 letters to Alcuin. — [Antoine] Godeau, 3 letters or pieces of poetry. — [Carlo] Goldoni, 8 letters to Madame de Pompadour. — Gournay (Mademoiselle de), 12 letters to Galileo; 14 letters to Cardinal Richelieu; 1 letter to Etienne Pasquier; 1 letter to Mathurin Regnier; 4 letters to Desportes; 2 letters to M. de Mauconys; 12 letters to [Joseph Justus] Scaliger; 3 letters to Montaigne; 3 letters to Cervantes; 14 letters to Shakespeare; 20 letters to various people; 4 pieces of poetry. — Graecinus (Julius), 1 letter to Rebilus, 1 letter to Seneca; 2 pieces of poetry; 2 letters to Jesus Christ. — Greban (Simon), 3 letters to Comines; 1 letter to the Duke d'Angoulême; 3 pieces of poetry; 1 lament and epitaph on Charles VII. — Gregory of Tours, 5 letters to Cassiodorus; 3 letters to Fortunatus; 2 letters to Queen Radegonde; 1 letter to Saint Felix of Nantes; 1 note about Saint Augustine. — Gregory XIII or XIV, pope, 1 letter to Desportes, abbot of Tiro. — [Jean Baptiste Louis] Gresset, 1 letter to [Étienne François] duc de Choiseul; 2 pieces of poetry. — Gringore (Pierre), 4 letters to Rabelais. — Griphius, 3 letters to Rabelais. — [Jean] Grolier, 10 letters to Rabelais. — Grotius, 3 letters to Galileo. — Guido d'Arezzo, 1 letter to Abbo. — Guido Cavalcanti, 5 pieces of poetry. — William of Chartres, 4 letters to Sire de Joinville; 6 pieces of poetry, list of knights, etc. — Guillaume de Lorris, 11 pieces of poetry or songs. — William III, 4 letters to the king of France. — Guise (the Duke de), 2 letters to M. de Bassompierre. — Guise (the cardinal [Charles] de), 1 letter. — Gustavus Adolphus, 2 letters to Cardinal Richelieu; 13 letters to Galileo; 2 letters to Mademoiselle de Gournay. — Gustavus Vasa, 2 letters to Rabelais; 2 letters to the king of France. — [Johann] Gutenberg, 5 letters to Jean Chartier; 1 letter to the Duke d'Angoulême; 20 letters to [Philippe de] Comines and to Charles d'Orléans.

HAMILTON (ANTHONY), 1 letter to Madame de Maintenon; 4 letters to Desmaiseaux; 4 letters to the king; 6 letters to various people. — Heinsius (Nikolaes), 3 letters to Pascal. — Heloise, 3 letters to Abelard; 1 letter to the pope; 1 letter to her beloved. — [Charles Jean François] Henault (the president [of the Chambre des Enquêtes]), 1 letter without name of addressee. — Henri II, 9 letters to Diane de Poitiers; 1 letter to Rabelais. — Henri III, 2 letters to

Phil. Desportes. — Henri IV [of France], 3 letters, of which 2 are to James I. — Henry VIII, 5 letters to various people. — Henrietta, Queen of England, 4 letters to the king of France; 3 letters to her son; 2 letters to her mother; 2 letters to the pope; 1 letter to Galileo. — Herod, 1 letter to Lazarus. — Hildebert, 1 letter to Queen Clotilde; 1 letter to Clotaire, king of Soissons. — Hilduin, 1 letter to the king. — Hipparchus, 1 letter to Anacreon; 1 letter to Gelon, king of Syracuse. — Hippocrates, 7 letters to Dexippus. — Hobbes, 3 letters to Galileo; 2 letters to Mariotte. — [Pierre Daniel] Huet, 1 letter to Cromwell; 2 epitaphs of Molière. — Hugh Capet, 1 letter. — Huygens, 7 letters to the king of France; 6 letters to Newton; 2 letters to Boyle; 2 letters to Pascal; 2 letters to Boulliau; 1 letter to Mariotte; 1 anecdote concerning Galileo.

IGNATIUS LOYOLA, 1 letter to Rabelais. — Irenaeus, bishop of Lyon, 1 letter. — Isidore of Seville, 2 letters to Redemptus of Aquitaine. — Isocrates, 78 precepts or notes; 7 letters to Euthymenes.

JAMES I, 11 letters to Henri IV; 19 letters to various people. — James II, 10 letters to Newton; 27 letters to the king of France; 2 letters to Brantôme; 1 letter to the pope; 1 letter to Mary de' Medici; 1 letter to Despréaux; 13 letters to Mademoiselle de Gournay; 15 letters to La Bruyère; 32 notes and character sketches. — Jamblichus, 5 letters to Ausonius. — Jamyn (Amadis), 1 piece of poetry. — John (the king), 3 letters. — John (Saint), apostle, 1 letter to Saint Peter. — John of the Cross, 2 letters. — John of Salisbury, 2 letters to the abbot Suger. — John of Bruges [Jan van Eyck], 1 letter to Thomas de Pisan. — Jean de Meung, 27 letters to Petrarch, to Dante, etc.; 52 pieces of poetry, of which 1 is a poem about the destruction of Troy the Great, etc. — Jeanne of Albrecht, 1 letter. — Joanna of Spain, 1 letter. — Joan of Arc, 6 letters to her father and to her mother; 1 letter to the Parisians; 1 letter to the Dukes of Bourbon and Berry; 3 letters to Agnes Sorel; 5 letters to the king; 12 letters to the Count of Dunois; 5 letters to Xaintrailles; 10 letters to various people; 34 accounts written by Agnes Sorel; 100 other accounts; 16 accounts in duplicate; 1 catalogue of knights, etc. — Saint Jerome, 31 letters to Sulpicius Severus; 2 lists of the names of the 70 disciples of Jesus Christ; 3 letters to Cassiodorus. — Joachim (George, called Rheticus), 2 letters to Ramus. — Joinville (Jean de), 3 letters to the king; 7 letters to William of Chartres; 1 letter to Jean, illuminator of manuscripts; 18 lays and pieces of poetry. — Joseph (brother), capuchin, 1 letter to Campanella; — Joseph II, 12 letters. — Judas Iscariot, 1 letter to Mary Magdalene. — Justus Lipsius, 1 letter. — Juvenal, 2 letters to Pomponius Mela.

KEPLER, 35 letters to Descartes; 2 letters to Father Mersenne.

LA BEAUMELLE, 9 letters to Desmaiseaux and others. — La Bruyère, 1 letter to Bayle; 2 letters to the bishop of Meaux; 11 letters to [Laurent] Bordelon; 18 letters to [Johann Franz] Buddeus; 1 letter to [François] Charpentier; 1 letter to [Henri Feydeau] de Brou; 1 letter to [Roger de] Bussy[-Rabutin]; 3 letters to Dangeau; 2 letters to Carlet de Chamblain; 1 letter to Du Clozet; 27 letters to Fontenelle; 25 letters to Hamon; 3 letters to Foucault; 6 letters to Madame de La Fayette; 2 letters to [François, duc de] La Rochefoucault; 135 letters to [John] Locke; 25 letters to Desmaiseaux; 9 letters to [Nicolas] de Malezieu; 31 letters to [George Brossin, marquis] de Meré; 16 letters to Monsieur de Messac; 6 letters to M. della Mirandola; 26 letters to M**; 2 letters to [Gilles] Ménage; 1 letter to [Jean] Ménard; 1 letter to [François Eudes] Mézeray; 16 letters to Molière; 22 letters to [Pierre] Nicole; 4 letters to Madame de la Sablière; 2 letters to [Marie de Rabutin-Chantal] Madame de Sévigné; 22 letters to Santeul; 98 letters to Saint-Evremond; 1 letter to [Sir William] Temple; 6 letters to the king; 5 letters to Monsieur de Villermont; 7 letters to Monsieur [François] Hébert; 123 letters to various people; 64 opinions about Molière; 52 unpublished notes, thoughts, verbal portraits; 4 poems, short treatises, etc.; 259 reflections, all signed; 580 character sketches, explications, notes, etc.; 1 conversation of Voiture and Costar. — Lactantius, 6 letters to Gennadius. — La Chambre, 2 letters to the king. — La Fayette ([Marie Madeleine Pioche de la Vergne] Comtesse de), 3 letters to the Duc de La Rochefoucault; 2 letters to Madame de Sévigné; 6 letters to Madame Scarron; 1 letter to Mignard. — La Fontaine, 6 letters to Molière; 10 letters to [Gastien de] Courtilz de Sandras; 1 letter to [Paul] Pellisson; 5 letters to de Vizé; 2 letters to Benserade; 1 letter to Mademoiselle de Scudéri; 1 letter to the king; 2 letters to Monsieur Fouquet; 4 letters to the Prince de Conti; 1 letter to his wife; 4 letters to Madame de la Sablière; 1 letter to Madame de Thianges; 1 letter to the Duchess de Bouillon; 1 letter to Madame [Antoinette du Ligier de la Garde] Deshoulières; 1 letter to Madame de Virville; 1 letter to Monsieur [Jacques] Vergier; 327 fables, rondeaux, epigrams, etc. — La Grange, 4 letters to Molière. — [Étienne Vignoles] Lahyre, 3 letters to the king; 3 letters to the Comte de Dunois; 1 letter to the dean of the church of Chartres. — Lalande, 3 letters to [Jean Charles] Borda. — Lambert Le Court, 2 letters to Alexander de Bernay, with the song of *El Cid*; 7 pieces of poetry. — Lampridus, 1 letter to Ausonius. — La Valette ([Louis de Nogaret d'Epernon, Cardinal] de), 5 letters to Galileo. — La Vallière (Mademoiselle de), 1 letter to the Prince [Armand de Bourbon] de Conti; 4 letters to Madame de Sévigné; 2 letters to the king; 17 letters to Madame de La Fayette; 3 letters to [Julie Lucine d'Angennes] Madame de Montausier and others. — Laisné (Jeanne), 1 letter to Comines. — [Anne Thérèse de Marguenat de Courcelles] Lambert (Mme. de), 1 letter. — La Rochefoucault, 45 letters to Father [René] Rapin; 2 letters to Mlle. De Sillery; 14 letters to Mme. de Maintenon; 44 letters to Mme. de La Fayette, maxims, etc.; 4 letters to Blondeau; 11 letters to Mme. de Sévigné; 31 letters to Mme. de la Sablière; 9 letters to Ménage; 1 letter to [Jean] Le Laboureur; 1 letter to [Charlotte Saumaise de Chazan] Comtesse de Bregy; 3 letters to M. [Jean] de la Barre; 4 letters to the Prince de Conti; 3 letters to M. de Brienne; 9 letters to various people; 16 miscellaneous pieces. — Lazarus, 25 letters to Saint Peter; 1 letter to Graecinus; 3 miscellaneous notes. — Lebeuf (the abbot), 5 letters to M. [Léonard] Garreau;; 3 letters to various people. — [Charles] Lebrun, 2 letters to Galileo. — Lefèvre [de la Boderie] (Gui), 1 letter. — Leibnitz, 27 letters to Malebranche, etc.; 5 letters to Rémond; 2 letters to Fontenelle; 12 letters to Desmaiseaux; 4 letters to Messieurs Perrier; 1 letter to Boulliau; 3 letters to various people; 31 notes and reflections. — L'Enclos (Ninon de), 59 letters to Saint-Evremond and Villarceaux; 11 letters to Molière; 4 letters to Mme. Scarron; 4 letters to Mme. de Sévigné; 2 letters to the king; 19 letters to Mme. de La Fayette. — Lentulus (Publius), 1 letter to Tiberius; 2 other letters. — [André] Le Nôtre, 2 letters to [Alexandre] Bontemps. — Leo X, 1 letter to the king of France. — Leonardo da Vinci, 11 letters to the king of France; 2 letters to Rabelais. — [Alain René] Le Sage, 34 letters to [Antoine de] la Roque; 2 letters to [Charles Rivière] Dufresny; 6 letters to the abbot [Jean-Marie] Henriau; 5 letters to [Aimé or Alexis] Piron; 2 letters to J. B. Rousseau; 2 pieces of poetry; 1 letter to Etienne Garreau; 4 letters to [François Antoine] Joly, about Molière. — [Eustace or Hubert] Le Sueur, 3 letters to Galileo; 1 letter to [Nicolas or Pierre] Mignard. — Leucippes, 1 letter to Theophrastus. — [Jean Baptise] Lhermite[, seigneur de] Souliers, 5 letters. — Liron (Dom), 7 letters. — Locke, 30 letters to Saint-Evremond, 14 letters to various people; 7 letters to La Bruyère; 4 notes. — Longueville ([Anne Geneviève de Bourbon-Condé] Mme. de), 1 letter to the Countess de Bregy. — Louis [I] Le Debonnaire, 1 oath of friendship with his brother. — Louis [II] the Stammerer, 1 letter. — Louis VI, the Fat, 1 letter to the pope. — Louis IX, 17 letters to the pope; 44 instructions, notes, or notable sayings. — Louis XI, 50 letters to Comines; 12 letters to various people; 22 quatrains. — Louis XII, 3 letters. — Louis XIII, 1 letter to [Maximilien de Béthune, duc de] Sully; 7 letters to Cardinal Richelieu; 3 letters to Simon Vouet; 2 letters to Saint Vincent de Paul; 9 letters to Galileo; 3 letters to Mlle. De Gournay; 4 letters to Descartes; 3 letters to the baroness de Chantal; 12 letters to Cardinal [Cornelio] Bentivoglio; 2 letters to Father [Samuel] Petit; 6 letters to the pope; 7 letters to the Comte de Noailles; 2 letters to Gabriel Naudé; 3 letters to Father Mersenne; 4 letters to Gassendi. — Louis XIV, 32 letters to Locke; 204 letters to King James; 41 letters to the same, about Descartes; 132 letters without name of recipient; 186 letters to Boulliau; 117 letters to [Giovanni Domenico] Cassini; 84 letters to Boulliau, regarding Galileo; 46 letters to Descartes; 20 letters to the abbot [Charles Irénée Castel] de Saint-Pierre;

24 letters to Pascal; 60 letters to Molière; 30 letters to La Bruyère; 43 letters to Despréaux; 33 letters to [Jean François] Regnard; 31 letters to the Chevalier [Jean Charles] de Folard; 63 letters to various people, concerning Newton; 47 letters to various literary figures; 145 letters to Mme. de Maintenon; 95 letters to Mlle. de la Vallière; 42 letters to Count Hamilton; 50 letters to Monsieur M**; 1 letter to Milton; 98 letters to various people; 984 letters to various people, such as the Dauphin, the abbot [Jean Paul] Bignon, [Jean Baptiste] Colbert, [Jean Baptiste] Lully, [Denis] Talon, [Marin Cureau] de la Chambre, Mignard, Bernouli, etc., etc.; 1 letter to Huygens; 1 letter to Milton; 80 pieces of poetry, 34 mottoes; 1 meditation on the art of kingship. — Louis XV, 9 letters to Mme. de Pompadour. — Louis XVI, 98 letters to [Philippe Henri] the Comte de Grimoard and others; 15 maxims, etc. — Louis of Savoy, 1 letter to Rabelais; 2 letters to his son; 3 notes or songs. — Loup, abbot of Ferrières, 1 letter to the king. — Luke (Saint), 1 letter to Seneca. — Lucan, 2 letters to Trogue Pompey; 3 pieces of poetry. — Luchet [Jean Pierre Louis, marquis] (de), 2 letters. — Lucretius, 1 letter to Divitiacus. — Lulle (Raymond), 2 letters. — Lully, 1 letter to [Paulo] Lorenzani; 2 letters to [Samuel] Chappuzeau; 15 miscellaneous pieces, letters, airs, notes. — Luther, 10 letters to Rabelais; 19 letters to Etienne Dolet; 3 letters to various people; 1 pamphlet *De tribus impostoribus* (of the three impostors).

[Niccolò] Machiavelli, 12 letters to Rabelais. — Magdalene (Mary), 3 letters to Saint Peter, to Lazarus, etc. — [Fernando] Magellan, 11 letters to Rabelais. — Mohammed, 1 letter to the king of France. — Maine ([Anne Louise Bénédicte de Bourbon] the duchesse du), 3 letters. — Maintenon (Mme. de), 12 letters to the king; 9 letters to her nephew and to her niece; 2 letters to the abbot [Jean Paul] Bignon; 5 letters to Ninon de L'Enclos; 3 letters to [Antoinette du Ligier de la Garde] Mme. Deshoulières; 3 letters to the Duc de Noailles; 9 letters to the bishop of Chartres; 1 letter to [Françoise Mariette Fréart] Mme. de Chantelou; 1 letter to the king of England; 2 letters to Bolingbroke; 3 letters to [Anthony] Hamilton; 1 letter to Monseigneur [Jean Baptiste] Massillon; 1 letter to [Françoise Athénais de Rochechouart] the Marquise de Montespan; 1 letter to Nantouillet; 1 letter to the Duc de Richelieu; 3 letters to Mme. de Villette; 1 letter to Mme. Brante; 2 letters to Mme. de Soubise; 12 letters to various people; 17 verbal portraits of the king, character sketches, etc. — [Nicolas] Malebranche, 10 letters to M. de Longueil; 6 letters to Saint-Evremond; 5 letters to [Guillaume François Antoine] the Marquis de L'Hôpital; 1 letter to Father [Charles] Porée; 4 letters to the abbot [Melchior] de Polignac; 6 letters to Leibnitz; 2 letters to Bernouli; 1 letter to M. de Belsunce; 16 notes; 1 observation on the *Réponse* [*a une dissertation de M. Arnauld contre un eclaircissement du "Traité de la nature et de la grace"* (1685)

— response to an essay of M. Arnauld against a clarification of the treatise on nature and on grace] of Father Malebranche. — [François de] Malherbe, 3 letters to Galileo; 21 letters to various people; one piece of poetry. — [Jacques] Mallet du Pan, 4 letters. — Müller [Johann], known as Regiomontanus, 5 letters to Comines. — Mamertinus, 1 letter to Ausonius. — Mansart, 1 letter; 16 descriptions in verse; the twelve months, etc. — [Jean Paul] Marat, 3 letters to M. de Boisjourdain. — Marcus Aurelius, 1 letter to Faustinus. — Marie de' Medici, 17 letters to Galileo, to Ronsard and others; 2 letters to various people. — Marie de France, 1 letter to Lambert Le Court; 1 letter to Guillaume de Lorris; 4 pieces of poetry. — Mary the Catholic, 1 letter to the queen of Navarre; 1 letter to Rabelais. — Marie Antoinette, 17 letters. — Mary Stuart, 22 letters to the Duchesse de Guisse; 6 letters to François II; 30 letters to various people; 33 notes, narratives, pieces of poetry, etc.; 166 emblems. — Marguerite d'Angoulême, 48 letters to Rabelais; 1 letter to [Emperor] Charles V; 4 letters to the king; 19 letters to Clément Marot; 12 letters to M**; 4 letters to [Bonaventure] Desperriers; 2 letters to M. de La Haye; 3 letters to Mme. de Lorraine; 10 letters to various people; 76 pieces of poetry; 29 coats of arms of flowers; 60 narratives of her adventures; 268 emblems and amorous devices; 1 poem, *La Création, ou comédie du monde* (the creation, or the comedy of the world); 1 poem, *La Vierge repentante* (the contrite virgin), a morality-play; 1 poem, *La Fille abhorant mariage* (the girl despising marriage), a morality-play. — Marigny (Enguerrand de), 2 letters. — Marinella (Lucrezia), 1 letter. — [Edme] Mariotte, 12 letters to Newton; 5 letters to Flamsteed; 1 letter to Boulliau; 3 letters to Huygens; 1 letter to Saint-Evremond; 1 letter to [Claude] Clerselier. — Martial, 4 letters to Trogue Pompey; 4 letters to Augurinus; 2 pieces of Latin verse. — Martianus Capella, 2 letters to Sidonius Apollinarius. — Marot (Jean), 3 letters to his son; 7 letters to various others. — Marot (Clément), 55 letters to Rabelais; 11 letters to Etienne Dolet; 2 letters to [Carlo] Sigonio; 2 letters to his beloved; 1 letter to M. de Villeroi; 1 letter to [Jacques de Beaune] the Baron de Semblançai; 13 letters to the queen of Navarre; 4 letters to the king; 52 epistles, songs, poems, etc.; 223 signed notes, entitled *Mes Fredaines* (my escapades). — [Edmond] Martène (Dom), 6 letters. — Masson (Papire), 1 letter. — Matthew (Saint), 2 letters to Montanus and to Castor. — Maupertuis, 7 letters to Fontanelle; 3 letters to Voltaire; 1 letter to d'Alembert; 2 letters to [Claude Adrien] Helvetius and to Desmaiseaux; 1 letter to de Jaucourt; 4 letters to the abbot Gerdil; 3 letters to Bernouli; 4 letters to La Beaumelle and to Montesquieu; 4 letters to the Marquise de Châtelet; 2 letters to Savérien; 3 letters to various others. — Maximin, 1 letter to Saint Avitus. — Maximilian, 1 letter. — Maynard, 6 letters to Galileo. — [Jean] Mairet, 1 letter to Corneille. — Maecenas, 6 letters to Trogue Pompey; 1 letter to Varro. — Lorenzo de' Medici, 2 letters to Melanchthon; 8 letters to Rabelais. — Mérovée, 1 letter to the king of the Visigoths. — [François Eudes] Mézeray, 1 letter to La Bruyère. — Michelangelo, 6 letters to Rabelais; 1 letter to the queen of Navarre; 1 letter to [Francesco] Primaticcio; 16 notes or maxims. — [Nicolas or Pierre] Mignard, 3 letters to Galileo; 1 letter to Molière; 4 letters to [Pierre] Puget. — [John] Milton, 5 letters to Mlle. de Gournay; 8 letters to the President de Brosses; 1 letter to [Antoine] Furetière; 16 letters to Molière; 5 letters to [Vincent] Voiture; 3 letters to Corneille; 4 letters to Mme. Perrier; 23 letters to Galileo; 1 letter to Julie d'Angennes; 14 letters to Pascal; 8 letters to [Claude] Nicole; 10 letters to Rotrou; 4 letters to the king of France; 25 letters to various people. — Molière, 34 letters to Saint-Evremond; 24 letters to the Prince de Conti; 36 letters or pieces of poetry; 16 letters to various people; 1,200 letters remaining at the house of M. Chasles; 1 comedy in one act, *Les Auteurs de bonne foi* (the sincere authors); 1 farce, *Le Docteur pédant* (the pedantic doctor); 1 grand ballet of *La Jeunesse* (youth); 1 group of scenes with one setting, *Le Vilain devenu médecin* (the scurvy fellow turned doctor); 1 masquerade, *Le Fagoteux* (the botcher or the faggot-maker); 1 farce, *L'Amoreux transi* (the bashful lover); 1 copy of the letter of M. de Vizé, about my comedy of *The Misanthrope*; 1 *Pensées libres d'un homme qui réfléchit quand il n'a rien à faire* (free thoughts of a man who reflects when he has nothing to do); 1 farce, *Les Médecins rivaux* (the rival physicians); 1 pastoral, *Les plaisirs champêtres* (the rustic pleasures); 1 *L'Avare amoureux* (the miser in love); 1 *Argon, ou le médecin amoureux* (Argon, or the doctor in love); 1 *Le Médecin volant* (the flying physician), comedy; 1 *M. de Pourceaugnac*, farce, partly in French, partly in Italian; 1 *L'Hypocronde, ou la femme qui ne parle point* (the hypochondriac, or the woman who says nothing), comedy in 5 acts. — Molinet (Jean), 2 letters to Jean Marot. — [Balthasar] Monconys, 3 letters to Boulliau; 1 letter to the cardinal of Lyon; 4 letters to Gassendi; 2 letters to Father Mersenne; 2 letters to Galileo; 1 letter to Mlle. de Gournay; 1 letter to [Henri de Lorraine] the Comte d'Harcourt; 1 letter to Bayle; 1 letter to Ninon de L'Enclos; 14 letters to various people. — Montaigne, 177 letters to Mlle. De Gournay; 24 letters to M. [Pierre] de Launay; 8 letters to [Étienne de] la Boëtie; 6 letters to Mme. de Duras; 125 letters to various people; 22 accounts of the affairs of [Eleanor of] Guienne; 238 maxims, pieces of poetry. — Montanus (Julius), 1 letter to Varro; 1 piece of Latin poetry. — [Count Raimondo] Montecuculli, 1 letter to Fontenelle; 3 letters to Louis XV. — [Françoise Athénais de Rochechouart, marquise de] Montespan, 1 letter to the king. — Montesquieu, 21 letters to d'Alembert; 10 letters to Bernouli; 18 letters to [Marc Pierre] d'Argenson; 4 letters to [Pierre] Barral; 13 letters to [Paul] Desforges-Maillard; 16 letters to Fontenelle; 152 letters to La Beaumelle; 45 letters to [Philip Dormer Stanhope,

4th earl of] Chesterfield; 22 letters to [Denis-François] Camusat; 48 letters to Desmaiseaux; 15 letters to Helvetius; 210 letters to [Charles Étienne] Jordan; 36 letters to Mme. de Pompadour; 260 letters about Ninon [de L'Enclos] to Mme. de Pompadour; 6 letters to Maupertuis; 72 letters his son; 42 letters to [Alexander] Pope; 3 letters to Savérien; 96 letters to M**; 157 to M**; 172 without name of recipient; 20 leaves, defense of *L'Esprit des lois* (the spirit of the laws); 1 manuscript of *Code de la nature* (law of nature). — Montmorency (M. de), 1 letter to Galileo. — Montpensier (the Duc de), 1 letter to M. [Henri de la Tour d'Auvergne] de Turenne. — More (Thomas), 23 letters to Rabelais; 3 letters to Suffolk. — [Ludovico Antonio] Muratori, 2 letters to [Bernard de] Montfaucon. — [Marc Antoine] Muret, 2 letters.

NASSAU (MAURICE OF), 1 letter to the pope. — [Claude de la Boisseliere] Nau, 4 letters to Galileo. — Naudé (Gabriel), 6 letters to Galileo. — Nero, 1 letter to Lucan; 2 letters to Zenodorus; 1 piece of poetry. — Nevers (the Duchesse de), 1 letter. — Newton, 1 letter to Asbon; 1 letter to Atterbury; 2 letters to [Edward] Bernard; 4 letters to Boulliau; 14 letters to Cassini; 1 letter to Chamberlayne; 7 letters to [Samuel] Clarke; 4 letters to Jean Baptiste Denis, physician; 74 letters to Desmaiseaux; 3 letters to Flamsteed; 171 letters to Fontanelle; 1 letter to [Nicolas] Fréret; 5 letters to Hamilton; 2 letters to Huet; 52 letters to Huygens; 2 letters to King James; 1 letter to La Bruyère; 3 letters to Malebranche; 8 letters to Mariotte; 6 letters to Maupertuis; 1 letter to Messange; 2 letters to Molière; 2 letters to Montesquieu; 11 letters to Pascal; 12 letters to M. Perrier; 2 letters to the Count de Polignac; 1 letter to Quenet; 3 letters to Oldenbury [sic; perhaps for Oldenburg; Henry Oldenburg was a secretary of the Royal Society]; 37 letters to the Duc de Rohan; 4 letters to [Joseph de] Saint Gery; 9 letters to [Pierre le Lorrain] Vallemont; 11 letters to [Pierre] Varignon; 2 letters to de Vizé; 75 letters without name of recipient; 88 notes, etc. — Nicole, 8 letters to La Bruyère; 1 letter to M. Perrier; 1 letter to Pascal; 2 letters to Father Arnaud; 6 letters to Montesquieu; 6 letters to the king; 4 letters to la Beaumelle. — Nonnius (?), 2 letters to Oronce Fine. — Noailles (the Duc de) 12 letters to Galileo; 7 letters to various people. — Nostradamus, 4 letters to the abbot [Giovanni] Rucellai; 39 letters to Rabelais.

OLIVET ([JOSEPH THOULIER] THE ABBÉ D'), 1 letter to Montesquieu; 1 letter to Desmaiseaux. — Orlandi (Guido), 3 pieces of poetry. — Orleans, (Charles of), 16 letters to his wife; 15 letters to various people; 42 pieces of poetry, ballads, etc. — Orleans ([Jean Dunois] the bastard of), 10 letters. — Oronce Fine, 6 letters to Rabelais. — Otto III, emperor, 2 letters to Gerbert. — Ossat (the cardinal [Arnaud] d'), 2 letters to Galileo. — Ovid, 2 letters to Varro; 1 letter to Trogue Pompey. — Oxenstiern, 15 letters to Galileo.

[ANDREA] PALLADIO, 7 letters to Jean Cousin, to Galileo, to Rabelais, etc.

— Paré (Ambroise), 4 letters. — Pascal (Étienne), 86 letters to his son, to Galileo, etc, — Pascal (Blaise), 12 letters to Arnaud; 27 letters to Barrow; 22 letters to Boulliau; 76 letters to Boyle; 2 letters to Cassini; 2 letters to [Pierre] Chanut; 1 letter to [Claude] Clerselier; 1 letter to Corneille; 12 letters to Descartes; 2 letters to Fermat; 139 letters to Galileo; 34 letters to Gassendi; 18 notes about Gassendi; 6 letters to Hamon; 33 letters to Hobbes; 6 letters to Hooke; 42 letters to Huygens; 51 letters to Jacqueline, his sister; 19 letters to La Bruyère; 2 letters to Louis XIV; 4 letters to Father Mersenne; 3 letters to Milton; 175 letters to Newton; 61 letters to Nicole; 1 letter to Oxenstiern; 4 letters to Perrault; 18 letters to Perrier; 16 letters to Petit; 1 letter to [Antonio] Pignatelli; 7 letters to Portes; 2 letters to Regnault; 7 letters to Roberval; 7 letters to [Isaac Louis Lemaistre] de Sacy; 51 letters to Father [Antoine] Singlin; 2 letters to Sorel; 2 letters to Torricelli; 1 letter to Viviani; 5 letters to [John] Wallis; 1 letter to [Sir Christopher] Wren; 107 letters to various people; 95 letters without name of recipient; 70 notes and other letters; 8 notes, charms, etc.; 186 other notes; 1 sonnet; 220 mathematical notes; 750 reflections; 4 treatises, each in a separate notebook. — Pascal's sisters, 127 letters to various people. — Pasquier (Etienne), 3 letters to M. Du Bellay; 9 letters to Mlle. De Gournay; 1 letter to Jean Cousin; 2 letters to Mlle. de Cailly; 3 letters to various people. — Paul (Saint), 1 letter to Montanus. — Paul V, pope, 6 letters to various people. — Paolo Giovio, 2 letters. — Paulinus, of Périgeaux, 1 letter to Sulpicius Severus. — Pellisson, 3 letters to Dangeau. — Desperriers (Bonaventure), 9 letters or pieces of poetry. — Pepin the Short, 17 letters to his son Charlemagne. — Perrault, 1 letter to de Vizé. — Petit (Samuel), 5 letters to Vossius; 3 letters to Boulliau; 2 letters to Huygens; 1 letter to the king; 1 letter to Viviani; 4 letters to Galileo. — Petrarch, 49 letters to Jean de Meung, Boccaccio, etc; 12 letters to Laura Chabiot, Flamel, etc.; 114 pieces of poetry, epistles, notes, etc.; 68 maxims; 15 miscellaneous pieces. — Petronius, 1 letter to Juvenal; 3 notes or pieces of poetry. — Peiresc, 1 letter to Galileo. — Phaedrus, the fabulist, 2 letters to Augustus. — Pherecydes, 1 letter to Pythagoras. — Philip, king of Castile, 1 letter to Montaigne. — Pico della Mirandola, 1 letter. — Philip II, Augustus, 4 letters. — Philip the Fair, 4 letters. — Philip IV (of Spain), 2 letters. — Philip, Duke of Chartres, 1 letter. — Peter the Venerable, 3 letters, to the king, to Heloise, etc. — Peter (Saint), 4 letters to Lazarus. — Pibrac ([Gui] du Faur de), 3 letters to the queen; 1 letter to the king; 3 letters to Jean de Tournes, printer. — Peter the Great, 1 letter to Fontanelle; 3 letters to Mme. de Maintenon. — Pilon (Germain), 5 letters to J. Cousin; 2 letters to Primaticcio and to Rabelais. — [Alexis] Piron, 1 opera, *Le Rôle de disenssion* (the role of discord). — Pisan (Thomas de), 1 letter to John of Bruges [Jan Van Eyck]. — Pisan (Christine de), 9 letters to the Duke of Burgundy; 7 pieces of poetry. — Pisseleu (Anne de) [Duchess of Estampes], 29 letters. — Pittacus, 1 letter to Pherecydes. — Plato, 3 letters to Archytas; 2 letters to Eucleides; 2 letters to Socrates; 3 letters to Euthymenes. — Pliny, 16 letters to Augurinus; 2 letters to Varro; 4 letters to Trajan; 1 letter to Urbius Gallus; 1 letter to Josephus; 4 letters to various people. — Plutarch, 2 letters to Augurinus. — Polignac (Cardinal de), 4 letters to Newton and to the Prince de Conti. — Polybius, 1 letter to Eratosthenes. — Pompadour (Madame de), 6 letters, of which 2 are to [Antoine Léonard] Thomas; 4 letters to Montesquieu; 9 letters to La Beaumelle; 1 letter to the king; 1 letter to the Marquise du Châtelet; 1 letter to d'Alembert; 3 letters to the abbot [Louis Maïeul] Chaudon; 1 letter to Paris [Joseph Guichard] Duverney; 4 letters to the Comtese de Lutzlbourg; 3 letters to the abbot Gerdil; 1 letter to Savérien; 1 letter to [Jean François Constant] Berrier; 6 letters to various people. — Pompey, 1 letter to Cato. — Pomponius Laetus, 2 letters to Castor. — Pomponius Mela, 5 letters to Augurinus; 5 letters to various people. — Pontius Pilate, 1 letter to Tiberius; 1 edict. — [Alexander] Pope, 3 letters to Fontanelle. — [Charles] Porée (Father), 2 letters to [André François Boureau] Deslandes. — Porphyry, 3 letters to Ausonius. — Poton de Xaintrailles, 5 letters to the Comte de Dunois; 1 letter to the king; 1 letter to the lords of state. — Pougens, 7 letters, of which one is to the king. — [Nicolas] Poussin , 13 letters to Claude de Lorraine; 5 letters to M. Desnoyers; 1 letter to Mignard; 4 letters to Galileo; 2 letters to various people. — Primaticcio, 2 letters. — [Pierre] Puget, 7 letters to Philip of Champagne; 1 letter to the king; 6 letters to Galileo; 1 letter to Mignard; 3 letters to [Charles] Lebrun; 2 letters without name to addressee. — Pythias, 4 letters to Anacreon; 1 letter to Aristotle; 4 letters to Theophrastus; 1 letter to Euthymenes. — Pythagoras, 16 letters to his daughter Damon; 4 letters to Aeschylus; 2 letters to Sappho; 2 letters to Pherecydes.

[PHILIPPE] QUINAULT, 1 letter to de Vizé; 3 letters to Mme. De Bregy. — Quintillian, 1 letter to Seneca. — [Angelo Maria] Querini (Cardinal), 3 letters to Desmaiseaux.

RABELAIS, 15 letters to M. de Châtillon; 17 letters to Copernicus; 32 letters to Etienne Dolet; 102 letters to Du Bellay; 32 letters to Erasmus; 17 letters to Luther; 108 letters to the queen of Navarre; 32 letters to Clément Marot; 51 letters to Nostradamus; 75 letters to Oronce Fine; 43 letters to the king; 21 letters to [Julius Caesar] Scaliger; 130 letters to ["]my comrade["]; 1 letter to [Henry Cornelius] Agrippa; 5 letters to Pietro Aretino; 2 letters to Alberti; 3 letters to Amerigo Vespucci; 6 letters to Guillaume des Autelz; 1 letter to de Beza; 1 letter to Jean Boucher; 1 letter to Amaury Bouchard; 2 letters to Guillaume Budé; 1 letter to Blondet; 1 letter to Comines; 2 letters to Burgensis; 4 letters to Calvin; 3 letters to [Jerome] Cardan; 4 letters to Cl.[aude]

Chappuys; 6 letters to G.[eoffroy] d'Estissac, bishop of Maillezais; 1 letter to Antoine Gallet; 1 letter to Pierre Gentil; 2 letters to [Sebastian] Gryphius; 1 letter to [Jean] Grolier; 3 letters to the Duchesse de Guise; 1 letter to [Étienne] Pasquier; 1 letter to Pontalais; 2 letters to Desperriers; 2 letters to [Nicolas] Denisot; 1 letter to Doribus; 2 letters to Zacharie Lilio; 3 letters to Leprevost; 1 letter to Montgoubert; 2 letters to Melanchthon; 2 letters to Michelangelo; 11 letters to Pailleron; 2 letters to Ramus; 5 letters to Raphael; 2 letters to Ronsard; 3 letters to Michael Servetus; 3 letters to [Niccolò] Tartaglia; 14 letters to G.[eoffrey] Tory; 3 letters to [Jean] de Tournes; 2 letters to [André] Tiraqueau; 1 letter to Leonardo da Vinci; 1 letter to [Blaise de] Vigenere; 1 copy of an autograph document of Gregory of Tours; 24 scientific reports; 89 notes, pieces of poetry, etc.; 156 notes entitled *Mes Fredaines* (my escapades); 151 other notes, jokes, etc.; 156 miscellaneous notes for a word-list. — [Honorat de Beuil de] Racan, 2 letters. — Racine, 5 letters to Nicole; 2 letters to de Vizé; 1 letter to [Claude] Brossette; 2 letters without name of recipient; 7 letters to [Jean Galbert de] Campistron; 2 pieces of poetry. — Ramus, 10 letters to Rabelais. — Raphael, 12 letters to Rabelais; 1 letter to King François I; 7 notes or letters to various people. — Rapin (Father), 1 letter. — [René Antoine Ferchault de] Réamur, 1 letter to M. Ganneau. — The Hermit of Moliens, 1 letter to John of Salisbury. — [Jean François] Regnard, 10 letters to Benserade; 13 letters to various people. — Regnier (Mathurin), 1 letter to Mlle. de Gournay; 10 letters or pieces of poetry addressed to [Pierre] Motin. — Reuchlin (Johann), 1 letter to Rabelais. — Remi (Saint), 2 letters to Clovis. — René of Anjou, 4 letters to Comines, to Queen Joan, etc.; 25 notes. — Renée de France, 1 letter. — Rey (Jean), 2 letters to Galileo. — Richelieu (Cardinal), 8 letters to Galileo; 22 letters to Rotrou, Cromwell, etc.; 3 letters to Mme. de Combalet. — Richer, 9 letters to Alcuin, Abbo, Gerbert, Fulbert, etc. — Richard the Lion Hearted, 4 letters to Blondel and to A.[nselm] Faydit; 27 pieces of poetry. — [Nicola Gabrini] Rienzi, 1 letter to Petrarch. — Robert (King), 4 letters to Gerbert; 1 treatise on the *Antiquité de l'Ecriture* (the antiquity of writing). — Robert of Anjou, 1 letter. — Robert de Sorbon, 1 letter to the king. — Robert Etienne, 18 letters. — [Jacques] Rohault, 2 letters to Newton. — Roland (the paladin), 1 farewell to his mother. — Ronsard, 19 letters to [Jean] Passerat; 19 letters to Philippe Desportes; 3 letters to Du Bellay; 1 letter to [Catherine de Clèves], the Duchess of Guise; 4 letters to the king; 4 letters to Sigonio; 5 letters to Pierre Gentil; 1 letter to the seneschal; 4 letters to Torquato Tasso; 1 letter to Palaprat; 1 letter to Hédelin [François Hédelin d'Aubignac]; 1 letter to Frédéric Morel; 37 letters to Baïf; 1 letter to Madame [the wife of] the High Constable; 1 letter to M. de Lorraine; 3 letters to his nephew; 18 pieces of poetry. — Roquelaure (the duc de), 1 letter to Prince

[Stanislas Heraclius] Lubomirski. — Rotrou, 46 letters to Pierre Corneille; 19 letters to [Guillaume] Colletet; 6 letters to Mlle. De Gournay; 113 letters to Cardinal Richelieu; 135 letters to Molière; 1 letter to M. [Jean Baptiste Budes] de Guébriant; 1 letter to the king; 1 letter to [Vincent] Voiture; 2 letters to [André] Félibien; 1 letter to [François le Metel de] Boisrobert; 2 letters to Regnault; 3 letters to Bellini; 25 letters to Galileo; 22 letters without name of recipient; 40 miscellaneous pieces. — Rousseau (J. B.), 1 letter to Ganneau; 2 letters to Dufresny. — [Peter Paul] Rubens, 1 letter to Mlle. De Gournay; 2 letters to Van Dyck; 4 letters to Gallileo; 1 letter to Malherbe; 1 letter to [Philippe de Croy] the Duke of Arschot. — Rutebeouf, 2 letters to the king; 7 letters or pieces of poetry to the queen.

SABLIÈRE (MME. DE LA), 2 letters to Father Rapin; 2 letters to La Fontaine. — [Johannes de] Sacrobosco, 1 letter to Sire de Joinville; 2 letters to various people. — [Giovanni] Sagredo, 11 letters to Peiresc and others. — [Jocopo] Sadoleto (the cardinal), 2 letters to the king. — Salel (Hughes), 2 letters. — [Francesco Saverio] Salfi, 3 letters to Mallet du Pan. — Salles (de), 1 letter to Galileo. — Sampieri (Dominico), 2 letters to Poussin. — Santeul, 2 pieces of poetry. — Sappho, 2 letters to Phaon; 3 letters to her friend Damon; 1 letter to her beloved. — [Jean François] Sarrasin, 3 pieces of poetry. — [Claudius] Salmasius, 2 letters to de Vizé. — Savérien, 3 letters to the king of Prussia; 1 letter to Bernouli; 1 letter to the Marquise de Pompadour; 1 letter to Thomas; 3 letters to President Montesquieu [Montesquieu was président à mortier — president for life — of the parliament of Bordeaux from 1716 until 1726, when he sold the office]; 8 letters to various people. — Saint-Aignan ([Paul de Beauvillier] duc de), 2 letters to Mme. de Maintenon. — Saint-Amand (the duc de), 2 letters. — Saint-Evremond, 12 letters to Hemart; 9 letters to La Bruyère; 10 letters to Molière; 11 letters to Ninon de L'Enclos; 3 letters to [Adrien] Baillet; 47 letters to various people. — Saint Peter (the abbot of), 3 letters to the king. — Saint-Gelais (Octavien de), 1 letter. — Scaliger, 20 letters to Rabelais and to Clément Marot. — Scarron, 1 letter to Mme. [Marie] de Hautefort; 2 letters to M. de Villarceaux; 1 letter to Marshall [César Phoebus] Albret; 1 letter to the Duc de Retz; 4 letters to Bertrand; 5 letters to Mlle. d'A.; 8 letters to Galileo; 3 letters to M. Carreau; 2 letters to Pellisson; 4 miscellaneous pieces. — Schwartz (Berthold), 1 letter to Roger Bacon. — [Johann] Schoner, 2 letters to Rabelais. — Shakespeare, 27 letters to Larivey; 43 letters about Montaigne; 34 letters to Mlle. De Gournay; 2 letters to Ronsard; 14 letters to Desportes; 5 letters to Florimond de Remond; 6 letters to Mlle. De Montchrestien; 6 letters to Montaigne; 8 letters to Galileo; 63 notes regarding Montaigne; 13 narratives; 39 sonnets and other pieces in English; 157 amorous devices; 205 reflections. — Scuderi (Magdalen de), 2 letters to the abbess of Poissy; 2 letters to [Jean] Chapelain; 2 letters to the Comte de Bussy. — Sébastien del Sarte, 1 letter to Rabelais. — Servetus (Miguel), 5 letters. — Sergines (Jean de), 1 letter. — Severus (C.), 7 letters to Trogue Pompey. — Sévigné (Mme. de), 35 letters to various people; 100 letters to the Comtesse de Brégy; 147 letters to Mme. de La Fayette; 44 letters to [George Brossin] the chevalier de Méré; 19 letters to Mme. de Grancey; 10 letters to de Vizé; 7 letters to Mme. de Marsy; 7 letters to Mme. de Louvois; 6 letters to the king; 6 letters to M. [Simon Arnauld, marquis] de Pomponne; 37 letters to M**; 8 letters to [Roger] the Comte de Bussy[-Rabutin]. — Seneca, 4 letters to Pomponius Mela; 3 letters to Petronius; 3 letters to Suetonius. — Simon, 1 letter to Graecinus. — Sidonius Apollinaris, 8 letters to Simplicius; 1 letter to Boethius; 1 note about Theodoric. — Socrates, 4 letters to Alcibiades; 3 letters to Plato; 1 letter to Euclid. — [Léonor Jean Christine] Soulas d'Allainval (the abbot), 9 letters to M. [Antoine] de la Roque; 1 letter to Juvenel; 1 letter to Barron; 1 letter to the abbot de Marsy. — Spinoza, 7 letters to Malebranche. — Spurina, 1 letter to Trogue Pompey. — Stella, 6 letters to Galileo. — Strabo, 2 letters to Quintilian, 1 letter to Juvenal. — Suger (the abbot), 7 letters to Yves of Chartres. — Sully, 4 letters to Galileo; 5 letters to the king. — Sulpicius Severus, 6 letters to Eutropus; 1 letter to Paulinus, bishop of Périgueux; 2 letters to Gennadius; 2 letters to Saint Jerome. — Suetonius, 8 letters to Augurinus. — Synesius, 2 letters to Boethius; 1 letter to Sulpicius Severus.

TABOUROT, 1 letter to Ronsard. — [Niccolò] Tartaglia, 9 letters to Rabelais. — [Torquato] Tasso, 5 letters to Montaigne, 1 letter to Mlle. De Gournay; 28 pieces of poetry. — [John] Talbot, 11 letters to the king, to the Duke of Bedford. — Tacitus, 5 letters to Augurinus. — Tasso (Bernardo), 1 letter to Rabelais; 20 notes and poems. — Thales, 4 letters to Ambigat; 8 maxims and pithy observations. — Tertullien, 2 letters to Irenaeus of Lyon; 4 letters to Saint Dionysius. — Theodoric, 1 letter to Boethius. — Théodulfe, 1 letter to the king. — Theophilus, 18 letters or pieces of poetry. — Theophrastus, 3 letters to the archon of ten; 2 letters to Alcibiades; 6 letters to Pytheas; 23 maxims. — Theresa (Saint), 1 letter to the queen of Navarre; 2 letters to Saint Ignatius Loyola; 2 sonnets. — Thibaud [Count] of Champagne, 15 items. — Thomas à Kempis, 1 letter to Jean Gerson. — Thomas, 1 letter to Savérien; 1 letter to La Beaumelle; 3 letters to various people. — Thou (Christophe de), 1 letter. — Tiberius, 2 letters to Antonius Castor; 1 to Graecinus; 1 letter to Pontius Pilate. — [Girolamo] Tiraboschi, 9 letters to [Pierre Louis] Ginguené, [Marie Charles Joseph] Pougens, and others. — Titian, 1 letter. — Tory (Geoffrey), 9 letters to Rabelais. — Trogue Pompey, 2 letters to Julius Caesar; 2 letters to Pomponius Mela; 1 letter to Virgil. — [Henri de la Tour d'Auvergne de] Turenne, 2 letters to Galileo. — Tycho Brahe, 28 letters to Cardinal [Jacques David] Duperron; 5 letters to Galileo; 1 letter to Mlle. De Gournay.

URBAN VIII, 7 letters to the king of France; 10 letters to Cardinal Richelieu; 11 letters to Mlle. De Gournay; 2 letters to the Duc de Sully; 1 biography of Galileo. — Urban XIII, 1 letter.

VARO, 1 letter to Galileo. — Varro (Terentius), 1 letter to Cicero; 2 letters to Virgil; 1 letter to Strabo. — [Sébastien le Prestre, Seigneur de] Vauban (Marshall of France), 1 letter. — Vercingetorix, 1 safe-conduct pass for Trogue Pompey. — Verloys (Roland de), 4 letters to d'Alembert and to Montesquieu. — Vignerod, 1 letter to Galileo. — Victorinus, 4 letters to Boethius; 1 letter to Fortunatus; 1 letter to Epiphanus. — [François] Villon, 30 letters and pieces of poetry, rondeaux, etc. — Vincent de Paul, 5 letters to Galileo; 3 letters to the king; 4 letters to Cardinal Bentivoglio; 1 letter to Mme. de Chantal; 1 letter to the bishop of Luçon; 1 letter to M. [Jean Jacques] Olier. — Vinci (Leonardo da), 1 letter to the king of France. — Vincent de Beauvais, 1 letter to Brunetto Latini. — Vitruvius, 1 letter. — Virgil, 6 letters to Varro; 1 letter to Trogue Pompey; 6 notes. — Viviani, 3 letters to Boulliau. — Vizé (de), 2 letters to the Comtesse de Brégy; 1 letter to the Duc de Luynes. — Voiture, 5 letters to Galileo; 1 account of Galileo; 4 letters to [Antoine] Godeau; 3 letters to the king; 2 letters to Mme. [de Souvré, marquise] de Sablé; 2 letters to [Pierre] Costar; 1 letter to M. de Bassompierre; 1 letter to M. [Claude de Mesmes] d'Avaux; 1 letter to Mlle. de Scudéri; 1 letter to Pascal; 1 letter to Mlle. de Gournay; 1 letter to Ménard; 2 letters to Rotrou; 1 letter to the Duchesse de Longueville; 1 letter to Scarron; 1 letter to Mme. De Rambouillet; 6 letters to various people; 7 pieces of poetry. — Voltaire, 4 letters; 11 pieces of poetry, etc. — Vouet (Simon), 12 letters, of which nine are to Galileo.

[JOHN] WINTHROP, 2 letters to the Chevalier Blondeau de Charnage.

YVES OF CHARTRES, 5 letters to Suger; 1 letter to Louis the Fat; 1 deed in French (on paper).

ZENODORUS, 1 letter. — Zeno, 1 letter to Leucippus. — Zozimus, 1 letter to Cassiodorus.

※※※※※※※※※

PIECES GIVEN BY M. CHASLES TO THE LIBRARY OF THE INSTITUTE

CASSINI, 1 account of Galileo. — Galileo, 1 letter to Louis XIII. — Louis XIV, 3 letters to Cassini; 2 accounts of Galileo; 1 letter to Milton. — Milton, 1 letter to Louis XIV; 2 letters to Molière; 2 letters to Voiture. — Pascal (Bl.), 2 letters to Boyle; 4 mathematical notes. — Rotrou, 2 letters to Cardinal Richelieu; 2 letters to Corneille.

ఌఄఌఄఌఄఌఄఌఄ

CATALOGUE OF AUTHENTIC PIECES PROVIDED TO M. CHASLES BY VRAIN LUCAS

Abstract of the schedule of interest payments from the accounts of the Masters of the Revels, signed [Nicolas Joseph] Foucault. (Authentic)

Order to pay a sum of money to Jacques known as Morel (authentic on parchment), signed François I.

Order to pay a certain sum to Jean Laguette, signed Henri (authentic on parchment).

Order to pay a certain sum to Gilbert d' Anglars, signed Anne de Montmorency, 28 February 1551 (authentic on parchment).

Letters patent signed Philip (king of Castile), containing articles of knighthood in favor of Nicolas de Villers, 20 April 1598 (authentic on parchment).

Order to pay a certain sum to Jehan Ruzé, signed Charles (IX), 14 February 1571 (authentic on parchment).

Order to pay a certain sum to Charles de Hautboys, bishop of Tournay, signed Louis (XII), 21 September 1510 (authentic on parchment).

Receipt to Jacques Burdelot, tax collector of the city of Avranche, given by Oudet d'Aydie, lieutenant to the Duke of Normandy (authentic on parchment).

Receipt of Charles de Ronsart, counselor and almoner to the king, 6 March 1578 (authentic on parchment).

Copy of letters patent of François I, granting a subpoena of the son of François Du Bellay against M. de Clermont, to determine inheritance. Paris, 1 December 1542 (paper).

Decree for the same purpose, 5 January 1542 (paper).

Sale of the land of Tallemond, made to the king of England in 1282 (authentic on parchment).

Letters patent of Henri III, containing the establishment of a new duty on the right to sell wine by the jug, 16 August 1589.

Certificate given by Henri de Bourbon, Prince de Condé, to Pierre de Bounault, Seigneur de La Forest, 5 July 1635.

Letter of Horatio Ruccellai to the king, 6 February 1605 (authentic).

The same to M. de Villeroy, 21 February 1605 (authentic).

Agreement between Claude de Lorraine, Duc de Guise, and the monks of Saint-Fuscien-au-Bois, 1533.

Three letters of La Viconterie, 20 January, 6 and 27 March 1736 (authentic).

Receipt given for his pledged goods by Henri d'Albret, Sieur de Miossens, 22 April 1591.

Act of faith and homage given to the king of England by the noble lord and baron Jean de Lalande, for the house of Lalande (copy collated with a document dated 15 March 1439).

Original letter of Charles-Louis, Duke of Bavaria, to the Comte de Bissy, 19 May 1689.

Letter of Casimir, king of Poland, addressed to one of his cousins (authentic).

Receipt of Jean-François Lalouette, prior of Blain, music-master of the cathedral of Paris, 19 May 1701.

Portrait of the aforementioned Lalouette, engraved by [Nicolas Henri] Tardieu.

Passport given by the Duc de Vendôme to a man by the name of Antoine Chatenay, called Saint-Aubin, dragoon of the regiment of Senneterre.

⁂

CATALOGUE OF COPIES OF THE 17th AND 18th CENTURIES THAT ARE NOT IN THE HANDWRITING OF LUCAS, BUT THAT ARE WORTHLESS

Essay of religious philosophy about ancient astronomical movements and about the intimate agreement of the zodiac with sacred theology (manuscript without the name of the author).

Les amours de Vanvres ou l'Ane perdu [the loves of Vanvre or the lost ass], comic opera.

Eulogy for Petrarch, pronounced at Vaucluse, the 15th of Fructidor, year XII [2 September 1804], by M. Renouard.

On mutability, from the exhortation of a rector.

Remarks on the reigns of Henri IV, of Louis XIII, and of Louis XIV (manuscript of 87 pages).

Letter of Father Gribourdon to Voltaire on the poem *La Pucelle* [the maid of Orleans, i.e. Joan of Arc].

Reflections on the monologue of Amaryllis.

La Robe de dissension, ou le Jaloux prodigue [the gown of discord, or the jealous prodigal], comic opera.

Report of the people of quality that the Academy must solicit for the solemn ceremony that it must hold.

Proposals to erect at Vaucluse a public monument to the glory of Petrarch (20 July 1804), by Citizen Piot.

On Saint-Evremond and Telemachus (small notebook in quarto).

New regulation of the Comédie-Française for the actors making up the board.

Research on the origin of the Celts.

Reflections of M. de La Rochefoucault.

Genealogy of the lords of the House of Orléans, copied according to the genealogies of the late M. Hubert.

On the journey of the king, in 1667, to the Flemish.

The death of the king of Ethiopia.

Various clear principles of morality, of philosophy, of metaphysics, and of physics.

Index alphabeticus carminum Gregorii Naziensis [alphabetical index of the songs of Gregory of Nazianzum].

Collection of poetry (a notebook in quarto).

Journal of the reign of Louis XV.

Les Noces sabines [The Sabine weddings], opera.

Principles on which the Nordic people based their settlements in Europe.

Letter to M. de Champfort, from [Claude Carloman] de Rulhière.

Stanzas on marriage, by Desportes.

Extract of a speech of Mr. Hook, 21 August 1684.

The cake of Virgil, in mock-heroic poetry.

Character sketch of Our Lord Jesus Christ, which Publius Lentulus, governor of Judea, sent to the Roman Senate, taken from the library of King Louis XIII.

۶

Catalogue of Pieces That Are Not in the Hand of Vrain Lucas, But That He Falsified By Additions or by Spurious Signatures

L'Hypocondre, ou la Femme qui ne parle point [the hypochondriac, or the woman who says nothing], a comedy in five acts. Added to the title page: *In the poetry of Molière, found in the portfolio of J. B. Rousseau.*

Reflections drawn from the essays of Montaigne, *signed La Bruyère*. With the endorsement, *unpublished manuscript of La Bruyère*.

Conversations of Voiture and of Costar. *Unpublished manuscript of La Bruyère*. And at the end: *Signature of La Bruyère*.

The Philippics against the Duc d'Orléans, Regent of France. At the front of the book one reads on a label printed with a coat of arms: *From the library of Julian Charles Boitet de Richeville*. Then, written by hand: *This manuscript was given to me by M.* [Joseph] *de La Grange-Chancel; the corrections are in his hand. Signed Boitet de Richeville*.

The life of M. Hamon. *Incomplete manuscript*.

Abstract of moral philosophy. At the front, in pencil: *unpublished manuscript of Pierre Charron, author of* [*Traité de*] *la Sagesse* [treatise on wisdom] . At the end: *Signature de P. Charron, theologal* [lecturer]. *Also, a note of Montaigne*.

Origin of Christianity among the Gauls and in Germany, or the fair weather of Catholicism. *Dissertation of which the title is in the handwriting of Lucas.*

Report on the body of least resistance, by M. de Saint-Jacques de Sylvabelle de Marville.

Law of Nature. *A work attributed to Montesquieu, and signed Montesquieu.*

The Vision of Sylvius Graphaletes, or the House of Fame. In the margin: *Very precious manuscript, in which is found a perfect evaluation of all the outstanding men.*

Des. Erasmi Roterodami in genere consolatorio de morte declamatio [Erasmus' a comfortable exhortation against the chance of death]. Printed, on which one reads: *Ex libris Rabelais,* and *Ex dono* [gift of] *Rabelesius* [Rabelais].

The most gracious declaration of her Majesty to all her affectionate subjects, urging them to assist her against the prince of Orange and his supporters. Printed. *Very rare piece, having been sought out and destroyed.*

The reasons that compelled the king of England to withdraw to Rochester. *Very rare item, having been sought out and destroyed.*

A sermon, signed *J. Benigne Bossuet.*

A satire on the subject of the taxations [of costs] of the Court of Justice of 1660. *Autograph manuscript of* [Guillaume de] *Brebeuf*

History of England. Bound volume, of 123 leaves. At the end: *These are my observations and thoughts on the history of Great Britain, that I certify* [are] *true and accurate. James, R*[*oi*].

Judgment against the memory of Charles, Duc de Bourbon. Copied at the end: *This is the true trial of Charles de Bourbon, who, after being covered with laurels, etc.... This 8 January 1669. Mezeray.*

Physica, etc. Volume in sheets, signed *Leibnitz.*

La Science, ou les Droits et les devoirs de l'homme [Knowledge, or the rights and duties of mankind], a work in four parts. *This manuscript corresponds to the notes that I provided to the copyist, who transcribed it. This 4 March 1752. Montesquieu.*

The Song of Songs of Solomon, with the explication of Monseigneur the bishop of Meaux. 1695. At the bottom of the title page one reads: *To the sister of Saint-Antoine Subtil.+ Benigne, bishop of Meaux.*

Reflections on the different governments. In the margin is written in pencil: *This manuscript of M. the P.*[resident] *Montesquieu is unpublished and very valuable. I traded it with M. the Chevalier de Charnage, in 1763, for other documents concerning the Jews. He appraised it for me at 200 francs. This manuscript was found among the papers of Mme. the Duchesse d'Aiguillon, along with that of the Persian Letters, to whom Montesquieu gave them before his death.* And at the end: *This manuscript, fruit of my reflections and meditations, is the product of more than twenty years of research and observations; I dedicate it to the friendship of Mme. d'Aiguillon, my friend. This 2 May 1750. Montesquieu.* This is a notebook in folio of 53 leaves.

Curious observations on the works of Master Fr.[ançois] Rabelais, doctor of medicine, etc., etc., or the heroic lives, deeds, and sayings of Gargantua and of Pantagruel. With a full account of the life and works of the author, etc. In the margin: *Found among the papers of Mlle. de Gournay.*

Division of the inheritance between Charles le Jars, Esquire, Sieur de Gournay, and others having the rights of heirs of the late Guillaume le Jars, Sieur de Gournay. 24 September 1598. *This deed was found in a bundle of papers of Mlle. de Gournay after her death, in which bundle there were also a good number of letters, notes, and rough drafts in the hand of Montaigne.*

Deed executed and authenticated by a notary relating to the Colletet family, dated 9 February 1662. In front: *Papers and Correspondence of Messieurs Colletet, father and grandfather.*

❧❧❧❧❧❧❧❧

Inventory of Printed Volumes or Manuscripts in the Possession of M. Chasles, To Which a False Value Was Added by Vrain Lucas

Noviciis adolescentibus … [*Sphaera mundi*] (Treatise on the globe, by Johannes de Sacro Bosco, annotated by Georgius Purbachius. Augsburg, 1485, in quarto) [This may actually have been printed in Venice by Erhard Ratdolt, who in the colophon signed himself "Augustensis" — a native of Augsburg, to which he returned in 1486. The caption title of the work begins "Noviciis adolescentibus" — for young initiates]. In the margins of this volume are several authentic notes, in various sixteenth-century hands. Below one of these one reads: *N. C.* added in the handwriting of Vrain Lucas, along with these words on the verso of the first leaf: *Ex libris Nicol. Copernic*[us]; then on the recto of this same leaf a long note in which Rabelais says that in the year 1545 he bought this book in Germany. This said note is signed *Rabelais*, and one reads again below, in a handwriting that appears older than the previous one: *This book is annotated by Copernicus.*

De adventu Henrici Valesii … in metropolim [of the arrival of Henri of Valois to the city, by John Stewart]. Paris[: Matthew David], 1549, in quarto.

Scipionis somnium [dream of Scipio]. Paris, 1550, in quarto.

Institutiones linguae graecae … auctore. Nic. Clenardo [organization of the Greek language, by Nicolaas Cleynaerts]. Paris, 1549, in duodecimo. On the title-page of each of these three volumes, Lucas wrote: *Ex libris Rabelais*, and, in addition, at the end of the last, a biographical note of sixteen lines about the author, signed, *Rabelais*.

Le rommant de la Rose [the romance of the rose]. Paris: Guill. Le Bret, 1538, in octavo, gothic letters. Bound in full red morocco. But it lacks, in the course of the volume, more than fifty pages. Added to the title-page: *Ex libris Rabelais.*

Traité excellent l'entretenement de santé [excellent treatise on preserving health], by Prop. Calanius. Paris, 1550, in 24mo. Bound in modern morocco, with gilt edges. At the end of the preface is an elegiac note and four lines signed *Rabelais*, and on the title-page is written: *Ex libris F. Rabelais.*

Commentarii in librum secundum Historiae mundi C. Plinii [commentary on the second book of Pliny's history of the world, i.e., Pliny the Elder's text with commentary by Jakob Milich], Hagenau[: Ex officina Petri Brubacchij], 1535, in quarto. On the title-page: *Ex libris Franciscus Rabelais.*

Platonis epistolae [letters of Plato]. Paris, 1555, in quarto. *Ex libris Rabelais.*

I trionfi de Petrarca [Petrarch's *Trionfi*], Venice[: Dominico Giglio], 1553, in quarto. On the end-paper and again on the title-page: *Ex libris Franciscus Rabelais.*

De Chyromantia per Joann. Dryandrum [of chiromancy, by Tibertus Antiochus, edited by Johann Dryander], Marburg[: Ivo Schoefer], 1538, in 18mo. On the title-page: *Ex libris Fr. Rabelesius.*

Divi Joannis Chrysostomi [*de orando Deum libri duo, Erasmo interprete* — the divine John Chrysostom's of praying to God, in two books, with commentary by Erasmus], Paris[: Christian Weckel], 1535, in 18mo. *Ex libris Franciscus Rabelesius.*

Bellum per Desiderium Erasmum [war by Desiderius Erasmus]. Paris, in 18mo. *Ex libris Franciscus Rabelesius.*

Artificium de applicatione astrologiae ad medicinam [the art of applying astrology to medicine, by Georgius Collimitius], Strassburg[: G. Ulricher], 1531, in 18mo. *Ex libris Franciscus Rabelesius.*

La décoration d'humaine nature [the ornamentation of human nature, by André Le Fournier], Paris, 1531, in 18mo. A small gothic book lacking the end, and it is without covers; but it is wrapped in paper, on which one reads: "This little book is in itself very rare, and in addition, that which renders it unique, is that it belonged to Master Fr. Rabelais. I traded it for a missal on vellum worth 100 francs. Mme. de Pompadour wanted this book and offered me 300 francs. I preferred to keep the book." In addition, there is on the title-page, *Ex libris Fr. Rabelais*[,] *doctor.*

De duplici copia verborum ac rerum D. Erasmi [of the abundance of both words and things, a commonplace book by Desiderius Erasmus], Lyon, 1538, in octavo. Across the title one reads: *Ex libris Fr. Rabelasius*, and on the verso an account of seventeen lines about the life of Erasmus, which notice was supposed to be in the hand of Rabelais.

Georgii Agricolae de mensuris & ponderibus Romanorum atque Graecorum [George Agricola's of measures and weights of the Romans and the Greeks], Basle[: H. Froben], 1550, in folio. On the title-page: *Ex libris Fr. Rabelesius.*

Breves in sphaeram meditatiunculae ... auctore Bartholomaeo [brief little thoughts about the globe by Bartholomaeo], Cologne, 1563, in duodecimo. On the title-page: *Ex libris J. Keplerus.*

Jamblicus, etc. [Venice:] Aldus, 1516, in folio. The title-page is lacking, but the volume ends with a page and a half in the hand of Galileo (Vrain Lucas), claiming to have received this volume as a gift from Aldus Manutius himself.

Eratosthenes Batavus [by Willebrodus Snellius, about geodocy], Leyden[: Apud Iodocuma Colster], 1617, in quarto, with: *Ex libris Galileo Galilei*, and a half page in his handwriting.

Amore innamorato [Cupid in love, by Lucrezia Marinelli], Venice[: G. B. Combi], 1618, in quarto. On the title-page: *Ex libris Galileo Galilei.*

Modo di formare [...] *le moderne battaglie* [Method of waging modern war, by Girolamo Cataneo], Brescia[: Francesco et Pietro Maria de' Marchetti Fratelli], 1571, in quarto. With: *Ex libris Galileo Galilei*, and a bibliographical note signed in the same way.

L'antibacinata di Leopardo [the anti-basin, a response to Ferrante Pallavicino's *Baccinata overo Battarella* noted below. *L'antibacinata* (Macerata: Agostin Grisei, n.d.) was written by Leopardo Leopardi Romano]. In quarto. With an *ex libris* removed by means of acid.

Beati Theodoreti (commentary on St. Paul [by Theodoret, Bishop of Cyrrhus]), Florence, 1572, in folio. On the verso of the title-page, a full page (in French, as always), signed, *Galileo Galilei.*

L'Ormondo di Francesco Pona [Ormond, by Francesco Pona], Padua[: Apud Bartholomaeum Merlum], 1635, in quarto. On the title-page: *Ex libris Gournay*, and attached to the beginning, a letter of Galileo to Mlle. de Gournay, to tell her that he was sending this book at her request.

Quintilien [Quintilian], a manuscript of the sixteenth century, on paper, 100 leaves. At the beginning: *Ex libris Galileo Galilei*, and on the end-paper a statement according to which this book was a gift of Galileo to Poussin; the aforesaid statement was in the hand of the latter, and signed *Nicolas Poussin.*

Jani Gulielmi [*F.*] *Laurenbergi antiquarius* [of Hans Villumsen Laurenberg, antiquarian, by Johann Laurenberg], Lyons[: I. Anard], 1622, in quarto. On the title-page: *Ex libris Galileo Galilei*, as well as a letter *of Mlle. de Gournay* writing to Galileo that she is sending him this book at his request.

L'usage de l'un et l'autre astrolabe [the use of the one and the other astrolabe, by Dominique Jacquinot], Paris[: J. Moreau], 1625, in duodecimo (two copies).

Discours parénétique sur les choses Turques [moral discourse on Turkish affairs], Lyons, 1602, in octavo, bound in full morocco, with gilt edges.

Les livres de Hierosme Cardanus [the books of Girolamo Cardano]. Paris[: Jean Houze], 1584, in octavo.

Il Petrarca spirituale [spiritual Petrarch] , Venice, 1575, in duodecimo. These four last works have on the title-page: *Ex libris Galileo Galilei.*

Arithmeticae practicae methodus [*facilis* — a simple method of practical mathematics, by Frisius Gemma], Cologne, 1592, in 18mo. *Ex libris Galileo Galilei,* plus a letter of Galileo offering this book as a gift to one of his correspondents whom he calls *my reverend father.*

Il Petrarchista[:] *dialogo di messer Nicolo Franco* [the Petrarchiad: dialogue of Mister Niccolò Franco], Venice[: Gabriel Gioli di Ferrarii], 1543, in 18mo. *Ex libris Galileo Galilei,* plus a letter of Galileo offering this book as a gift to Mlle. de Gournay.

Cinque cariti [actually *canti*] *di Camillo Camille* [Five songs of Camillo Camilli], Venice, 1604, in quarto. At the bottom of the title-page: *Ex libris Galileo Galilei,* plus a letter of Galileo to Rotrou offering him this book as a gift; in addition a note of Rotrou confirming the fact, and confirming as well that one manuscript note located at the beginning of the volume and another at the end, are indeed in the hand of Galileo.

Traité de la composition et fabrique de l'astrolabe [treatise on the construction and manufacture of the astrolabe, by Johann Stoffler], Paris[: Guillaume Cauellat], 1560, in duodecimo. On the title-page: *Ex libris R. Descartes.*

Il primo libro della Eneida [the first book of the *Aeneid*], Padua, 1564, in quarto. *Ex libris M.-L.-J. de Gournay.*

Le Roman de la Rose [the romance of the rose], manuscript in quarto, on paper, of 1,107 pages. It is entirely in the hand of Lucas, and supposedly, according to him, was in the hand of *Mathurin Regnier,* who supposedly added, at the beginning, a preface of his own, of fourteen pages, under the title of *Exposition morale du roman de la Rose* [moral exposition of the romance of the rose]. Moreover, the volume concludes with a supposed letter of *Mlle. de Gournay,* signed.

Les gymnopodes ou [*de*] *la Nudité des pieds* [gymnopods, or of the nakedness of the feet], by Sebastien Roulliard, Paris, 1627, in quarto. *Ex libris Rotrou.*

Le retorica di M. Bartolomeo Cavalcanti [*The Rhetoric* of Bartholomeo Cavalcanti], Venice[: C. and F. Franceschini], 1574, in quarto. *Ex libris Montaigne.*

Les Regrets and other poetic works of Joachim Du Bellay. Paris, 1565, in quarto.

Le premier livre des antiquitez de Rome[the first book of the antiquities of Rome], by Joachim Du Bellay, Paris, 1562, in quarto.

Receuil d'aucuns mensonages de Calvin, etc. [collection of certain errors of Calvin, etc.], Paris, 1561, in octavo.

Ample discours au Roy ... [full discourse to the king], by Michel de L'Hospital [translated into French by Joachim Du Bellay], Paris, 1570, in octavo. The last four items with *Ex libris Montaigne.*

Le prince de Nicolas Machiavelli [*The Prince* of Niccolò Machiavelli], Paris[: Charles Estienne], 1553, in quarto. A very dirty volume, the title-page defective, without covers, but at the end a note signed by Montaigne, saying that this precious volume was given to him by his friend Master Remy Belleau.

Briefve et facile réfutaton d'un livret au nom de J. de l'Espine, se disant ministre [brief and simple refutation of a pamphlet bearing the name J. de l'Espine, so called minister], by M. René Benoist, Paris, 1564, in octavo. At the beginning: *Ex libris Montaigne,* and at the end, a long note of Montaigne about the book and the author.

Les Epistres dorées de dom Antoine de Guevare [the golden letters of Dom Antonio Guevara], Lyon[: Benoist Rigaud], 1588, in octavo. *Ex libris Montaigne,* and on the verso of the title-page: "This book full of sense is one of those that give me the greatest pleasure I am delighted to acknowledge to it this benefit." *Montaigne.*

De l'Office et préséance de l'Ecclésiastique et du Magisrat [of the duties and priorities of the clergyman and magistrate], 1591, in octavo. On the verso of the title-page: "This book is heretical; Luther, under the pretext of attacking the undertakings of the clergy, destroys all hierarchical authority." *Montaigne.*

Arminius ou les Frères ennemis [Arminius, or the hostile brothers], by [Georges de] Scuderi. Paris[: T. Quinet and N. De Sercy], 1644, in quarto. *Ex libris Corneille.*

Clavis philosophiae naturalis [key to natural philosophy, by John Ray], Leyden[: John and Daniel Elzevier], 1654, in quarto. On the middle of the title-page: *Ex libris Pascal.* And on top: "Tribute of friendship to the young Newton." *Pascal*

Lettre à une jeune personne de condition sur les jansénistes [letter to a young person of quality on the subject of the Jansenists], in quarto.

Sentence de l'archevêque de Paris, portant approbation du miracle de Port-Royal du 24 mars 1556 [Decision of the archbishop of Paris, certifying the miracle of Port Royal of 24 March 1556], in quarto.

Seconde lettre de M. [Antoine] *Arnauld* [second letter of M. Antoine Arnauld], Paris, 1655, in quarto.

Traicté de la Sphère du monde [treatise on the globe of the world], by Sieur [Jean] Boulenge. Paris[: Jean Moreau], 1620, in duodecimo. These four items bear on the title page: *Ex libris B. Pascal.*

L'Artisan de la fortune [the fortunate artisan], Paris, 1640, in 18mo. Across the title-page: *Ex libris Pascal.*

Les Oeuvres spirituelles et dévotes de D. Seraphin de Ferme [the spiritual and devout works of Dom Seraphin de Ferme], Paris, 1614, in duodecimo.

Abrégé de la Perfection chrestienne [abstract of Christian perfection, by Alfonso Rodriguez], Paris, 1613, in duodecimo.

Brief traicté de la conversion et fructueuse penitence [brief treatise on conversion and profitable repentance], Paris, 1613, in duodecimo.

Traicté de la cognoissance et victoire de soy mesme [treatise on self-knowledge and self-control], Paris, 1613, in duodecimo. The last four items are small volumes without covers, but each carrying on the title-page: *Ex libris Pascal*; and, on the last page, a note signed by *Pascal,* who therein recommends reading the work. (There is a fifth example, lent by M. Chasles to the abbot Moigno.)

Lettre à M. [François du Val, marquis] *de Fontenay Mareuil sur le trépas de Monseigneur le cardinal de Richelieu* [letter to M. de Fortenay Mareuil on the death of Cardinal Richelieu], Paris, 1642, brochure in duodecimo, with: *Ex libris Rotrou.*

Relations de la mort de plusieurs saints religieux de la Trappe [accounts of the deaths of several holy monks of the monastery of La Trappe], 143 leaves in octavo. A filthy-looking manuscript, on the end-paper of which is written in pencil, in the hand of the supposed old man: *This manuscript is by the abbot* [and reformer of La Trappe, Jean le Bouthillier] *de Rancé.*

Les Mémorables journées des François [the eventful days of François, by Antoine Girard], Paris[: Jean Henault], 1647, in quarto. *Ex libris De Lafontaine.*

La Poétique d'Aristote [Aristotle's *Poetics*], Paris, 1672, in quarto. *Ex libris De Lafontaine.*

Cento favole bellissime de piu illustri antichi et moderni autori [one hundred most beautiful stories by the most illustrious ancient and modern authors, by Giovanni Mario Verdizotti], Venice[: Alessandro Vecchi], 1613, in octavo (detailed in the report). *De Lafontaine.*

Lettres de M. Descartes [letters of M. Descartes], Paris[: Henri le Gras], 1659, 2 volumes in quarto. A copy filled with notes added on small slips of paper; and supposedly in the hand of Boulliau. The work was supposed to be in three volumes; Boulliau's notes on volume III, which is missing, are in a separate folder.

Another copy of the same edition, complete, three volumes. At the beginning: *Ex libris Boulliau,* and marginal notes by the same.

P. Terentii … comoediae [Terence's comedies], Venice[: Apud Hieronymum Scotum], 1569, in folio. *Ex libris, J. B. P. Molière.*

Les tragédies de Rob. Garnier [the tragedies of Robert Garnier], Lyon, 1615, in 18mo.

Les Conversations (du maréchal de Clérembault et du chevalier de Méré) [the conversations of the Marshall de Clérembault and of the Chevalier de Méré, by Antoine Gombault, chevalier de Mere], Paris, 1669, in 18mo.

Les Folies de Cardenio [the extravagances of Cardenio, by Pichou], tragi-comedy dedicated to M. de S. Simon. Paris[: François Targa], 1630, in duodecimo.

Guisiade, a new tragedy [by Pierre Matthieu], Lyon, 1589.

Les intrigues de la loterie [the schemes of chance, by Jean Donneau de Vizé], Paris[: E. Loyson], 1670, in 18mo.

La Celimène, comedy of Rotrou, Paris[: Guillaume de Luyne], 1661, in 24mo. The last six works, with the signature of Molière.

Le Mausolée [the mausoleum], tragi-comedy by A.[ndré] Mareschal. Paris[: Quinet], 1642, in quarto. *Ex libris J. B. Poquelin*

[*La maladie de M. Guillaume morfondu au] voyage de l'autre monde* [the illness of M. Guillaume chilled during his voyage to the other world], Paris, 1612, in duodecimo. *Ex libris J. B. Poquelin.*

Las Coplas de don Jorge Manrique [the couplets of Don Jorge Manrique], Madrid[: Luis Sanchez for Juan Berrillo], 1598, in 24mo. *Ex libris Molière.*

Les Entretiens du philosophe Saturnin [the conversations of the philosopher Saturnin], Paris, 1696, in duodecimo. Bound in red morocco. On the verso of the title-page: *Ex libris Anne de Lenclos.*

La Critique désintéressée sur les satyres du temps [disinterested critque of the current satires, by Charles Cotin, who was responding to satires directed against him by Molière and Boulliau. Paris: L'Hermite de Paris, à la correction Fraternelle, 1666]. Brochure in octavo. On the title-page: *Ex libris Labruyère.*

La Cour [the court]. Dialogues. Paris. On the title-page: *Ex libris la m. de Sévigné.* And on the back: "This book is very entertaining, and it delights me thus to congratulate its author." *la m. de Sévingé.*

Receuil de poésies françoises [collection of French poetry], 1676. Manuscript paper notebook in duodecimo bound in red morocco. At the end, the signature of [Antoine] *Furetière.*

Remonstrances au roy Louis XI sur les libertés de l'église gallicane en 1609 [remonstrances to King Louis XI concerning the liberties of the French Church in 1609], in quarto. At the end: *Ex libris J. Benigne, Bishop of Meaux.*

Baccinata overo Battarella [the battle of the basins, by Ferrante Pallavicino] in quarto, [s.l.: s.n.,] 1642. Volume preceded by a bibliographical notice of two pages, written and signed by *Louis XIV.*

A manuscript on paper. containing *Meditations pieuses* [pious meditations], written in verse, 1629 (88 pages) without covers. On the last page one reads: "This manuscript, containing the speeches, discourses, lessons, and good advice of the Reverend Mother Prioress of the girls of the [order of nuns of the] Visitation [of Our Lady] of Saint Mary of Chaillot, was given to me by her when I entered this convent after the death of King Charles I, my husband, whom may God forgive ... — *Henrietta Maria of France, former queen of the English.*

Traité de la Géographie [treatise on geography], by P.[ierre] du Val, Paris, 1680, in 18mo. *Ex libris Isaac Newton.*

Dialogue sur la Musique [dialogue on music, by François de Castagneres, abbé de Chateauneuf], Paris[: N. Pissot], 1725, in 18mo. *Ex libris Isaac Newton.*

Commentarius in universam Aristotelis physicam [commentary on the whole of Aristotle's *Physics*], a small manuscript of the seventeenth century. *Ex libris Isaac Newton.*

Description de l'aimant qui s'est formé à la pointe du clocher [neuf] *de N. D. de Chartres* [description of the magnet that formed on the tip of the new bell of Our Lady of Chartres], by Pierre Le Lorrain, abbé of Vallemont, Paris[: Laurent d'Houry], 1692. *Ex libris Is. Newton.*

Bibliothèque Angloise ou Histoire littéraire de la Grande-Bretagne [English library, or literary history of Great Britain, vols. 1-5 edited by Michel de la Roche, vols. 6-15 by Armand Boisbelland de Montrésor], Amsterdam[: La veuve de Paul Marret, etc.], 1717. Two parts, each having at the beginning: *Ex libris Is. Newton.*

Nouvelles de la République des Lettres [news from the republic of letters], May, 1702; September, 1703; May, 1704. Each of these three volumes bears at the beginning: *Ex libris Is. Newtonis*

Les [lettres] *Provinciales* [provincial letters, by Pascal], Cologne, 1700, two volumes in duodecimo. At the beginning of each volume: *Ex libris Newton.*

Manuscript of the eighteenth century, without title-page, at the front of which Newton is supposed to have written: "True key to philosophy, with something special." *Is. Newton.*

Commentarius in Aritotelis physicam [commentary on Aristotle's *Physics*]. In front is the *Ex libris de Newton*, with this note of his: "This manuscript is the work of a scholar, and therefore very valuable for metaphysics."

Nouveaux Mémoires pour servir à l'histoire du Cartésianisme [new memoirs to serve as a history of Cartesian thought, by Pierre-Daniel Huet], Paris[: Raymond Mazieres], 1711, in 18mo. On the title-page: *Ex libris Newtonius.* On the verso of the first end-paper, a note of fifteen lines, in which Newton announced having drafted these memoirs with Desmaiseaux. In addition, these words on the verso of the flyleaf: *Paid in 1772, 1200 francs, because of the enclosed letters and notes since they reveal the true authors of these memoirs, which were first published in 1692 under the name of M. G. de La., which is to say M. Giles de*

Launay. And at the very beginning: *Paid 1200 francs. An Englishman had offered 1000 francs for it.*

Rudiments de la philosophie péripatéticienne [rudiments of Peripatetic, i.e., Aristotelian, philosophy], manuscript in octavo, seventeenth century, of about 300 pages. Bound in black morocco in compartments. One reads at the end: 1712, *vu. Malebranche, P. D. Lo.*

Das Christliche Fürst [the christian prince], Ratisbone, 1730, in quarto. On the first fly-leaf: *Ex libris Montesquieu.*

Pensées philosophiques [philosophical thoughts, by Denis Diderot], The Hague[: Au depens de la compagnie], 1746, in 18mo. Bound in half morocco, green. Across the title page: *Ex libris Montesquieu.*

Restablissement du commerce [restoration of trade]. 1 volume in folio, 18th century. The preface, dated 1715, carries the signature of *Law.* And at the bottom of the first leaf: *Gift of M. Law. Montesquieu.*

L'Ouvrage de la Création. Traicté physique du monde [the work of creation, a treatise on the physical properties of the world], by [Claude] Mallement [,seigneur] de Messange, Paris, 1679, in duodecimo. At the beginning of the volume four pages in the hand of Newton, preceded by five lines in the hand of Louis XIV, which says that he received this volume from the abbé de Polignac.

La Chronologie des anciens royaumes [*corrigée* — the chronology of ancient kingdoms amended, by Isaac Newton], translated from Newton [by François Granet], Paris[: Gabriel Martin et al.], 1728, in quarto. *Ex libris des Maizeaux.*

Traité de la Fortification [treatise on fortification], manuscript of the eighteenth century, of about 200 pages in quarto. The last page is filled with an historical note written and signed by King *Louis XV.*

Les six [*premières*] *comédies facécieuses* [the first six facetious comedies], by Pierre de Larivey. Paris[: Abel L'Angelier], 1579, in 24mo. On the title-page: *Ex libris la m. de Pampadour.*

Le Morfondu [the frozen one], the fourth comedy, by Pierre de Larivey. Paris, 1519 [i.e., 1579]. On the title-page: *Ex libris la m. de Pampadour.* This volume and the preceding one bear on the covers a coat-of-arms of three towers, which were in fact the arms of the marquise.

Volume I of *Mercure Britannique* [British Mercury], by Mallet du Pan, London[: W. and C. Spilbury], 1798, in octavo. At the beginning of the volume is a supposed letter of Mallet du Pan to M. the count (de Boisjourdain). To this letter is attached a note, also by Mallet du Pan, about a collection *of 1240 pieces for sale, documents from the collection of a man of taste ... but making them public must necessarily offend the self esteem of a certain people and a certain sect.*

Découvertes de M. Marat, docteur en médicine, des gardes du corps de Monseigneur le comte d'Artois, sur le Feu, l'Électicité et la Lumière [discoveries of M. Jean Paul Marat, doctor of medicine, of the bodyguard of Monseigneur the count d'Artois, on fire, electricity, and light], Paris[:Clousier], 1779, in octavo. A brochure preceded by a supposed letter of Marat, and signed by him, in which he thanks M. the count (de Boisjourdain) "for the services you have rendered me in communicating to me your precious documents."

꙼ꙮ꙼ꙮ꙼ꙮ꙼ꙮ꙼

Appendix 1
Scolastica

———◦◉◦———

[THIS STORY BY ANATOLE FRANCE was first published as "Histoire des deux amants d'Auvergne"—story of the two lovers of Auvergne—in *Le Temps*, 8 December 1889, and reprinted in *L'Étui de Nacre* [the mother-of-pearl box] in 1892. As the conclusion of the story reveals, this piece was inspired by the forgeries of Vrain-Denis Lucas. Imitating Lucas, France took this story from Gregory of Tours's *Historia Francorum*. This anecdote appears in *Histoire des Francs. Livres I-VI* (Paris: A. Picard, 1886), 1:25]

In that time, which was the fourth century of the Christian era, the young Injuriosus, only son of the senator of Auvergne (thus the municipal officers were called), sought in marriage a girl by the name of Scolastica, like him the only child of a senator. She consented. And the marriage ceremony having been celebrated, he led her into his house and shared his bed with her. But she, sad and with her head turned toward the wall, wept bitterly.

—What troubles you? Tell me, I beg of you.

And as she remained silent, he added:

—I beg you, by Jesus Christ, Son of God, to reveal to me plainly the cause of your wailing.

Then she turned towards him:

—If I were to weep all the days of my life, she said, I would not have enough tears to express the immense sadness that fills my heart. I had resolved to keep absolutely pure this feeble body and to offer my virginity to Jesus Christ. Alas for me, whom He so abandoned that I am unable to accomplish what I desired! O day that I might never have been obliged to see! Here, divorced from the celestial bridegroom who promised me paradise for my dowry, I have become the bride of a mortal man, and this head that should have been crowned with undying roses is adorned or rather sullied with these roses that are already losing their petals. Alas! This body that, beside the fourfold stream of the Lamb, should have been dressed with the stole of purity, wears as a vile burden the wedding veil. Why was the first day of my life not the last? Oh! I had been fortunate if I had been able to pass through the gate of death before drinking one drop of

145

milk! And if the kisses of my gentle nurses had been placed on my coffin! When you hold out your arms to me, I think of the hands that were pierced with nails for the salvation of the world.

And, having spoken these words, she cried bitterly.

The young man gently replied to her:

—Scolastica, our parents, who are noble and rich among the inhabitants of Aurvernes, have on your side only one daughter, and on my side only one son. They wished to unite us to continue their families, for fear that after their deaths a stranger would inherit their wealth.

But Scolastica said to him:

—This world is nothing; riches are nothing; and this life itself is nothing. Is it living when one merely waits for death? Only those truly live who, in eternal blessedness, drink the light and taste the angelic joy of possessing God.

At this instant, touched by grace, Injuriosus exclaimed:

—O sweet and plain words! The light of eternal life shines before my eyes! Scolastica, if you wish to remain true to what you have promised, I will remain chaste along with you.

Half reassured and already smiling through her tears [she replied]:

—Injuriosus, she said, it is hard for a man to allow such a thing to a woman. But if you arrange matters so that we live without stain in this world, I will give you a portion of the dowry that was promised to me by my husband and lord Jesus Christ.

Then, strengthened by the sign of the cross, he said:

—I will do what you wish.

And holding each other's hand, they went to sleep.

And thereafter they shared the same bed in incomparable chastity. After ten years of steadfastness, Scolastica died.

According to the custom of the period, she was carried into the basilica in festive clothing and with her face uncovered, amid the chanting of psalms, and followed by all the people.

Kneeling close to her, Injuriosus pronounced these words in a loud voice:

—I thank you Lord Jesus, for giving me the strength to preserve your treasure intact.

At these words, the dead woman raised herself from her funeral bed, smiled, and murmured softly:

—My friend, why do you say that which no one has asked of you?

Then she resumed her eternal sleep.

Injuriosus soon followed her in death. He was buried not far from her, in the basilica of Saint Allire. The first night that he lay there, a miraculous rose bush, emerging from the coffin of the virginal bride, encircled the two graves with its floral branches. And the next day the people saw that the lovers were bound together by chains of roses. Recognizing by this sign the saintliness of the blessed Injuriosus and of the blessed Scolastica, the priests of Auvergne pointed out these graves for the veneration of the faithful. But there were still pagans in this province, which had been evangelized by Saints Allire and Nepotian. One of them [the pagans], named Silvanus, worshipped the fountains sacred to the nymphs, hung pictures on the branches of an old oak tree, and preserved by his hearth small clay figures representing the sun and the fertility goddesses. Half hidden in the foliage, the god of the gardens protected his orchard. Silvanus spent his old age in the composing of poems. He wrote eclogues and elegies in a style somewhat unpolished, but of a clever turn and into which he introduced the verses of the old poets whenever he found the opportunity. Having visited with the crowd the tomb of the Christian spouses, the good man marveled at the rose bush that adorned the two graves. And, since he was pious in his own way, he recognized therein a heavenly sign. But he ascribed the prodigy to his gods, and he did not doubt that the rosebush bloomed by the will of Eros.

—The unfortunate Scolastica, he said to himself, now that she is no more than an empty shadow, misses the period of love and lost pleasures. The roses that emerge from her and that speak for her tell us: "Love, you who are alive." This wonder teaches us to taste the joys of life while there is still time.

Thus the simple pagan thought. On this subject he composed an elegy that by the greatest of chances I found in the public library of Tarascon, on the end-paper on the sixteenth-century Bible, catalogued: Michel Chasles Collection, F *n*, 7439 17⁹ *bis*. The precious leaf, that until now had escaped the notice of scholars, contains no fewer than eighty-four lines in a quite legible Merovingian cursive hand, that must date from the seventh century. The text begins with this verse:

Nunc piget; et quæris, quod non aut ista voluntas
    Tunc fuit …
[Now displeasure arises; and you seek what you once rejected]
and concludes with these words:
Stringamus mæsti carminis obseqio.
[We weave a sad song by way of compliance]

I shall not fail to publish the complete text as soon as I have finished deciphering it. And I do not at all doubt the M. Léopold Delisle[1] will himself undertake to present this priceless document to the Academy of Inscriptions.

---

1 Léopold-Victor Delisle (1826–1910), member of the Académie des inscriptions et belles-lettres and director at *De Bibliothèque nationale.*

Related Documents of Interest in the Lucas Affair

——— ➤((◉))◄ ———

I
Newton Ousted

Athenæum, #2077, 17 August 1867, pp. 209-210

ewton[g.] *dépossédé!* [NEWTON DISPOSSESSED]— The *Indépendance*, a Brussels paper, informs us that a few days ago M. [Michel] Chasles came before the French Institute, proofs in hand, to dispossess Newton, in favour of Pascal, of the discovery of the great law of universal attraction. Some notes, and two letters to Robert Boyle, leave no doubt of the priority. The first of these letters, dated May 8, 1652, contains nothing: the second, of September 2, without a year, is as follows:—

> "Le 2 septembre:
> "Monsieur, Dans les mouvements célestes, la force agissant en raison directe des masses et en raison inverse du quarré des distances [De Morgan's insertion: formule exacte des lois de l'attraction, adds the newspaper] suffit à tout, et fournit des raisons pour expliquer toutes ces grandes révolutions qui animent l'univers. Rien n'est si beau, selon moy: mais quand il s'agit des phénomènes sublunaires, des ces effets que nous voyons de plus près et dont l'examen nous est plus facile, la vertu attractive est un Protée qui change souvent de forme. Les rochers et les montagnes ne donnent aucun signe sensible d'attraction. C'est, dit-on, que ces petites attractions particulières sont comme absorbées par celle du globe terrestre, qui est infiniment plus grande; cependant on donne comme un effet de la vertu attractive la mousse qui flotte sur une tasse de café, et qui se porte avec une précipitation très sensible sur les bords du vase. Est-ce là votre sentiment? Je suis, Monsieur, votre très affectioné,   PASCAL.
> "Note.—Le corps, en vertu de la tendance au mouvement que l'attraction lui imprime, est capable de parcourir un espace donné dans un tem[p]s donné. Sa vitesse initielle sera donc proportionelle à

l'intensité de l'effort ou de la tendance imprimée par la puissance attractive; et cette intensité sera elle-même proportionelle à la masse attirante, à égale distance, et à différentes distances comme la masse attirante divisée par les carrés de ces distances.

PASCAL."[1]

Supposing these letters genuine, it is to be observed that Pascal, in repeating what had been said before him, does not write in so clear a way as he had written sixteen years before, when explaining what he then thought on the same subject. But first: Newton is liable to this sort of attack so long as his claim is stated in the incorrect way which prevails both at home and abroad. The *savants* [scholars] of the French Institute, though they will, of course, record these letters and give due honour to the ingenuity of Pascal's guess, will smile at the newspaper idea of Newton's being *dispossessed:* there are *sous-savants* [literally, under-scholars, i.e., the less knowledgeable] who might take it up in earnest. It was the common notion, before Newton wrote, that attraction is the probable explanation of the celestial motions, and that it is most likely as the inverse square of the distance. But the question was, how to demonstrate that such an attraction gives observed phenomena for its necessary consequences: who would show that this law of attraction will make a body *describe an ellipse* about the centre of force? This is what Newton did: assuming *universal* gravitation, that is, attraction of every *particle* on every other, he showed that spheres attract one another as they would do if they were collected in the centres, which is not true for any other inverse law; and that *this* attraction of sphere on sphere is as the inverse square of the distance. He established the ellipse as the undisturbed orbit, and made good progress in pointing out the effects of the distur-

---

1   2 September.:

Sir, Among celestial movements, the force operating in direct proportion to the masses and in inverse proportion to the square of the distances [between them] [De Morgan's note: the precise formula of the laws of gravity, adds the newspaper] suffices for all, and furnishes the grounds for explaining all these great revolutions that propel the universe. Nothing is so beautiful, from my point of view: but when it comes to sublunary phenomena, to the effects that we see from a shorter distance and the examination of which is easier for us, the attractive force is a Proteus that often changes its shape. Crags and mountains do not exhibit any observable evidence of gravitational attraction. This is because, one may say, these small particular gravitational forces are as it were absorbed by that of the terrestrial sphere, which is infinitely greater; nevertheless, one gives as an effect of gravitational force the froth that floats on a cup of coffee and proceeds with most perceptible haste towards the side of the vessel. Is that your opinion?

I am, Sir, you most affectionate,   PASCAL

Note.—A body, because of the tendency towards motion that gravity imparts to it, is able to travel a given distance in a given time. Its initial speed will therefore be proportional to the exertion of the pull or the tendency imparted by the gravitational force; and this force will itself be proportional to the attracting mass, at a constant distance, and at varying distances directly proportional to the attracting mass divided by the square of the distances [between objects].

PASCAL

bances of the other planets. When the newspaper writer dispossesses Newton by help of two sentences of Pascal, it is because those two sentences contain *all he knows about Newton.*

Kepler (died 1630), who was one of the first who advanced the doctrine of attraction, took it that the attractions of the heavenly spheres were inversely as the distances. Bouillaud [Ismaël Boulliau], the countryman of Pascal, in his "Astronomia Philolaica," published in 1645, [Paris: S. Piget] made the next step. He says (p. 23),—

> "That corporeal virtue by which the sun takes hold of or grasps the planets, which is to it in the place of hands, emitted through all the amplitude of the universe, revolves with the body of the sun, *quasi species solis* [as it were a sort of sun]. Being corporeal, it is diminished and extenuated in greater space and interval, but the ratio of this diminution is the same as that of light, that is, in the ratio of the squares of the distances, but inverse."

Pascal himself, in conjunction with [Giles Personne de] Roberval, wrote to [Pierre de] Fermat a letter (Aug. 16, 1636), which is printed in Fermat's "Opera Varia" [Toulouse: Johann Pech, 1679]. A question put by Fermat requires the consideration of attraction, and Pascal admits three possible suppositions. The attraction may be an effort of the so-called attracted body to *seek* the attracting body; it may be an attraction towards the body which draws— *like the earth*; it may be a mutual attraction, like that of the magnet and the iron. Pascal has no idea of the stone *and the earth* mutually attracting one another. Neither has he (1636) any notion of a *law* of attraction. Perhaps he got both from Bouillaud nine years later. Any one who reads the chapter of Bouillaud will see, in spite of various errors, a great quantity of suggestion for such a mind as Pascal's.

[Christian] Huyghens, before Newton published, but not before he discovered, published a step in the theory. He gave in his celebrated "Horologium Oscillatorum" ([Paris: F. Muguet,] 1673), a full account—without demonstration—of the law of centrifugal force in circular motion. Now this centrifugal force is also the tension of the string, which of course might be replaced by a centripetal force. Huyghens states that this force is as the radius inversely and the square of the velocity directly.

It is very obvious that Pascal had been preceded by Bouillaud. All who wish to preserve to Newton what he *can* claim, must take care not to load him with what he *cannot.* The anagrams of the Budget of Paradoxes should be remembered: as to the notion and law of attraction Newton is *not new:* but he *went on.* Remember also that Bouillaud and Pascal *guessed:* that Newton *demon-*

strated, having first invented the branch of mathematics which was wanted. M. Chasles, the geometer—(who must not be confounded with M. Philarète Chasles, his cousin, well known to our readers),—is an historian of science distinguished by research and acuteness. We shall perhaps have to give our readers his reasons for thinking these letters genuine: but we confess that to us, and as yet, his sanction is the strongest circumstance in their favour. We put together a point or two at short notice, being the most prominent of those which require his attention.

We do not see anything like Pascal's style: the last sentence of the note is either bad grammar or mathematical solecism. We cannot find any proof of communication between him and Boyle. The long life in the five-volume folio edition of Boyle's works does not show us any evidence of such communication. The first of the letters above mentioned is in a style of familiar acquaintance. The writer asks for communication of experiments, and ends with "Je suis, Monsieur, comme toujours, votre très humble et très affectionné serviteur." [I am, Sir, as always, your most humble and most affectionate servant.] But Boyle's mention of Pascal, when subsequently criticizing his writings on fluids, is distant, complimentary, and of an antagonism unrelieved by any reference to personal acquaintance. And Pascal, who in 1652 is so cordial a correspondent, has no other phrase for Boyle in or after 1660, than "un gentilhomme Anglais nommé Monsieur Boyle" [an English gentleman named Mr. Boyle]. Add to this that in 1652 Boyle was a young man of twenty-six, who published nothing until 1660. In 1652 he was in Ireland. His elementary chemical studies began in 1646: but we do not trace him into original investigation until about 1654.

The explanation of the froth of the coffee moving towards the side of the cup by attraction, be it of the cup or of the distant mountains—it is not clear which—is not like Pascal. But this is not the only difficulty. Pascal is sure, of course, that his English correspondent will understand him: and he himself, equally of course, has often seen the phenomenon. But there are great difficulties in the way. The letter is presumed to be written in or near 1652. Now in 1652 coffee was, it is said, first introduced into England. By 1657, [Edward] Phillips [author of *The New World of English Words*, London: Printed by E. Tyler, for Nath. Brooke, 1658] says, "Coffa, see Cauphe," and Cauphe is "a kind of drink among the Turks, made of a brown berry; much in use now in these parts." There is some record of coffee having been tasted at Marseilles in 1644; but a coffee-house was not opened there until 1671. As to Paris, the first recorded coffee is that brought by [Jean de] Thevenot the younger from the East in 1657. It was only drunk at the houses of M. Thevenot and some of his friends until 1669, when the Turkish ambassador brought in a large quantity, distributed it in presents, and established the custom of drinking it. Two years afterwards an Armenian, *of the name of Pascal,* set up a coffee-house, but met with little encouragement, and migrated to London, where coffee-houses were in vogue, for they were (for a few days) suppressed by a royal edict in 1675. They were taxed in 1660, and subjected to licence in 1663. Curiously enough, Edwards, the Turkey merchant, who first brought coffee into England in 1652, brought with him a Greek *named Pasqua,* who knew how to roast and boil it, and who set up a shop in George Yard, Lombard Street. Many thanks to *Notes and Queries.*

We find no mention of coffee in Molière's plays (1653-1673): in the very last, the "Malade Imaginaire" [hypochondriac], we should have expected that when Toinette, *en médecin* [in the guise of a doctor], regulates all the details of the old fool's diet, Molière could hardly have resisted something about the new beverage, unless it had been so new as not to be generally intelligible. The Dictionary of the Academy (1694) has the word of course, and its derivatives; but in one of the examples there is a hint of newness: *café,* a coffee-house, is exemplified by "Il y a beaucoup de cafés à Paris et à Londres" [there are many coffee-houses in Paris and in London].

These and some other little matters furnish presumptions against the letters which no one is better qualified than M. Chasles to rebut, if it can be done. These newspaper mares'-nests are useful: they tend to call public attention to exact specification of discoveries, of which there is, we believe, not one which was not preceded by some hint, guess, conjecture, surmise, *aperçu,* or conceit. When the straws which show the way the wind blows are proved to be the ships which the wind impels, Newton will run some risk of being dispossessed by Bouillaud and Pascal. The second is a great name, to those who know his writings: greater still to those who remember that he died at the age of thirty-nine, after many years of bodily and mental depression.

Since writing the above, we see by a newspaper paragraph that there are more letters, and one from young Newton, who was learning his elements at Trinity College [Cambridge], as an undergraduate, when Pascal died. Of these we can say nothing: and in any case we should prefer to wait for next mail, which will probably bring Pascal's answer to young Newton, communicating the theory of the universe.

We hear that the French *savants* make very light of the Pascal papers; and the name of a hoaxer is freely mentioned [Guglielmo Libri—see the next entry].

[Augustus de Morgan]

II
Foreign Intelligence

Times (London), 14 September 1867, 10a

—

FRANCE
(From our Own Correspondent)
Paris, Friday, Sept. 13, 7 A.M.

You are probably already acquainted with the Pascal-Newton controversy—with how M. Chasles, of the Academy of Sciences, contends that Pascal preceded Newton in his great discovery of the laws of gravitation, and with the fact that letters, alleged to be written by Pascal and by Newton himself, have been brought forward in support of this theory. By all impartial persons who have investigated the affair the letters in question are set down as clumsy forgeries, of which they contain internal evidence. Newton's age at the time when he is alleged to have written the letters falsely attributed to him, the allusion to things not in general use at the time (as, for instance, to coffee)[,] the style of the letters attributed to Pascal, and various other reasons sufficiently refute the authenticity of the correspondence. With reference to this affair I have received the two following letters, written originally in French for circulation in this country, and which I hope some of the French papers will have the candour and courage to publish, in justice to a man long and cruelly persecuted by political enemies:—

"To Monsieur Chasles, Member of the Paris Institute.
"London, Sept. 7, 1867.
"Sir,—They write to me from Paris that after your refusal to make known the origin of the false autographs of Pascal which you presented to the Institute, your friends, to get you out of the scrape, have dared to utter and even to print my name, and to strive to throw upon me the responsibility of those absurd and silly fabrications. This affair, it is added, makes a noise and scandal in France.

"Nobody knows better than I how the credulity of the Parisians may be played upon. Nevertheless, after having been, in 1848, from personal motives, the victim of a proscription against which all Europe protested, and which had for its effect to make a place for you at the Institute, it may appear strange that 19 years later I should be exposed to new calumnies, having for sole object to cover your responsibility. [In 1851 Chasles assumed Libri's seat at the Institute. Libri had been accused and then convicted in absentia of massive thefts of documents from French libraries. Despite his guilt, Libri maintained that he was innocent.] In the Old Testament, there where the scapegoat is spoken of, it is not said that the same victim can serve twice; but I should be wrong to complain of such repetition, for the absurdity of the present calumnies is a fresh proof of the absurdity of the former ones.

"From the beginning, on the mere inspection of the first documents you presented to the Institute, and which I saw by chance in a Brussels journal, the *Indépendance*, I understood that those papers were but a clumsy fabrication. The annexed letter, from an illustrious man of learning, Professor De Morgan, written originally in English, and of which he has seen and approved the translation, can leave no doubt on that point.

"I need not add that I have never had anything to do with those false autographs, of which I learnt the existence only from the *Indépendance*. If I am desirous that the origin of them should be known, it is not for my sake but for yours, Sir, since your scientific authority would be very much diminished if you delayed longer to make known in an indubitable manner how those papers got into your hands. A man who writes on the history of sciences has often to cite documents which the reader has no means of verifying, and it is more important to him than to any other person not to allow a doubt to rest upon the authenticity of the proofs upon which he bases his assertions.

"G.[uglielmo] LIBRI."

M. De Morgan's Letter to M. Libri.

"91, Adelaide-road, N.W., Sept. 6, 1867.

"My dear Sir,—Towards the 10th of August you showed me the *Indépendance* of the 3d, containing two letters attributed to Pascal. You strongly expressed your opinion that they were forgeries. I took the paper saying that I would send an article to the *Athenæum* on the subject. My article appeared in the number of the 17th of August. The remark that 1652 was too remote a period for any one to speak in that way of coffee was made by you. Since then we have had several conversations on that amusing subject. The assertion that the forgery in question is due to you is a stupidity worthy to figure in company with the other stupidities relating to Pascal.

"Yours sincerely,

"A.[ugustus] DE MORGAN."

III
Newton or Pascal.

Times (London), 20 September 1867, 9c-d

—

TO THE EDITOR OF THE TIMES

Sir,—The documents respecting Newton and his discoveries which have been recently communicated to the French Academy of Sciences by M. Chasles, and printed in the *Comptes Rendus* [proceedings], have naturally excited some degree of interest in this country. If we are to believe the statements contained in these papers, the real discoverer of the law of gravitation is not Newton but the French philosopher Pascal. Newton is also dethroned from the position which he occupied as the inventor of the infinitesimal calculus, since it would appear, according to the same authority, that he was indebted for this great achievement mainly to assistance which he privately received from his confidential friend Pascal.

The direct tendency of the numerous statements contained in these Pascal documents is to degrade Newton from the high position he has heretofore occupied as a natural philosopher and a mathematician. He is represented as not only receiving instruction in science from Pascal, but also as obtaining from him a great number of important results in physical astronomy, which he afterwards gave forth to the world as his own in the *Principia*. His correspondence with the French philosopher is alleged to have commenced in the year 1653, when he was only 11 years old, and to have continued down to near the time of Pascal's death in 1662. Nor is it to Pascal alone that Newton would appear to have been indebted for the great discoveries in science with which his name is associated. He is presented to be constantly sitting at the feet of Descartes and deriving inspiration from his writings, concealing, however, his obligations to the French philosopher, whose merits he studiously endeavours to ignore, except in one instance, in which he is forced to acknowledge, with all the humility of a kneeling penitent, "that Descartes is undoubtedly the greatest genius of the 17th century." Indeed, it would be difficult to say whether the tendency of the papers communicated by M. Chasles is more to degrade Newton than to elevate Pascal and Descartes. But this is not all. It would appear, if we are to give credence to the same documents, that Newton had also in his possession unpublished manuscripts of Galileo, Kepler, and Leibnitz, which he freely availed himself of in the preparation of the *Principia*. Need we be surprised that with all this surreptitious aid, he succeeded in palming himself off upon the world as the greatest of philosophers and mathematicians? Indeed, according to a French writer the wonder is that he took so long a time to digest the treasures which he had so assiduously collected from so many different sources, and which he so basely appropriated to the purpose of his own personal aggrandisement.

Those astounding documents have formed the subject of grave discussion in the French Academy of Sciences. When they were first communicated by M. Chasles, a committee, consisting of some of the most eminent members of the Academy, was appointed to inquire into their authenticity. The committee have since delivered their report. They state that the information before them is insufficient to enable them to decide upon the question whether the documents are true or false. Few persons, we think, will concur in the justness of this view of the matter. The materials accessible to the committee were abundantly sufficient to lead them to the conclusion that the entire mass of the documents communicated by M. Chasles are gross fabrications, and it is to be regretted, since the Academy had lent the high sanction of its authority to the publication of papers so injurious to the memory of Newton, that the question of authenticity, once entertained, was not carried out to its logical issue.

In Newton's own country men of science have not hesitated to denounce the documents communicated to the French Academy of Sciences by M. Chasles as pure forgeries. Sir David Brewster has shown by the most conclusive evidence that they are not genuine, and he is strongly supported in this view of the matter by the authority of Mr. [Augustus] De Morgan, who is so eminently capable of discussing any question of scientific history. It is right also to state that in France M. [Armand Prosper] Faugère, though not a member of the Academy, has very pointedly exposed the falsity of the so-called Pascal papers.

But there are certain numerical results contained in these documents which do not appear to have been yet subjected to examination, "although they are capable" of furnishing a decisive test in the investigation of the question of the authenticity of the documents. It is in reference to these results that I would beg your permission for a few remarks.

According to the papers communicated by M. Chasles, Pascal determined the masses of the Sun, the Earth, Jupiter, and Saturn, the densities of those bodies, and the force of gravity at their surfaces. I shall now show that the results thus attributed to the French philosopher are pure forgeries of the corresponding numbers contained in the third edition of the *Principia*.

Let us commence by citing a few dates which bear upon the question. Pascal was born in 1623, and died in 1662. The first edition of Newton's great work, the *Principia*, was published in 1687, the second in 1713, and the third in 1726. The third edition was the last published during the life of Newton, who died in 1727.

Madame [Gilberte] Perrier, the sister of Pascal, who has written an account of her brother's life, asserts distinctly that at the age of 30 he abandoned all secular pursuits; that during the next five years he devoted himself wholly to religious studies, and that during the four years which preceded his death he was utterly incapable of occupying his mind with any subject, whether religious or secular. Notwithstanding this statement I shall give the year 1662 as the date of Pascal's so-called discoveries in physical astronomy.

When the theoretical astronomer proceeds to ascertain the numerical values of the results of his abstract researches he calls to his aid the practical astronomer, who supplies him with observations adapted to the special subject of research in which he is engaged, and which he employs as absolutely necessary materials in the formation of the physical groundwork of his calculations. The more accurate such observations are, of course, the more accurate will be the ultimate numerical results. Now, the observations made by astronomers in one age will be found, generally speaking, to differ in precision from those made by astronomers in any other age. Improvements in the principles of observation, and in the construction and use of instruments, the superior abilities of the observers, and other causes will necessarily produce this result. The latter half of the 17th century will be for ever memorable in the history of astronomy, for the complete revolution which was effected in the principles and practice of observation. The heavenly bodies were scanned with telescopes of unwonted power, and micrometers were applied to them for making minute and delicate measures. The Observatories of Greenwich and Paris were established, and observations for ascertaining the exact positions of the celestial bodies were now made exclusively in the meridian by means of carefully divided instruments furnished with telescopic sights. It is not too much to assert that, during the period to which I refer, more was done for promoting the precision of astronomical observations than all else that has been accomplished from the time of the establishment of astronomy as a strict science by the Greeks down to the present day.

This would be the proper place for pointing out the particular kind of observations which the theoretical astronomer requires for calculating the masses of the sun and planets, their densities, and the force of gravity at their surfaces; and the question would then naturally offer itself for examination, what was the precision of the observations accessible in Pascal's time for determining the numerical results to which I refer. But in a journal intended for general circulation any such discussion would be out of place. I shall therefore content myself with one or two brief statements.

In Pascal's time the great improvements in practical astronomy to which I have referred had not yet come into operation. No practical astronomer of note had appeared since the days of Tycho Brahè, and indeed the only mass of observations available for ascertaining the exact position of the heavenly bodies were those due to the Danish astronomer. But for computing the masses and densities of the sun and planets other delicate observations are required, such as measurements of the apparent diameters of those bodies. The highest authority for such measures in Pascal's time was the celebrated Dutch astronomer [Christian] Huyghens. In the following table I have given a comparison between the diameters of the Sun, Jupiter, and Saturn, as deduced from the measures of Huyghens and the diameters which Newton has given in the first and third editions of the *Principia* as derived from measures executed in the one case by [John] Flamsteed, the first Astronomer Royal; and in the second, by [the Reverend James] Pound and his nephew, the celebrated [James] Bradley:—

	The Sun.	Jupiter.	Saturn.
Pascal (1662)	10,000	1,818	1,351
Newton (1687)	10,000	1,063	889
Newton (1726)	10,000	997	791

The corresponding results of modern astronomers may be represented by the numbers—10,000—986—898. The numbers for 1662 show how widely Huyghens erred in such delicate measurements.

For determining the earth's mass an element of great importance is required—the solar parallax. Now, the most trustworthy value of this element which was available in Pascal's time was that derived by Kepler from Tycho Brahè's observations. It amounted to 1 min. 1 sec. But when an improved system of observations had been prosecuted for some years at Greenwich, it became evident that the value of the solar parallax was much less than Kepler had assumed it to be. Newton, in 1687, assumes the value of the solar parallax to be 20 sec.

In 1726 he assumes it to be only 10½ sec. According to modern researches the value of this element amounts to 8 min. 9 sec.

In the Pascal documents no astronomer is mentioned as having supplied the observations upon which the calculations contained in the documents are founded. I have cited the authority of Huyghens merely as the best which was accessible in Pascal's time for minute and delicate measures. Newton has candidly stated the astronomers to whom he was indebted for the observations which formed the groundwork of his researches. In 1687 he employed the observations of [Giovanni Domenico] Cassini and Flamsteed. In 1726 the observations he used were those of Cassini, Pound, and Bradley. It deserves to be borne in mind that the observations which thus formed the groundwork of Newton's calculations were all made subsequently to the death of Pascal in 1662.

I now proceed to compare the results communicated by M. Chasles to the Academy of Sciences, with the corresponding results of Newton's researches as contained in the editions of the *Principia* of 1687 and 1726.

Let us first compare the masses of the Sun, the Earth, Jupiter, and Saturn. We have thus:—

	The Sun.	The Earth.	Jupiter.	Saturn.
Pascal, 1662	1	$\frac{1}{169,282}$	$\frac{1}{1,067}$	$\frac{1}{3,021}$
Newton, 1687	1	$\frac{1}{28,700}$	$\frac{1}{1,100}$	$\frac{1}{2,360}$
Newton, 1726	1	$\frac{1}{169,282}$	$\frac{1}{1,067}$	$\frac{1}{3,021}$

An inspection of these numbers will show at a glance that one of two conclusions is unavoidable. Either some nameless observer must have supplied Pascal with elements of computation absolutely identical with those which Newton obtained in 1726 from Cassini, Pound, and Bradley, and Pascal must have used the very same value of the solar parallax which Newton employed in 1726—viz, 10½ secs., or the numbers communicated by M. Chasles to the Academy of Sciences must be pure forgeries. The first of these conclusions cannot be admitted. We have seen from the sample which I have given of Huyghens' measures how inadequate they are to stand the test of a comparison with the corresponding measures which Newton employed in 1726. Besides, when extreme precision is aimed at, no two astronomers even in the same age have arrived at absolutely the same results in such delicate measures. Difference of instruments, difference of climate, difference of skill on the part of the observers, and many other disturbing causes, will necessarily produce minute discordances in the final results. Again, as I have already remarked, the determination of the earth's mass depends upon the solar parallax; but what right had Pascal for assuming a solar parallax of 10½ sec. at a time when practical astronomy had not advanced beyond the condition in which it existed in the days of Tycho Brahè? Finally, it is to be remarked that the numbers communicated by M. Chasles are not merely approximations to those given in the earliest edition of the *Principia*, but are absolutely identical with the numbers stated in the third and most perfect edition of that work, which last numbers were based on measures executed by astronomers who were not born at the time of Pascal's death. Taking these circumstances into consideration, it is impossible to avoid the conclusion that the numbers communicated by M. Chasles are gross forgeries of the corresponding numbers contained in the third edition of the *Principia*.

Let us next institute a comparison between the densities of the Sun, the Earth, Jupiter, and Saturn, as communicated by M. Chasles to the French Academy, and the densities as given by Newton in 1687 and 1726:—

	The Sun.	The Earth.	Jupiter.	Saturn.
Pascal, 1662	100	400	91½	67
Newton, 1687	100	387	76	60
Newton, 1726	100	400	91½	67

Here, again, notwithstanding that the apparent diameters enter as elements of calculation, the numbers communicated by M. Chasles are absolutely identical with those given by Newton in the third edition of the *Principia*. Of course, the observations which form the basis of computation must have been identical also—for we must reject as utterly incredible the idea of an absolutely exact balance of errors in so many instances. But whence arises this peculiar affection of Pascal for the observations of Pound and Bradley, when it is considered that neither of these astronomers was born at the time of Pascal's death? M. Chasles, in the discussions at the meetings of the Academy of Sciences, takes up some purely mathematical parts of the *Principia*, and working out, by the use of a few symbols, the corresponding so-called notes of Pascal, he points out triumphantly the identity of the results with those given by Newton in the *Principia*; but he would perform a vastly more extraordinary feat, and would give greater satisfaction to the world, if he would show how the identity arises in the case of the numbers which I have given above.

Finally, let us institute a similar comparison in respect to the intensity of gravity at the surfaces of the bodies:—

	The Sun.	The Earth.	Jupiter.	Saturn.
Pascal, 1662	10,000	435	943	529
Newton, 1687	10,000	805½	804½	536
Newton, 1726	10,000	435	943	529

The elements of computation being the same in this as in the preceding case, it might be expected that the numbers for 1662 and 1726 would be identical also. The question, however, still remains for solution, how does the identity arise in either case?

There is only one possible solution to the difficulties which I have proposed, and it is this:—The entire mass of the documents communicated to the Academy of Sciences by M. Chasles are pure forgeries.

I am, Sir, your obedient servant,
The Observatory, Glasgow, Sept. 18.   R.[obert] GRANT.

IV
The Pascal-Newton Forgeries

Times (London), 18 February 1870, 9e

The sixth Chamber of the Correctional Police of Paris, commenced on Wednesday the investigation of charges of fraud and misrepresentation imputed to a man named Lucas Vrin [sic], and, indeed, to a great extent admitted by him. The defendant is the man who supplied M. Chasles, an eminent member of the Académie des Sciences, with a number of alleged autograph letters by Blaise Pascal, the contents of which, if true, would have transferred to the writer the fame which Newton had acquired for his discoveries in natural science, and converted the latter into a mere plagiarist from Pascal. The controversy which was provoked by the introduction of these letters resulted in their being proved to be forgeries, as their author ultimately admitted them to be. Subsequent investigation proved that from the same source had proceeded many thousands of pretended autograph letters of distinguished personages, including Charlemagne, Petrarch, Raphael, Gabrielle d'Estrées, Rabelais, and others. The author of these forgeries, Lucas Vrin, is a man aged 52, described as imperfectly educated, but with a wonderful natural talent for invention. He admits that he imposed upon M. Chasles, but pleads that he included with the forgeries he sold authentic documents of value fully equal to the sums he received. The hearing is not yet concluded.

———————— ◄◄((●))►► ————————

V
The Pascal Forgeries

Times (London), 19 February 1870, 8b

The prisoner Vrin Lucas [sic], who is charged with forgery and fraud, was examined on Wednesday by the Judge of the Sixth Chamber of the Police Correctional in Paris. His avowals were of a most extraordinary character. He admitted that he had sold to M. Charles [sic], at different times, no less than 27,000 documents, for which he had received from that gentleman 140,000f. Of the 27,000 documents which he sold to M. Charles only about 100 were genuine, the rest being productions of his own pen, although purporting to be written by Julius Caesar and other Roman Emperors, by Apostles, and by poets and statesmen of all ages, and had all been manufactured by himself, without the aid of any other person. In order to complete the deception he had forged annotations upon old books and documents, purporting to be made by former possessors of the manuscripts, which he palmed off upon M. Charles, and also had recourse to various expedients to give an appearance of antiquity to the papers, by submitting them to the action of heat and by mixing colouring matter with the ink he used. M. Charles, upon being examined, said he was a member of the Académie des Sciences, and was 76 years old. He could not fix the date when Lucas first came to him, but it was a long time since. He introduced himself with a letter from a collector of curiosities known to M. Charles, and produced several documents, which the latter purchased. From that time these dealings became frequent until they reached the enormous figure admitted by the prisoner. For an alleged letter of Molière M. Charles paid 500 francs, and for a first letter of Rabelais 200 francs, afterwards purchasing at various prices upwards of 2,000 bearing the same signature. Lucas also obtained money from him on different pretences of pressing need, and had also obtained books, which he never returned. Being asked by the Judge how he explained the production of such documents in such numbers, M. Charles replied that the letters explained each other. Thus, Alcuin wrote to Charlemagne upon documents which he found at the Abbey of Tours. Rabelais was sent to that same abbey by

Francis I., from which place he wrote the letters included in the manuscripts sold by Lucas, which comprised 100 letters from Alcuin, and more than 2,000 from Rabelais. The detection of the prisoner's fraud arose from M. Charles's apprehension lest Lucas should dispose of any of his valuable manuscripts out of France, and he therefore directed the attention of the police to the man's actions. Having sent a pretended letter of Galileo to Florence for examination by a commission of *savants* there, it was returned to him as a forgery. He then complained to Lucas, who gave him another letter, telling him the owner of the collection from which those documents came was a M. de Boisjardin [sic]. After the Académie des Sciences had decided that the Pascal letters were forgeries Lucas said his employer had consulted him, and he thought the best thing would be to restore the purchase money and take back the documents, "but this," said M. Charles, "I would not do, as I believed in their authenticity." The prisoner was interrogated by the Court as to what he had done with the large sums of money received from M. Charles, but he persisted in saying that he had but 2,000 or 3,000 francs left, and refused to give any account of his expenditure of the remainder. Several experts were called, as it seems rather unnecessarily, to prove the methods employed by the prisoner to give the appearance of age to the forged writings, and the further hearing was then adjourned for a week.

——————⟫⟪(❰❱)⟫⟪——————

VI
"The Pascal Forgeries in the French Academy"

The Penn Monthly 1 (April, 1870): 151-158

Our age of reconstruction seems bent on a rereading of all history, a rehabilitation of all the scamps of antiquity, and the dragging of honored forms down from the niches and pedestals which Clio has assigned. Mr. [Thomas] Carlyle has much to answer for, and his chief disciple, Mr. [James Anthony] Froude, has closely followed the example set by the eulogist of Mirabeau, Marat, and Frederick [the Great]. Small men have done worse, misled by the petty instinct of indiscriminate contradiction, and have gravely asked us to accept kings John and Richard III as examples of all that is noble and excellent. One of the most amusing and curious scenes of this drama of historic reconstruction was enacted in the French Academy of Sciences during the past three years; M. Chasles, a member of the Academy, being the magician who, at a sweep of his wand, was to transfer the laurel crown from the head of Sir Isaac Newton to that (not bare) of the great theologian and metaphysician Pascal.

On the 8th day of July, 1867, M. Chasles, at the request of President [Michel-Eugène] Chevreul, promised to anticipate his forthcoming book on "The Discovery of the Laws of Attraction by Pascal," and to lay before the Academy the letters on which his views were based. At the next meeting (July 15) he read two letters and four scientific memoranda addressed by Pascal to Sir Robert Boyle, in the year 1652, in which the law of gravitation was fully stated. The date at which Sir Isaac Newton was alleged to have discovered the same law is 1689 [the first edition of the *Principia* appeared in 1687]. We quote from one of these letters of Pascal to Boyle:

"In the movements of the heavenly bodies, the force acting in the direct ratio of the mass, and in the inverse ratio of the square of the distance, suffices for every thing, and furnishes reasons for explaining all the great revolutions which animate the universe."

In the latter part of the letter he illustrates the action of the same force on the surface of the earth by speaking of "the foam which floats on a cup of coffee, and which moves with a very sensible impetus towards the sides of the cup." In one of the memoranda, Pascal gives, for proportional values of the masses of the Sun, Jupiter, Saturn, and the Earth, the following numbers, as derived by induction from the general law of gravitation:

$$[\text{The Sun.} \quad \text{Jupiter.} \quad \text{Saturn.} \quad \text{The Earth.}]$$
$$1 \qquad \frac{1}{1067} \qquad \frac{1}{3021} \qquad \frac{1}{169282}$$

He gives no proof of the accuracy of these figures, nor does he indicate the method by which he arrived at them.

We may here anticipate M. Chasles' subsequent statements (September 13, 1869) by saying that he had obtained these letters and memoranda from a person calling himself a palaeolographic [sic] archivist, who furnished them during the six preceding years, together with some thousands of others, professing to come from the pens of Galileo, La Bruyere, Moliere, Montesquieu, Copernicus, Christopher Columbus, Calvin, Melanc[h]thon, Luther, Machiavelli, Raphael, Michael Angelo, Shakespeare, Montaigne, Cervantes, Dante, Petrarch, Boc[c]accio, and a host of others. This marvelous collection extends back to the first centuries of our era, including epistles from the Apostles, St. Jerome and St. Augustin. This precious and rare assemblage of documents, the archivist assured him, had been carried to America in 1791, from which country their present possessor had brought them, and he was now perusing them at his leisure, so that he would only dispose of them to M. Chasles piece by piece; and that gentleman felt a great delicacy about mentioning his name at the meetings of the Academy, as it might cut off posterity and the public from the rest of the documents, and inflict an irreparable loss upon literature.

During the two years between M. Chasles' first statement and this last disclosure a warm controversy agitated the Academy, and extended to England and Italy. In the Academy only a few members, and those the least distinguished as men of science, took ground in favor of the genuineness of the pretended discoveries. One after another of the great *savan[t]s* came forward to impugn the letters as forgeries. It is not the least notable fact in the discussion that as fast as any point of M. Chasles' story was impugned, new documents were forthcoming to substantiate his statements, all of which, he solemnly averred, were in his possession from the commencement. For instance, M. [Hervé-Auguste-Étienne-Albans] Faye (July 22, 1867) objected that the calculations necessary to reach the conclusions given in the letters were impossible until Newton had invented the calculus of fluxions, which was not until long after the date of the supposititious letters to Boyle. Thereupon a letter appears in which Pascal acknowledged to Boyle the receipt from Newton (then eleven years old) of "a treatise on *the* calculus of the infinite," and other papers of an equally profoundly scientific nature. At the same meeting M. [Jean-Marie-Constant] Duhamel had objected that even if these letters were genuine, Newton would still have the glory of establishing the great law of universal gravitation.

At the next meeting (July 29) M. Chasles produced a dozen letters of a character to show that Newton had been in direct communication with Pascal in regard to these very questions. The first, addressed to "the young Newton, studying at Grantham," in May, 1654, must have reached the author of the "Principia" in his twelfth year, and must have been read by that not very precocious youth in the intervals of "hound and hare," or top-whipping, or their equivalents in the middle of the seventeenth century. The following is an extract:

> "MY YOUNG FRIEND:—I have learnt with what care you seek to initiate yourself into the mathematical sciences and geometry, and that you desire to thoroughly master in a scientific way the works of the late M. Descartes. I send you several of his papers, which were given to me by a person who was one of his most intimate friends. I send you also several problems which were formerly the objects of my study, concerning the laws of attraction, in order to exercise your genius. I pray you to tell me your opinion of them."

Others of this batch of the letters are from Newton to Pascal and to Robault [i.e., Jacques Rohault], and must have been written in his eighteenth, twentieth and twenty-sixth years. They are written in beautiful French, while Sir Isaac never possessed the ability to compose fluently in that language. They also, as English critics pointed out, contain anachronisms in regard to the name of Newton's mother, and many small inaccuracies which a critical eye would at once detect. It is notable, as M. Benard pointed out, that Pascal's letters to Newton are full of English idioms rendered into French words. Others of the blunders were pointed out by Sir David Brewster, in a letter to President Chevreul, which was read August 12. He had re-examined all the correspondence and papers of Newton preserved at Hurtsbourne Park;[2] he declares that no paper or letter to or from Pascal to Newton, nor any piece containing the name of Pascal, exists in that collection.

M. [Armand-Prosper] Faugere (August 26) called attention to the instance given by the pseudo Pascal in 1652 to illustrate the law of attraction—namely, the attraction of foam on the surface of a cup of coffee to the sides of the cup. The way in which coffee is spoken of implied its common use in 1652, while not until 1669 did Soliman Aga, the Turkish ambassador to the Court of Louis XIV, teach the French the use of that beverage.

The second letter from England was from Robert Grant, of the Glasgow Observatory, who took up the numbers of the pseudo Pascal, which we have given as expressing the relative masses of the Sun, Jupiter, Saturn, and the Earth. M. Benard had already pointed out that the necessary data for the calculation as regards Saturn could not have been in Pascal's possession at the date of the letter, (January 2, 1655,) as the satellite from whose revolutions they are derived was not discovered until March 25 of the same year, and the first tables of those revolutions, by Huyghens, were not published until 1659. Mr. Grant followed up this blow by pointing out that the numbers of the pseudo Pascal were more accurate than any that Newton himself could reach until near the close of his life. The editions of the "Principia" of 1687 and 1713 give a different and a less accurate set of numbers; but in the last edition published during his own life, that of 1726, the numbers contained in M. Chasles' documents were inserted. These numbers were based upon observations made by [James] Pound and [James] Bradley with a telescope of new construction and unexampled power. The elder of these associate astronomers was born in 1669, or seven years after Pascal's death. To this M. Chasles gravely replied by charging Newton with changing Pascal's correct figures in his earlier editions of the "Principia," to prevent the detection of his plagiarism, and then returning to the exact fig-

---

2   Hurtsbourne Park was the seat of the Earls of Portsmouth, related to Isaac Newton and therefore possessors of Newton's papers.—translator's note

ures in his third edition, after a lapse of forty years; or else, he suggests, Newton had not Pascal's accurate data, and did not like to adopt his results without verification, which he did attain to before publishing the edition of 1726.

In the meantime the palæographical archivist had heard of Huyghens and his importance to the controversy; so at the same session of the Academy letters were forthcoming from Mynheer Huyghens to Pascal, Newton and Boyle, showing that Pascal had communicated his discoveries to that great savan[t], with whom they met with but a cold reception, as being likely to overthrow all branches of physics as then received and taught. M. Duhamel keenly retorted that these additional letters show that if the Chasles documents were genuine, then the alleged discoveries of Pascal had been made a subject of discussion and gossip in the scientific circles of Europe, without ever finding their way into print until 1867, a fact only to be accounted for on the supposition that they had never obtained a recognized place or standing by a rigorous proof of their truth. In any case the glory of the discovery remains with Newton. The clumsiest inventions of the Chasles documents were those presented at this meeting as written by the exiled James II to Newton, and from Newton to Louis XIV. The exiled king writes from St. Germain, in the new *role* of patron of science and of the whig Newton, whom his successor made Master of the Mint. In the midst of his preparations for an armed expedition to Ireland he finds time to busy himself with a Pascal-Newton controversy elsewhere unrecorded, which had sprung up in France, provoked by some offensive expressions used by Newton in regard to Pascal. He urges him, by his memory of old kindnesses—also unrecorded elsewhere—to retract his words and acknowledge his indebtedness to Pascal, of which abundant documentary evidence had been discovered. Newton complies, and in a letter to *le Grand Monarque* eats his own words with edifying gravity. The first letter is dated 1689, the second 1685, at a date when James was still Duke of York and a loyal subject of his brother, Charles II, little expecting to be an exiled king at St. Germain. Later in the controversy a whole host of these royal letters appear, all in regard to the interest which these much misunderstood monarchs took in the history of scientific discovery and the claims of Pascal. The archivist, it is evident, thought that he had made a good point here.

At the session of October 7 another illustrious astronomer comes on the scene. M. Huyghens' Saturnian discoveries proving too late in their date for the basis of Pascal's calculations, the archivist brings forward the great Italian, Galileo, as the first discoverer of the satellite which bears the name of Huyghens. He speaks, in autograph letters dated 1641, of a treatise received from Pascal, in which the numbers quoted above were demonstrated from astronomical data furnished by Galileo himself. These numbers, be it remembered, could only be reached by the calculus of fluxions, which even the pseudo Pascal first heard of in 1654, when Newton, then eleven years old, invented and communicated that mathematical process. In 1639, we may also note, a Roman inquisitor certified that Galileo had gone stone-blind, and all his authentic letters after that date are written by his disciples, and so signed, while those of M. Chasles are in autograph. At the next meeting a letter was read from M. Faugere, asking a formal investigation of the genuineness of these documents, by comparison with others from the same pens, preserved in the Bibliotheque Imperiale, and of undisputed genuineness. To this M. Chasles gave his cordial assent.

As a first step to this, we presume, he laid before the Academy, at its next meeting, (October 28,) a list of documents received through the archivist from the unknown collector, which have a bearing on the controversy. Although covering, as was afterwards ascertained, but a small part of the whole mass of documents, this list astonishes one by its extent and its audacity.

Sir David Brewster, appealed to by M. Chasles, in regard to the genuine papers and correspondence of Newton, declared that none of them contained the name of Pascal. He had previously pointed out the entire dissimilarity of the handwriting of the pseudo Newton to that of the genuine letters of Sir Isaac. He conjectured that [Pierre] Des Maizeaux, one of M. Chasles' authorities, as a correspondent of Liebnitz, was the real forger of these documents, in which he assigned to them a much more ancient origin than they could really claim. The correspondence is largely traced by its last possessors to Des Maizeaux, who must have had it in 1734–40, when he aided in the compilation of the "General Dictionary."[3] This work contains elaborate biographies of the men whose letters are now produced, but in no place does he record a single one of the startling facts revealed in them. Of the nine volumes of his correspondence preserved in the British Museum, not a single letter contains the name of Pascal.

Mr. Robert Grant, of the Glasgow Observatory, whose previous letter had necessitated the Galileo forgeries, now came forward to demolish the hypothesis based upon them, showing that even if Galileo had given Pascal data for the discovery of the mass of Saturn, still that would not account for the accuracy of his other figures, as no data possessed by Galileo would have enabled him to arrive at the numbers given in regard to the mass of the Sun, Jupiter and the Earth. M. Chasles' reply to these hard knocks from *perfide Albion* [treacherous England] is very amusing. His method has an attempt at

---

3   The reference is to the English edition (London: J. Bettenham, 1734-1741) of Pierre Bayle's *Dictionaire historique et critique.* Desmaiseaux became associated with this work for the fourth edition (Amsterdam: P. Brunel [etc.], 1730).

logic, but logic is not his main reliance. As Mahomet used to get a special rev-
elation to lift him out of any little difficulty with his public, so M. Chasles is
always succored by his archivist. Dividing up one of Mr. Grant's arguments
into three parts, he responds by presenting three series of letters, one of them
especially designed to overthrow the argument derived from Galileo's blindness
for three years before he wrote to Pascal. His faithful disciples are made to testify that his blindness was only by fits, and partial, so that he could write with
some difficulty. In the meantime the letters of the pseudo Galileo had been
noticed in Turin, and Signor [Gilberto] Govi writes to sustain Mr. Grant. He
shows that Galileo never wrote in French, the language of the pseudo Galileo.
His MSS. in the National Library at Florence contain not a line of French, and
when a French name appears in them it is generally "disfigured." When
Frenchmen wrote, it was, with the single exception of the Comte de Noailles,
in Italian or Latin, and his answers are always in the same languages. His disciples do not ascribe to him any knowledge of French, and mention no correspondence with Pascal, through themselves, according to the Chasles manuscripts. His blindness began in 1632, and the Inquisitor reported in 1639, "*Io l'ho
ritrovato totalmente privo di vista, e cieco affatto;*" i. e., "I have found him entirely deprived of sight and completely blind;" a statement confirmed by his correspondence and by other reports of the Inquisitor. After 1637 he wrote nothing, except once or twice his signature. These statements are confirmed by a letter from the Padre [Pietro Angelo] Secchi, of the Roman Observatory, read at
the session of December 16, who also points out minor inaccuracies. He especially notes that Galileo confined his studies to mechanics in his years of blindness, abandoning that of astronomy. M. Chasles' answer to these Italian opponents is amusingly inconsequent. At this point of the discussion M. [Antoine
Jérôme] Balard moved that the documents so liberally furnished by M. Chasles
be no longer published in the *Comptes Rendus* [proceedings] of the Academy.
This led to a discussion, participated in by a large number of the members.
Although the general sense of the Academy was decidedly against the genuineness of the documents, yet the desire for fair play prevailed, and the motion was
rejected; so that M. Chasles continued to hold the lists against all comers.

The Penn Monthly 1 (May, 1870): 191-200

The Chasles controversy spreads itself over four volumes of the Reports
of the Academy, each volume representing a period of six months. The first
period, which we have already chronicled, and in which the supposititious documents were first brought to light, shares with the last of the four in the depth
of interest excited, and the number of the combatants who come forward,

while the year that lies between them is rather deficient in both respects. The controversy had found its way into literary journals and books—a fact which rather diminished the importance of its discussion in the Academy itself. The most patent objections to the authenticity of the MSS. had been urged and answered, and the savan[t]s had begun to grow impatient of each other's stupidity in regard to the force of the objections, or of the answers to them. Sharp words begin to be heard instead of the suave and courteous periphrases in which, at an earlier stage, one side had insinuated that the documents were unhistorical, and the other had politely rejoined that excessive scepticism was unworthy of unprejudiced men of science. The self-love of the contestants had been enlisted, and nothing so freely excites the tongues, of even learned men, as does that deepest infirmity of the human character.

If the first six months was the period of Newton and Pascal, the second was that of Galileo Galilei, the Florentine astronomer and the inventor of the telescope. It will be remembered that the discoveries necessary as the basis of the calculations ascribed to Pascal were described in autograph letters ascribed to Galileo, and dated at a period in which history describes "the Tuscan artist" as completely blind, incapable of writing the letters, much less of making the observations in question in regard to the satellites of Saturn. On this single point the whole controversy for the time being now turns, the position of Chasles being defended by himself, and his Palæographical Archivist, and by Signor [Paolo] Volpicelli, but assailed by Padre Secchi, of Rome, Signor Govi, of Turin, and M. Th.[omas] H.[enri] Martin, of Rheims. It was conceded by the former that the language used by the Roman inquisitor, and by Galileo himself, in regard to the state of his sight, was, if strictly truthful, not consistent with their own theory. But they urged: What more likely than that he and his friends exaggerated the facts, with a double aim: to secure his liberation from the custody of the Inquisition, and to excuse him from an extensive correspondence, which would be inconsistent with the pursuit of his special studies. Quite an ingenious defence of this theory was made by collating undisputed letters of different dates. Thus, in a letter bearing the date, January 30, 1637, Galileo speaks of himself as dreaming in darkness, now upon one effect of nature, now another, and as unable to make calculations, because he could not trace figures and reason upon them. His sight was not, indeed, gone entirely, but "a perpetual rain of tears" prevented his engaging in his accustomed work. Yet, in a later letter, (April, 1637,) he speaks of his right eye alone being inflamed, and of his fears that he must lose it. Unless his disease was of an intermittent type, (M. Chasles reasoned,) the language of the first letter must be interpreted by that of the later one, showing that for *some* reason the Italian did exaggerate. If it was intermittent, then there may have been periods of relief and partial recovery at a still later date, at which the alleged discovery of the satellites of Saturn was made, and the letters to Pascal were written. This ingenious argument he followed up with a long string of documents from the never-failing repertory of the Archivist, from which it would appear that half Europe was agitated and concerned at the state of Galileo's eyes, "the royal caste" being especially forward in anxious and sympathetic interest. Urban VIII., Charles I., of England, Queen Christine, of Sweden, Richelieu, St. Vincent de Paul, St. Francis de Sales, and the Cardinal [Guido] Bentivoglio, vie with [Daniel] Elzevir and [Simon] Vouet in their concern for the physical welfare of this republican enemy to orthodox science. The Archivist evidently felt that there was much at stake here, and hurried forward his heaviest artillery to defend an imperilled position.

At one blow, Signor Govi demolished the authentic basis on which the whole argument had rested. The letter in question, he conceded, was indeed dated *January* 30, 1637, and did describe Galileo as almost entirely blind, while it is admitted that his blindness was but very partial until the beginning of the following year. But then, the true date of the letter was *January* 30, 1638. Galileo was writing in answer to a letter dated January, 1638, which is still preserved in his correspondence, and wrote 1637 because he retained the old Florentine style, in which the year began with the 25th of March. Even M. Chasles was obliged to admit the force of the answer, and we can hardly conceive of any one more impervious to the force of logic than this would-be reconstructor of the history of science. The observation of Govi cleared away all objections to the legitimate force of Galileo's own words in regard to his blindness. He says, (January, 1638,) that "he can see no more with his eyes open than with his eyes shut," and that "the entire light of his eyes is extinct," (*oculorum meorum lux omnis est extincta.*) He speaks, indeed, of writing briefly, but either because the pain forbade the protracted use of an amanuensis, or because he could write a short letter—as any one could—in the dark. To [John] Deodati, the Italian reformer, he writes, (January 2, 1638,) that he is irreparably blind, and that the world, which he has aggrandized so much, is for him reduced to his own body, and that he had especially lost the right eye, with which he had made his great discoveries. In a less careful letter of the following July, he seems, indeed, to say that he is not totally blind, and that he had lost the left eye only. But the whole genuine and undisputed correspondence of Galileo tells an utterly different story from that contained in these supposititious documents. Nor is his biography, by [Vincenzo] Viviani—his chosen disciple and the companion of his later years of darkness—less explicit, as he speaks of him as totally blind from 1637. Signor Volpicelli brings forward letters of the Padre Battista Borghi (February, 1638) which show that Italian surgeons had promised to restore the sight of the astronomer; and, again, Borghi speaks of some actual amelioration by the use of sugar candy, but the testimony of Viviani must be taken as final as to the failure of the powerful and recondite medicament to work the change anticipated.

Passing from the blindness to the studies of Galileo, we find the Chasles theory equally untenable. Signor Volpicelli indeed managed to find a statement in the *Allgemeine Encyclopædie*, (Leipsic, 1846,) to the effect that a letter from Galileo to Fermat contains "the germs of Newton's discoveries." M. Chasles adduced a passage from the astronomer's works to show that in 1640 he was occupied with the study of Saturn, and in defending the Copernican theory of our system; also an undisputed letter of Descartes, saying that Gassendi claimed to have Galileo's telescope, and expresses wonder whether its excellence is as great as the Tuscan had claimed. The story of the supposititious letters, that Galileo had sent his telescope to Pascal, with an account of the discovery of the satellite of Saturn, was not therefore improbable.

Secchi in turn demanded the proof from his acknowledged works and letters, that Galileo had ever busied himself with the subject of gravitation as implied in the letters of the pseudo-Galileo. His later works are occupied entirely with mechanics, although he speaks of many other subjects in letters. He writes to [Benedetto] Castelli, in 1640, that he has not seen Saturn for three years. As to what Descartes wrote of Galileo's telescope, it is well ascertained that Italian opticians of that day sent telescopes to all parts of Europe, calling them Galileo's telescopes, although he had never looked through them, much less made or used them. We find him in his period of blindness sending back an objective to its maker, because unable to use it. His own telescope he declared he reserved for his friend and patron, the Duke of Tuscany, as a souvenir of the great discoveries of which it had been the instrument. Equally futile was the objection that Copernicus had already discovered the law of gravitation; the passage appealed to proved nothing of the sort. M. H. Martin pointed out a genuine letter of 1639, in which Galileo enumerates the discoveries made by himself and his disciples in regard to Saturn; he repeatedly mentions the planet's ring, but never its satellites.

We pass by some minor details of this curious controversy, which involved the whole circumstances of the Tuscan astronomer's declining years. His personal relations—rather of the old Italian sort—were dragged into the arena, when the Archivist, finding that he had made a blunder of some thirty years or so, at once rushes to the rescue with a deluge of letters, as if to carry his point by a *tour de force*. Another blunder was the representing the Cardinal Bentivoglio—one of Galileo's enemies and judges—as profoundly interested in his well-being and in the progress of his revolutionary discoveries. The keen

French eye—in another instance—detected the Archivist in putting a slipshod phrase of modern French into the mouth of a king of France, of the seventeenth century. In another case the Archivist made Bentivoglio write when Galileo had been some months dead, as if he were still alive.

Little else than the Galileo side of the controversy was touched on during this year. The exceptions were a masterly paper by M. [Gustave Doulcet] Pontécoulant, showing that Pascal could not have reached the conclusions arrived at in the letters ascribed to him, and that the writer of those letters must have had before him the rigorous proofs of Newton. The Academy evinced their satisfaction with this paper, by voting to print it, although its size exceeded the limits fixed for admission to their report. M. Chasles' documents are handled without gloves, and finally pronounced "apocryphal" and "unworthy of examination." M. Faugère followed up his previous attacks on Chasles with an extensive pamphlet, reviewing the whole discussion, attacking every part of the new "discoveries," and giving his readers a humorous dialogue between M. Chasles and the Roman Inquisitor, who had certified to the total blindness of Galileo. The title of his pamphlet was admirably chosen: A Defence of Pascal and Incidentally of Newton and Others, Against the False Documents of M. Chasles.[4] M. Chasles' reply appears in the reports, but exhibits nothing new in fact or argument, not even a batch of new letters. M. [François Pierre Charles] le Baron Dupin—at a later session—had the honor of being the first French savan[t] who avowed his faith in the new documents, calling upon their custodian to publish them all and entire, as the best proof of their genuineness—a proof which must highly "conduce to our national glory." M. Chasles' feelings seem to have overpowered him as he rose to reply, and he at once rewarded his confiding adherent with a gush of documents on the Galileo question, mostly from the pens of the royal caste of Europe.

———

The last period of the controversy, and that in which the *coup de grace* was given to M. Chasles' discoveries, opens with the prolongation of the Galileo controversy. Signor Volpicelli published a work (in reply to a pamphlet of Padre Secchi) in which he maintained that the Tuscan did not become totally blind until after the middle of 1638. Signor Govi retorted by producing a nuncupative will of Galileo, dated August 21, 1638, in which the notary describes Galileo as deprived entirely of eyesight, (*privo in tutto della luce degli occhi*,) giving this a reason for the nuncupative character of the instrument, as

---

4 *Défense de B. Pascal et accessoirement de Newton, Galilée, Montesquieu, etc. contre les faux documents présentés par M. Chasles à l'Académie des sciences* (Paris: L. Hachette, 1868).

the testator was unable to write. M. Chasles replied by reiterating his theory that Galileo was saying all this for effect, and in order to secure his own discharge from custody. At this Signor Govi waxed wroth, and retorted a month later that it was no use to produce documentary evidence where it was at once set aside as containing false statements, and he might have added the proverb about people who live in glass houses. M. Chasles' Archivist had now had time for another batch of fiction, so his principal at once defended his position by presenting a new series of documents, in which, among other things, Galileo writes to Louis XIII, confessing that he is not entirely blind, but is shamming to secure his freedom. He speaks of his pretence as "the sweet illusion which is the ægis of his liberty."

The next blow to M. Chasles' pretences was the first of a fatal series. M. [Paul-Émile] Breton de Champ (April 12, 1869) called attention to the source upon which the Archivist had drawn in his Pascal forgeries. [Alexandre] Saverien's "History of Modern Philosophers,"[5] pub. 1761-7, (vol. iv, p. 14,) contains a statement in regard to the theory of gravitation which corresponds almost word for word with that put into the mouth of the pseudo-Pascal, in that letter to Fermat which contains the famous comparative magnitudes of the sun and three of its planets. The same volume, which is mainly devoted to Newton's "Principia," contains the letter of the pseudo-Galileo to the pseudo-Pascal referring to the same figures. These letters had been manufactured out of the philosophical discussions of Saverien. The Archivist was almost equal to even this critical occasion, and at the next session M. Chasles was furnished with a series of documents to prove that Saverien had drawn upon the letters of the pseudo-Pascal and Galileo. One of the new letters from Saverien to that illustrious and excellent blue-stocking, Madame de Pompadour, thanking her for the use of two hundred letters of Pascal, Newton, Galileo, &c., and returning them to her custody. But the daring inventor neglected to find some explanation of the fact that Saverien, with all these documents before him, still ascribed to Newton the honor of discoveries which he must have known were first made by his countryman Pascal.

The final explosion of the pretensions represented by M. Chasles, and defended by Signor Volpicelli and le Baron Dupin, began June 21, with the reading of the report of a commission which the Academy had appointed in 1867 to take cognizance of the whole matter. The eminent astronomer, [Urbain Jean Joseph] Le Verrier, on behalf of the commission, read their report, which occupied part of almost every session until July 26. It reviewed the whole course of the controversy, which had now lasted for nearly two years, and then proceeded to the merits of the case. It pronounced that there was no authentic evi-

---

5 *Histoire des philosophes modernes* (Paris: Brunet, 1761-1767).

dence that Pascal had ever corresponded with Galileo or with Newton; that the documents of M. Chasles had been proved devoid of authenticity by a comparison of the handwriting and the style with those of the undisputed letters of the same persons. [author's insertion: As to the paper and ink used, some discussion took place in the Academy, the conclusion reached being that they possibly were old, but most probably had been made to appear yellow and faded by chemical processes.] As to the origin of these documents, the commission note that M. Chasles had hitherto refused to say from whom he obtained them, and then prove by printing the passages in parallel columns that the forger drew on Saverien's work for a large number of the letters and scientific memoranda ascribed to Pascal, Galileo, &c. They had been copied almost word for word, the third person being changed to the first, and a few connecting words left out so as to make of the disconnected letters and memoranda a connected argument. Still others of these pseudo-Pascal MSS. had been taken in the same way from a "Dissertation on Attraction,"[6] by Father [Giacinto Sigismondo] Gerdil, (Paris, 1754,) and from the "Universal Dictionary," (Paris, 1810.) A few others of the Chasle[s] letters are then taken up and individually exploded. As to the much mooted question of Galileo's blindness, it is decided that by all authentic documents it was total from 1638. As to the main issue presented by M. Chasles, the claim of Newton to the great discoveries associated with his name and that of Huyghens to the discovery of the satellites of Saturn are fully vindicated. The commission thus sum up the case: "The letters produced by M. Chasles have no internal evidence of authenticity; they contradict each other; they do not agree in any particular with other documents, whose veracity does not admit of the least question…. The documents attributed to Galileo, Pascal, Huyghens, Newton, and their co[n]temporaries, whose object is to overthrow the authentic history of astronomy, are the work of a culpable speculation. Science and the Academy have a right to know who are the authors of this speculation."

At the session of September 13, 1869, M. Chasles made his answer to this last demand, an answer which we have partly anticipated. His reluctance to say how he came by the MSS. was purely in the interests of science. The Archivist had begun to bring them to him in 1861, and had assured him that they were at present in the possession of a gentleman who wished to read them carefully before disposing of them. To have told M. Le Verrier this when he asked it, in 1867, would have been to incur the blame of all world for compromising the fate of the rest of the collection. He called the Academy to witness how freely he had submitted the MSS. for inspection to all who took any interest in

6 *Dissertation sur l'incompatibilité de l'attraction et de ses différentes loix…* (Paris: Desaint & Saillant, 1754).

them, and declared that he had never visited the house of the Archivist, nor sent any one thither, for any document. The latter had visited him, at noon or in the evening, bringing his wares. For himself, M. Chasles had had full confidence in their authenticity, until the report of the Florentine commission on one of Galileo's letters made him uneasy, and then he had asked the aid of the police in investigating the matter. The house of the Archivist was visited, in the hope of finding the mass of documents, of which he had palmed off mere copies on M. Chasles, as well as other documents due to that gentleman but not yet delivered. The Archivist himself was arrested, but only some blank papers, registers, pens and a flask of ink was discovered, where the valuable documents were looked for. The audacious scamp confessed that he had forged every one of the letters, etc., which he had sold to M. Chasles—some 20,000 in number; and that he had been engaged in the business since 1861. M. Chasles still persisted in his credulity. "Had not the Archivist obtained valuable papers from le Comte de Menou, in 1861?" "Yes, but only some sixty." But (says Chasles) a note found among his papers shows that he had received at least 1,020 valuable documents from the papers of that nobleman. That a single man could have forged a mass of documents so extensive and so technical in their contents he declined to believe. To give the Academy some notion of their contents, he specifies a number of the authors of these supposititious papers, (beginning with Julius Caesar and the Apostles,) and proceeds to track the possible history and growth of the collection, beginning with Alcuin and the Abbey of Tours, and coming down through Rabelais and Foucault. The inventor, if they were forged, must have been a wonderful man. "Such as they are, it is certain that their composition, if they are not genuine, must have required long labor and numerous materials; and if one considers how they harmonize with others of every period down to the last century, and of what various subjects they treat, one cannot believe that they are the work of a single individual, a single forger, who, for one thing, knew neither Italian nor Latin, nor any thing of the sciences which are treated in a large number of them. There is a mystery to be penetrated, and until this is done no certain conclusion can be reached."

This paper of M. Chasles gave so much dissatisfaction to his colleagues, that M. Dumas, the Secretary, urged him to withdraw it from the reports, and substitute a simple declaration on the state of the question; warning him that, if he did not, the next session would witness an emphatic protest against his conduct. M. Chasles insisted on its publication as it stood; so, at the next session, MM. Dumas and Chevreul, in behalf of a considerable number of the members of the Academy, protested against the conduct of M. Chasles in declining to explicitly retract the slanders which he had promulgated against

Newton and Huyghens, on the authority of documents which had been proved false to the satisfaction of all the world. Justice to these philosophers and the dignity of the Academy had been outraged by the halting language with which M. Chasles had closed his communication.

M. Chasles replied briefly. His closing words had been misunderstood. They meant that the origin of the documents was still hid in mystery. As regards the matters discussed in them, he had no assurance as to the authenticity of any one of the 20,000 which would justify his impugning the glory of Newton or of Huyghens. With this session the discussion closed.

Such is this latest chapter in the "Curiosities of Literature." Seldom has a great literary forgery been so daringly conceived, or so cleverly executed, but once again has it been seen that only omniscience could render such an undertaking successful. No keenest insight into the circumstances and events of any age can suffice to render historical fiction perfect in its ver[i]similitude. Some point will be missed; some Achilles' heel will always be vulnerable. A lie cannot consist with the truth, and reality will always vindicate itself. It was fortunate that the interest excited by the Chasles mss. led to a thorough and immediate investigation; and the scientific world may well be proud of the acuteness, the unselfishness and the simple love of truth and fact, so publicly exhibited by savan[t]s, where mean motives would have made mean men—Dupins and such—eager to detract from the honor of foreigners and to add undeserved laurels to the brows of their compatriots.

━━━━➤)(◖)(━━━━

VII
Sketch of Michel Chasles

Popular Science Monthly 18 (April 1881): 840-842

"In the death of Michel Chasles," said M. J.[oseph-Louis-François] Bertrand, in his funeral eulogy of the deceased mathematician, "France has lost one of its glories, and the members of the Academy of Sciences have lost an excellent friend, who, devoted without reserve to the beautiful studies which made his fame, showed an equal and active kindness to all who traveled in different directions along the highways of sciences." "As far back as the present generation can remember," says Mr. R. Tucker in "Nature," "Chasles has been a prince of geometers, and it has come upon many of us as a surprise to hear that he was still walking and working in our midst.... To many," says the same writer, "the man who had surpassed in age Leibnitz by seventeen, [Leonard] Euler by eleven, [Joseph Louis] Lagrange by ten, [Pierre Simon] Lapalce and [Karl Friedrich] Gauss by nine, and Newton by two years, was a *venerabile nomen*,' but yet a *'nomen'* only."

M. Chasles was born at Epernon, France, November 15, 1793, and died December 18, 1880. His mathematical tastes were exhibited at a very early age; while a pupil in elementary mathematics in the Imperial Lyceum, he was accustomed to communicate to the students in the rival colleges the problems and exercises of each week, asking them, in return, to furnish him the questions proposed by their masters. He entered the École Polytechnique in 1812, and passed out from it with a diploma in engineering in 1814, after having taken his place in the defense of Paris. He was about to go to Chartres to bid farewell to his mother before proceeding to duty at Metz, when he was waited upon by the father of one of his comrades, who asked him to resign in favor of his son, who had failed to obtain a position, pleading that he had made great sacrifices, which he could not afford to repeat, to prepare the youth for a career suited to his taste. Young Chasles made no reply, but went on to Chartres and told his mother he would stay with her. He returned to the École Polytechnique in 1815, but voluntarily renounced public employment, and went to Chartres to spend ten years working quietly at mathematical occupations. "Always," says M. Bertrand, "passionately fond of geometry, he worked out elaborate problems, discovered elegant theorems every day, invented general and fruitful methods, without attracting the attention of the masters of science, or pretending to do so.... Without grieving or complaining of his obscurity, or being discouraged by it, he pursued his studies for the love of them, and found glory without having done anything to secure it except to produce great works."

M. Chasles was elected a corresponding member of the Academy in 1839, was appointed Professor of Mechanics and Geodesy in the École Polytechnique in 1841, and was elected the first occupant of the newly created chair of Modern Geometry in 1846. He resigned his position in the École Polytechnique in 1851, in consequence of the introduction into the school of changes of which he did not approve. He was chosen a foreign member of the Royal Society in 1854, was awarded the Copley medal in 1865, and was elected in 1867, the first foreign member of the London Mathematical Society.

M. Chasles's life was one of active, uninterrupted work in his favorite field, from the time he left the Lyceum till he was eighty-seven years old—a period of sixty-eight years. His contributions of papers to scientific societies and journals are estimated to number nearly two hundred and forty, on subjects which range "over curves and surfaces of the second and any degree, geometry, mechanics (and attractions), history, and astronomy."

Of his greater works—"masterpieces that commanded attention"—the earliest was the "Aperçu Historique," or "Historical View of the Origin and Development of Methods in Geometry," which, says M. Bertrand, "under a title that is more than modest, remains the most learned, the most profound, the most original work that the history of science has ever inspired." It was published in 1830, being an elaboration of a paper contributed several years before to the Royal Academy of Brussels, and was reprinted in 1875, with a preface, giving a short historical account of the book. It is, says Mr. Tucker, a perfect mine of geometrical facts, and is to the present day a high authority on the subject of which it treats.

The courses of lectures delivered by M. Chasles as Professor of Modern Geometry were embodied in 1852 in the "Traité de Géométrie supérieure," or "Treatise on the Higher Geometry," a work which, of late years scarce and high, has recently appeared in a second edition. This was followed by a sequel, a treatise on conic sections ("Traité des Sections Coniques, faisant suite au Traité de Géométrie supérieure" [treatise on conic sections, constituting a sequel to the treatise on higher geometry][)], the first volume of which appeared in 1865. The second volume has not been published, but the materials for it have been given from time to time in the "Comptes Rendus" [proceedings].

In 1863 M. Chasles published his "Three Books on the Porisms of Euclid," which was the origin of a short controversy with M. P.[aul-Émile] Breton. The question of attraction was presented to M. Chasles under several points of view, and gave occasion to a number of memoirs extending even to the consideration of the general problem of the attraction of a body of any form. [Louis] Poinsot said of one of these papers that it offered a remarkable example of the elegance and light that geometry could shed on the most obscure and difficult questions; and M. Bertrand has said of them that they gave demonstrations and results admirable as models of elegance and generality.

M. Chasles gained notoriety a few years ago by his connection with a number of manuscripts and autographs purporting to be by distinguished men of the past, among them Galileo, Pascal, Sir Isaac Newton, and even Julius Caesar and other Roman emperors and the apostles, which he bought of one Irène [sic] Lucas and which proved to be nearly all forgeries by that adventurer. Among them were some which claimed for Pascal the merit of Newton's most celebrated discoveries. M. Chasles earnestly defended the authenticity of the documents, of which he was fully and honestly convinced, and was sustained by some eminent members of the Academy, until Lucas was unmistakably shown to have fabricated them. Out of twenty-seven thousand papers which he bought, only about a hundred were genuine.

M. Bertrand, summing up the mathematical work of M. Chasles, says that more than once, without abandoning the geometric method, he "has shown with a rare felicity how all mathematical truths are connected by a close and mysterious bond. We owe to him, in one of the highest and most difficult theories of the integral calculus, elegant theorems admired by analysts; he has added to mechanics a chapter which has become classic on the displacement of solid bodies; he has found in the theory of attraction beautiful and general theorems which have revived the theory of static electricity…. All geometricians, without distinction of nationality or school, have bowed before this venerable old man; all have admired his inventive power, his fertility, which age seemed to rejuvenate; his ardor and his zeal continued into his latest days."

———=◉)◉(◉=———

VIII
Michel Chasles

Nature 23 (23 December 1880): 174

The news of the death of Michel Chasles, perhaps the oldest and best-known mathematician in Europe, will be everywhere learned with deep regret. For the fifty-five years over which his writings extend he has devoted himself with persistent industry to the history of geometry and to the perfection of those geometrical methods with which his name will be always associated. The "Aperçu historique sur l'Origine et le Développement des Méthodes en Géométrie," which in fact forms an elaborate history of the subject from the time of Thales and Pythagoras to the beginning of the present century, is the best known of his works; it was first published in 1837, and a second edition appeared only a few years ago. His restoration of the Porisms of Euclid was published in 1860. The last great work of Chasles related to the investigation of the number of conics satisfying any five conditions: the special method which he invented for these researches, termed by him geometrical substitution, involved the consideration of the characteristics of systems of conics, *i.e.* of the numbers of conics satisfying four common conditions and (1) passing through an assumed point; (2) touching an assumed line.

In 1865 Chasles received the Copley medal of the Royal Society; this medal has, since its foundation in 1731, been given only five times for discoveries in pure mathematics, viz., in 1784 to [Edward] Waring, in 1814 to [James] Ivory, in 1841 to [Jacques Charles François] Sturm, in 1865 to Chasles, and in the present year to [James Joseph] Sylvestyer,

In 1846 Chasles was appointed to fill the new Chair of Modern Geometry, founded by the Faculty of Sciences at Paris; and as a professor he exerted personal influence over the younger geometers of that time, which has since been apparent in their writings, although the effect of the geometrical methods to which he devoted his life is chiefly visible in the works of the Italian and German mathematicians. He was the inventor of the term "anharmonic ratio," but not of course of the ratio itself, which was known to the ancients. Chasles's memoirs on the attraction of ellipsoids are well known to English mathematicians and physicists; and a translation of his memoirs on Cones of the Second Order, and Spherical Conics, was published in Dublin in 1841 by Dr. [Charles] Graves, now Bishop of Limerick.

Most of our readers will remember how in 1866 Chasles was deceived by M. Vrain Lucas by what were called the Pascal forgeries, and they will also remember how honourably he extricated himself from the matter, and did all in his power to repair the mischief done. The forger was convicted and sentenced to two years' imprisonment; and not a shadow of suspicion was ever thrown upon the honour or good faith of Chasles.

Scientific visitors to Paris will miss a well-known face at the Academy and a kind and hospitable friend. Till quite recently Chasles seemed as active as ever, both mentally and physically, and it was only last September that he issued a new edition of his "Géométrie supérieure." He was a Foreign Member of the Royal Society and of the Cambridge Philosophical Society.

⟻⟺⟺«(❖)»⟺⟺

IX
Michel Chasles
Born November 15, 1793, Died December 18, 1880

Nature 23 (6 January 1881): 225-227

"Know ye not that there is a prince and a great man fallen this day?" might well have been the thought of the President [Alexandre-Edmond] Becquerel when he announced to the Academy on the 20th ult. that Chasles was dead. To many the man who had surpassed in age Leibnitz by seventeen, Euler by eleven, Lagarnge by ten, Lapalce and Gauss by nine, and Newton by two years, was a "venerabile nomen," but yet a "nomen" only.

As far back as the present generation can remember Chasles has been a prince of geometers, and it has come upon many of us as a surprise to hear that he was still walking and working in our midst. A few years back a telegram was sent to him from Boston conveying congratulations, and expressing the hope that the illustrious mathematician might see the close of the present century, in which event he would have surpassed the years of Pythagoras. Length of days is not always a boon, but Chasles's was a pleasant old age, and he died in harness: in such a case he might say with one of old, "nihil habeo quod incusem senectutem."[7] "La vie de M. Chasles a été heuresuse et simple; il a trouvé dans la Science, avec les plus grandes joies, une gloire qui sera immortelle, et dans la vive affection de ses amis, dans leur assiduité empressée aux réunions où il les conviait avec une grâce si aimable, dans leur respectueuse déférence en toute circonstance, la consolation de sa vieillesse."[8]

Born at Epernon (Eure-et-Loir), he entered the École Polytechnique in 1812. At this early date he would communicate to students in the rival colleges the problems and exercises of the week, asking in return the questions proposed by their masters: "Dans cet échange organisé par le jeune lycéen, on peut croire aisément que le futur géomètre avait souvent la meilleure part."[9] After taking

---

7 I have nothing for which I may condemn old age.

8 The life of M. Chasles was fortunate and straightforward; he found in learning, along with the greatest happiness, a glory that will be immortal, and in the strong affection of his friends, in their eager assiduousness at gatherings to which he invited them with so amiable an air, in their respectful deference in every circumstance, the consolation of his old age.

9 In this exchange organized by the young schoolboy, one can easily believe that the future geometrician often had the greater profit.

his place in the defence of Paris in 1814 he passed out in engineering, but he re-entered the school in 1815. And this is the reason: Chasles was on the point of leaving for Chartres to show his uniform and to bid farewell to his mother before going to Metz, when he was waited on by the father of one of his comrades. "Mon fils," said the father, "est le premier des élèves qui n'ont pas obtenu de place; vous avez hésité, je le sais, à accepter l'épaulette; votre refus aurait assuré à votre camarade une carrière qui lui plaît et pour laquelle j'ai fait les derniers sacrifices; il m'est impossible de les continuer pour lui en préparer une autre."[10] Chasles made no reply: he went to Chartres; on his arrival his choice was made, and he told his mother he would stay with her. The army lost him as an officer, the world gained him as a geometer. On finally leaving the establishment, in spite of the high position he held amongst his companions, he voluntarily renounced public employment (Larousse states however: "Fut agent de change et plus tard aux affaires pour les sciences"[11]) and went to Chartres, where he spent some ten years. He was working quietly however: "Toujours passionné pour la géométrie, il résolvait de beaux problèmes, comme au collège, trouvait chaque jour d'élégants théorèmes, inventait des méthodes générales et fécondes, sans attirer l'attention des maîtres de la sciènce et sans y prétendre. 'Que de talent perdu!' disaient les plus bien-veillants, sans songer même à traiter d'égal ce jeune homme obstiné à approfondir les théories élémentaires et qui bientôt peut-être devait, par elles, s'élever bien au-dessus d'eux."[12] Elected a Corresponding Member of the Academy in 1839 ("decorated" the same year), he was made "Professeur de Machines et de Géodésie"[13] at the École Polytechnique in succession to Savary in 1841. This chair he occupied for ten years, when, in consequence of some alterations ("profondes et très regretables"[14]), he sent in his resignation, and ever afterwards did all in his

---

10 My son is the first of the students who have not obtained a situation; you hesitated, I know, to accept a commission; your refusal would assure to your comrade a career that would please him and for which I made the utmost sacrifices; it is impossible for me to continue them to prepare him for another career.

11 He was an exchange-broker and later a general agent for scientific matters.

12 Always passionately fond of geometry, he solved eleborate problems, as he had in school, discovered each day elegant theorems, invented general and fruitful methods, without attracting the attention of the masters of science and without seeking to do so. 'What lost talent!' said the most alert, without even dreaming of treating as an equal this young man intent on studying thoroughly the elementary theories and who soon perhaps must, through them, have risen far above them [i.e., "the most alert"].

13 Professor of mechanics and geodesy.

14 profound and most unfortunate [Tucker's note: Note, p. 583, to the admirable "Discours d'Inauguration de Cours de Géométrie Supérieure de la Faculté des Sciences de Paris [inaugural lecture of the course of advanced geometry of the science faculty of Paris] (December 22, 1846), which follows the second edition of the "Traité de Géométrie Supérieure" (1880)]

power to combat these, as he thought, dangerous reforms. His affection how-ever continued unabated: "C'est ainsi qu'il acceptait avec tout d'empressement la présidence du Comité de la Société amicale des Anciens Élèves; c'st ainsi qu'il entrait au conseil de perfectionnement, et que, tout récemment encore, malgré son grand âge, il acceptait le renouvellement de son mandat, avec le désir, dis-ait-il, de continuer jusqu'à son dernier souffle à entretenir ce foyer de travail, d'honneur et de dévouement au pays."[15] With the ardour which so distin-guished him, M. Chasles had undertaken to write a history of the school; an extract from this history he recently published: "Exposé historique concernant le Cours de Machines, dans l'Enseignement de l'École Polytechnique"[16] (see notice in NATURE, vol. xxiii. p.75). M. Laussedat informs us that the veteran's wish is in great part attained, and that it was with great pleasure Chasles learned before his death that the *Journal de l'École Polytechnique* is to be revived, and that the revision of the "programmes de l'enseignment"[17] was decided upon. In France the professional chairs are *special.*[18] Poinsot was, for some years, desirous that a chair should be appointed for the Modern Geometry, and in 1846 this chair was created by the Faculté des Sciences, and Chasles was elected to be the first occupant. In 1851 he was elected a Member of the Academy, and in the same year, as above stated, gave up his appointment at the Polytechnic. In 1854 he became Foreign Member of our Royal Society, in 1865 he was awarded the Copley medal, and in April, 1867, he was elected the first (and for some time the only) Foreign Member of the London Mathematical Society. His honours of membership were numerous, and are printed on the title-pages of his works. The Pascal-Newton controversy has already been alluded to in these pages, and we willingly leave it here untouched.

"M. Chasles a poursuivi son oeuvre sans interruption depuis sa sortie du Lycée jusqu'à l'âge de quatre-vingt-sept ans. Soixante-huit années séparent la première note de l'élève Chasles, insérée dans la *Correspondance sur l'École Polytechnique*, du dernier mémoire présenté à l'Académie des Sciences. Tous les géomètres, sans distinction de nationalité ni d'école, se sont inclinés devant ce vénérable vieillard; tous ont admiré sa puissance d'invention, sa fécondité, que

---

15 It is thus that he accepted with complete alacrity the presidency of the board of the benevolent society of alumni; it is thus that he embarked on the plan of improvement, and that, quite recently again, despite his great age, he accepted the renewal of his mandate, with the desire, he said, to continue until his last breath to maintain this focus of work, of honor, and of devotion to his country.

16 Historical exposition concerning the course of mechanics, in the curriculum of the Polytechnic School.

17 programs of instruction

18 Tucker's note: "Toutes les chaires ont un titre special." "Rapport sur les Progrès de la Géométrie," Paris, 1870, pp. 219, 376 [All the chairs have a particular title. Report on the progress of geometry].

l'âge semblait rejeunir, son ardour, et son zèle, continués jusqu'aux derniers jours."[19]

A mere recital of the titles of M. Chasles' numerous papers would fill several columns. In the "Catalogue of Scientific Papers" will be found the titles of 177, and from the slight examination we have been able to make we have little doubt that the number published since 1873 would bring the total to nearly 240. The subjects range over curves and surfaces of the second and of any degree, geometry, mechanics (and attractions), history, and astronomy. Amongst his earliest papers are those which were translated by the present Bishop of Limerick [Charles Graves] in 1841, under the title "Two Geometrical Memoirs on the General Properties of Cones of the Second Degree, and on the Spherical Conics." "These possess strong claims on the attention of mathematicians, whether they are considered merely as exercises of pure geometry, exhibiting its elegance and power in a remarkable degree, or as a rich and early contribution to the theory of spherical curves."

Chasles himself remarks in his *Rapport*[20] (which perhaps furnishes the best key to his writings), "On peut s'étonner que, jusque vers la fin du premier tiers de ce siècle, on n'ait eu l'idée d'étudier ni les propriétés des cônes du second ordre qui servent à engendre les coniques, ni celles des courbes qui tiennent sur la sphère le rang des coniques sur le plan"[21] (p. 75).

In reply to the question, "On demande un examen philosophique des différentes méthodes employées dans la géométrie récente et particulièrement de la méthode des polaires reciproques,"[22] was written, "Mémoire de Géométrie sur deux Principes généraux de la Science, la Dualité, et l'Homographie"[23] (January, 1830, to the Académie Royale of Brussels), preceded by some historical researches. This work subsequently took the form of the famous

---

19 Mr. Chasles pursued his work without interruption from the time he left the lycée until the age of eighty-seven. Sixty-eight years separate the first note of the student Chasles published in the correspondence concerning the polytechnic school from the final memoir presented to the Academy of Sciences. All geometricians, without regard to nationality or school, bowed their heads before this venerable old man; all admired his power of invention, his productivity, that age seemed to rejuvenate, his ardor, and his zeal, that continued until his final days.

20 Tucker's note: Pp. 72-126, 220-280, contain an account of the author's own contributions to geometry.

21 One may be surprised that, until almost the end of the first third of this century, no one had the idea of studying either the properties of cones of the second order that are useful for generating conic sections, or those of curves that have in regard to the sphere the status of conic sections with regard to the plane.

22 One asks for a philosophical (i.e., scientific) examination of the different methods used in modern geometry and particularly the method of polar reciprocals.

23 Memoir of geometry concerning two general principles of the discipline, duality and homography.

"Aperçu historique sur l'Origine et le Developpement des Méthodes en Géométrie ... suivi d'un Mémoire ... sur deux Principes généraux ...et l'Homographie." This work appeared in 1837, and having become exceedingly scarce, was reprinted verbatim in 1875, with the addition of a short preface giving a brief historical account of the book. In the *Rapport* (p. 80) we are told "c'est cette troisième partie (the memoir on Duality and Homography) "qui à donné lieu à la composition de l'ouvrage. La théorie des figures homologiques et celle des polaires reciproques qui sont la base des beaux travaux de l'illustre Général Poncelet donnèrent une heureuse impulsion aux recherches de pure géométrie."[24] These two methods were susceptible, he says, of generalisation, and the progress of the science demanded it. The *Aperçu*, which has been translated into German (except the third part) by [Ludwig Adolph] Sohncke, is a perfect mine of geometrical facts, and is to the present day a high authority on the subject of which it treats. In some places too great reliance on [Jean Étienne] Montucla (see Dr. [George Johnston] Allman on "Greek Geometry from Thales to Euclid," p. 171, cf. also p. 202 [papers published initially in *Hermathena* and collected under the same title in 1889]), and in others nonacquaintance with German ("nous éprouvons un vif regret de ne pouvoir citer ici leurs ouvrages, qui nous sont inconnues, par suite de notre ignorance de la langue dans laquelle ils sont écrits,"[25] p. 215) may slightly detract from its merits, but after all deductions it exhibits a vast amount of research and originality, and well merits the title of *ouvrage classique*.[26]

The appointment to the Chair of Modern Geometry necessitated a course (or courses) of lectures, and in 1852 these were embodied in the "Traité de Géométrie supérieure" [treatise on advanced geometry], "an elaborate and masterly treatise," which of late years has been rarely attainable, and only at a very high price. M. Chasles, hardly two months before his death, had the satisfaction of seeing a second edition, accompanying which is (pp. 547-585) the excellent "Discours d'Inauguration" (referred to above). The three fundamental principles of this work are "Anharmonic Ratio of Four Points," "Homographic Divisions," and "Involution" (*Rapport*, p. 220).

In 1865 appeared the first volume of the "Traité des Sections coniques, faisant suite au Traité de Géométrie supérieure" [treatise on conic sections writ-

---

24 It is this third part (the memoir on Duality and Homography) that gave rise to the composition of the work. The theory of homological figures and that of polar reciprocals that are the basis of the fine works of the illustrious General [Jean Victor] Poncelet will give a fortunate impetus to research in the field of pure geometry.

25 We feel a deep regret at being unable to cite here their works, which are unkown to us, because of our ignorance of the language in which they are written.

26 Classic work. [Tucker's note: De Morgan says, "A work of great importance in the historical point of view."]

ten as a sequel to the treatise on advanced geometry]. As its title indicates, constant application is made in it of the principles of pure geometry unfolded in the earlier work. It thus differs considerably not only from analytical treatises, but from geometrical treatises also: "Ces trois théories primordiales s'appliquent avec une extreme facilité à toutes les recherches concernant les sections coniques"[27] (*Rapport*, pp. 266-9).

Mathematicians have long looked for a second volume, materials for which have appeared in the *Comptes rendus* [proceedings]. In the *Rapport* (pp. 257-266) will be found an account of the method of *geometrical substitution* and a definition of the *elements* (or *characteristics*) of a system of conics (*Comptes rendus*, 1864-7). Numerous applications are made of this remarkable theory (for further accounts the English student may refer to Dr. [George] Salmon's "Higher Plane Curves," pp. 360, &c., and "Conics," p. 368; see also later papers in the *Comptes rendus*, vol, lxxviii.[28] p. 577, &c., vol. lxxxv. p. 362, pp. 460-6).

We must now go back to the year 1863, when Chasles published his "Les trois Livres de Porismes d'Euclide, rétablis pour la première Fois, d'après la Notice et les Lemmes de Pappus, et conformément au Sentiment de R.[obert] Simson, sur la Forme de Enoncés de ces Propositions."[29] In 1838 he had contributed a paper, "Sur la Doctrine des Porismes d'Euclide" [on the tenets of the porisms of Euclid], to [Lambert Adolphe Jacques] Quetelet's *Corresp. Math.* X (pp. 1-23). We must content ourselves with referring to the *Rapport*, pp. 155, 233-42; the *Aperçu*, pp. 39, &c. (He cites Montucla as to the profoundness of the Porisms, gives high praise to Simson, and shows that there is in Pappus's Lemmas what is in effect the projective property of the anhamonic ratio of four points). The publication of this work led to a short controversy with M. P.[aul-Émile] Breton ("Question des Porismes—notices sur les débats de priorité auxquels a donné lieu l'ouvrage de M. Chasles sur les porismes d'Euclide,"[30] Paris[: madame veuve Bouchard-Hazard], 1865; and a second part, Paris, 1866 [The National Union Catalogue gives the date for part two as 1872]). M. Chasles comments on these in the *Rapport* (cf. reff. above).

We turn now for a moment to the subject of attraction. "La question de l'attraction presenta-t-elle à l'auteur sous plusieurs points de vue, qui donnèrent

---

27 These three primary theories easily apply to all studies regarding conic sections.

28 Tucker's note: "Considerations sur le caractère propre du principe de correspondance," "S'applique avec une très grande facilité à une infinité de questions." [considerations on the proper character of the principle of correspondence applies very easily to an infinity of questions].

29 The three books of porisms of Euclid, restored for the first time, according to the account and lemmas of Pappus, and agreeing with the ideas of R. Simson, on the form of the expression of these propositions.

30 Question of porisms—accounts of the debates of priority to which the work of M. Chasles gave rise concerning the porisms of Euclid.

lieu à divers mémoires et s'étendirent même au problème général de l'attraction d'un corps de forme quelconque"[31] (*Rapport*, p. 101); on p. 103 he gives a history of [Colin] Maclaurin's theorem (of which [Isaac] Todhunter—"History of the [Mathematical] Theories of Attraction," &c., vol. i. 260, writes: "Chasles is correct"); on p. 105 we read: "Mais il restait toujours à désirer une démonstration directe et rigoureuse du théorème de Maclaurin;"[32] and he cites an extract from Poinsot's report on his paper (*Mémoires* sur divers Savants [memoirs concerning various scholars], t. ix. 1846): "Ce mémoire remarquable nous offre un nouvel exemple de l'élégance et de la clarté que la géométrie peut répandre sur les questions les plus obscures et les plus difficiles"[33] (*Comptes rendus*, t. vi. 1838, pp. 808-812).

This, the first *synthetic* solution (of General [Edward] Sabine's address on presenting the Copley Medal) was published, if we mistake not, in 1837. M. Bertrand, in his *éloge* [praise] of [Gabriel] Lamé (January 28, 1878, *Mémoires* de l'Académie des Sciences), says "M. Chasles obtenait, en la transportant à la théorie si souvent étudiée de l'attraction des ellipsoïdes, des démonstrations et des résultats admirés comme un modèle d'élégance et de généralité."[34]

We have no space left, having perhaps already dwelt too much in detail upon the complete works, to give an account of the numerous papers we referred to above. This is the less necessary as the results of many are already incorporated in the larger works. We must however just mention the important mechanical principle founded upon the proposition "quand deux polygones égaux sont placés d'une manière quelconque dans un plan, il existe toujours un point du plane qui est également distant de deux sommets homologues quelconques des deux polygones, le point est semblablement placé par rapport aux deux polygones."[35]

The applications of this, under Poncelet's form of enunciation, are fully treated of by Richard in his "Note sur un nouveau principe de cinématique sur son emploi et sur la Théorème de M. Chasles" [note on a new principle of kine-

---

31 The question of attraction presented itself to the author from many points of view, which will give rise to various memoirs, and even will extend to the general problem of attraction of a body of any shape whatever.

32 But there always remained lacking a complete and rigorous demonstration of the theorem of Maclaurin.

33 This remarkable memoir offers us a fresh example of the elegance and light that geometry can shed upon the most obscure and difficult questions.

34 M. Chasles obtained, in extending the theory so often studied of the attraction of ellipsoids, proofs and results admired as a model of elegance and general application.

35 When two identical polygons are placed in any manner whatsoever on a plane, there always exists one point on the plane that is equidistant from any two homological apexes of the two polygons, the point is similarly placed with respect to the two polygons.

matics concerning its use and concerning the theorem of M. Chasles] (Paris, 1856).

In the closing lines of the *Rapport* M. Chasles indignantly condemns the modern system which has for its supreme and immediate object *des applications pratiques* [practical applications]; and which is "caracterisée suffisamment par l'idée fatale de *bifurcation*."[36] These remarks we pass over, but gladly draw attention to a wish he strongly expresses, viz. that a defect should be remedied by the creation of two chairs, one for "Géométrie infinitésimale et analytique" [infinitesimal and analytical geometry] and the other for "Analyse transcendante" [calculus]. If these chairs do not now exist, it would be a fitting compliment to his memory to establish one or both. One other wish we have which we repeat, and that is, following the fashion of the time, that a collected edition of his papers be issued, for at present they are scattered over a very wide area.

In this notice we are indebted to the funeral speeches pronounced over M. Chasles's grave (*Comptes rendus*, xci. No. xxv., December 20, 1880) which, and M. Chasles's own remarks, we have freely cited in their original language, thereby securing conciseness of expression.

> We must however linger no longer by the grave, but turn to the "living present," after repeating M. Dumas's last words, "Adieu, Chasles, adieu!"
>
> R. Tucker

---

36 Sufficiently characterized by the notion of bifurcation.

UNE FABRIQUE

DE

FAUX AUTOGRAPHES

OU RÉCIT DE

L'AFFAIRE VRAIN LUCAS

PAR

M. HENRI BORDIER

Avocat, ancien archiviste aux Archives nationales

ET

M. EMILE MABILLE

Attaché au département des Manuscrits de la Bibliothèque impériale

PARIS

LÉON TECHENER, LIBRAIRE

RUE DE L'ARBRE-SEC, 52

1870

Original French Title Page

A FORGING

of

FALSE AUTOGRAPHS

OR AN ACCOUNT

OF THE AFFAIR VRAIN LUCAS

by

M. HENRI BORDIER

Lawyer, former archivist of the National Archives

and

M. ÉMILE MABILLE

Associated with the Department of Manuscripts of the Imperial Library

— — — — — —

ACCOMPANIED BY FOURTEEN FACSIMILES
Of the Principal Documents Placed in Evidence during the Trial

— — — — — —

Price: 10 Francs

— — — — — —

PARIS
LÉON TECHENER, BOOKSELLER
52 RUE DE L'ARBRE-SEC
— — — — — —
1870

Translation of original French advertisement

Original Preface
to the 1870 French Edition

———————————

This work contains the diverse pieces of evidence relative to the collection of false autographs sold to M. Chasles by the forger Vrain Lucas:

First, the work of the experts requested by the judge to aid him with their special knowledge; not their verbatim report, because documents of this type do not leave the confines of the tribunal to which they are addressed, but a summary of all the facts comprising the substance of this report, a summary that has already appeared, though abridged, in the *Revue Contemporaine* of the past 1 March;

Second, the inventory of the various pieces making up the collection of false autographs sold to M. Chasles: (1) the list of scientific letters and notes; (2) the list of authentic manuscripts and of those that, to be sold to M. Chasles, were fraudulently filled with false autograph annotations intended to raise their price; (3) the list of printed books in the same collection given false provenances;

In the third place, the proceedings of the affair as it was tried in the Tribunal of the Seine (6th chamber), in the sessions of 17 and 24 February 1870;

Finally, the text of the decision by which this literary affair was closed and resolved.

Some specimens of the false autographs over which the discussion was conducted will finish giving the reader the complete profile of this singular case.

Index

—————⚙—————

[The index does not include the inventory of forgeries, nor does it contain entries for Vrain-Denis Lucas, Michel Chasles, or the Academy of Sciences because these names appear on virtually every page. An *n* following a page number indicates the reference is in a footnote]